DEBATING VALUES

MICHAEL D. BARTANEN
Pacific Lutheran University

DAVID A. FRANK
University of Oregon

GSP

Gorsuch Scarisbrick, Publishers
Scottsdale, Arizona

Editor	John W. Gorsuch
Consulting Editor	Gerald R. Miller
Production Manager	Carol H. Blumentritt
Copyeditor	Carolyn Acheson
Cover Design	Cynthia Maliwauki
Typesetting	Laserworks
Printing & Binding	BookCrafters

Gorsuch Scarisbrick, Publishers
8233 Via Paseo del Norte, Suite F-400
Scottsdale, Arizona 85258

10 9 8 7 6 5 4 3 2

ISBN 0-89787-341-6

Printed in the United States of America.

Contents

4

—————————— **Section Two** ——————————

Applying the Theory

5

6

Appendix A

Appendix B

Preface

Academic debate is one of the most valuable educational experiences. Skills in creating, researching, and defending debate positions prepare students for a lifetime of citizenship as well as career success and satisfaction. The challenge of standing up in a competitive debate and "jousting" with another student is stimulating, and it is a way of building courage.

No other society compares to the United States in the amount of time and energy spent on learning to debate. Each year thousands of high school and college students participate in debate competition. Although debate training is particularly valuable in preparing for a career in law, many professionals in other areas recognize debate training as important to success in their chosen field. A remarkable number of public figures give credit to debate training in their preparation for public service.* We also should not overlook the societal importance of debate in providing the systematic means to debate important fact, value, and policy questions that confront us in everyday life.

This is a book about value debate, an area of interest that has grown rapidly in the past twenty years. Each year thousands of college students participate in college debate tournaments and classroom debates on value resolutions. Many of these students have had no prior experience in either college or high school debate. Others have had experience in policy debate but are unsure of how value debate works. This book is directed toward both groups of students.

Value debate is different from policy debate. It involves different kinds of issues. It has a different language. It has different audience expectations. This book tries to identify and lay out those differences.

This text also takes a philosophical position about debate. We think debate ought to be "audience-centered"; it ought to stress good communication skills and teach students to adapt to different kinds of audiences. This theme is repeated at various points within the text.

* From Kent Colbert and Thompson Biggers, "Why Should We Support Debate?" *Journal of the American Forensics Association* 21 (1985): 237–240.

We discuss structural and situational elements of the debate process; we devote a chapter to audience concerns such as delivery; and we include individual chapters on the debate judging paradigms and on ethics.

The first four chapters are primarily theoretical in nature, laying out the groundwork of a theory of debating values. Chapters 5 through 7 deal primarily with application, relating the theories to the context of academic debate. The final three chapters integrate theory and practice, examining issues that arise out of participating in competitive academic debate.

Our purpose in this book is to give students the necessary knowledge to use debate to prepare for the lifelong challenges of careers and citizenship. The book covers the fundamentals of debate, the characteristics of debating values, and propositions of judgment, and it suggests some effective debate strategies. Learning to debate well is not easy. It requires mastering technical language, learning the "rules of the game"; and understanding the subject area of the debate resolution. To completely master these skills, readers should go beyond the material presented herein and should practice debating either in class or in debate tournaments.

We are indebted to the meaningful suggestions of Clark D. Orr, Arizona State University, and Diana Prentice, University of Kansas, reviewers of this text. We also recognize the substantial theoretical contributions of many of the scholars in the emerging field of Cross-Examination Debate Association (CEDA) debate scholarship.

We think the readers' experience in debate will be similar to ours. The chance to participate in debate was one of the most challenging and meaningful experiences of our lives.

The Theory of Debating Values

1

Introduction to Value Debate

☐ Define *debate* and differentiate debate from garden-variety arguing.

☐ Identify the important characteristics of the debate format.

☐ Understand the background of debate study in the United States and why debate training is valuable.

Academic debate is different from other debate forms. It is more complicated than the unorganized arguing we do every day, and very different from organized methods such as political debates or debates conducted in court cases. Although academic debate has some aspects in common with other arguing forms, it is unique in many ways because of its special educational requirements.

THE DEFINITION OF DEBATE

We define academic debate in the following way:

> A debate is a competitive speaking activity between two or more people arguing about a proposition of policy or judgment under mutually agreed-upon rules in front of a listener(s) who has the responsibility to decide who did the better job of debating using whatever criteria the listener deems important.

We will develop this definition as the book unfolds. It suggests several important debate characteristics.

CHARACTERISTICS OF DEBATE

Debate characteristics include equal speaking time, use of a resolution, a particular format, specific responsibilities for the speakers which include adapting statements to the listener, and commitment to fair play.

Equal Speaking Time, A Resolution, A Format

Each speaker in a debate has the same amount of speaking time in the framework of a format the participants know ahead of time. A debate consists of speakers on two sides of the resolution: the affirmative side, which argues in favor of the resolution, and the negative side, which argues against the resolution. Debates typically use one of three formats: cross-examination style, Oxford style, or Lincoln-Douglas style. Table 1.1 shows the order of speeches for each format.

The *cross-examination* style is the prevalent format of team debate used in the United States.[1] Oxford style was the original format used in academic debates, and the Lincoln-Douglas style is commonly used in high school and college debates alike.

Specific Responsibilities

Each speaker in the debate is expected to carry out certain duties during his or her speaking time. Contemporary debate builds on the legal system model of presumption and the burden of proof. In most contexts we expect that "they who assert must prove" and that there is a corresponding presumption against people advocating a change in the status quo (things as they are) or arguing against the values accepted by most people. For example, if someone is arrested and indicted for a crime, he or she is presumed innocent unless proven guilty beyond reasonable doubt.

Table 1.1   Speaking Order for Common Debate Formats

	Cross Examination	Oxford	Lincoln-Douglas
aff constructive	8 minutes	10 minutes	6 minutes
C-x by neg	3 minutes	---	3 minutes
neg	8 minutes	10 minutes	7 minutes
C-x by aff	3 minutes	---	3 minutes
aff	8 minutes	10 minutes	---
C-x by neg	3 minutes	---	---
neg	8 minutes	10 minutes	---
C-x by aff	3 minutes	---	---
neg rebuttal	5 minutes	5 minutes	---
aff rebuttal	5 minutes	5 minutes	4 minutes
neg rebuttal	5 minutes	5 minutes	6 minutes
aff rebuttal	5 minutes	5 minutes	3 minutes

C-x = cross-examination
aff = affirmative
neg = negative

These general principles are used in academic debate. The affirmative fulfills its burden of proof by presenting a *prima facie* case justifying the resolution. A prima facie case is one that "stands on its own merits," similar to the prosecutor providing sufficient evidence to form a case against a defendant. The negative has the burden of rejoinder, which is an ensuing duty to refute the assertions and claims presented by the affirmative. (Chapter 2 addresses these difficult and sometimes confusing concepts in more detail.) Listeners expect all speakers in the debate to clash with the assertions and claims presented by the other side. This expectation contributes to the popular notion of a debate as a "he says yes, she says no" activity in which participants try to overcome all or at least most of the opposing statements.

Adapting Statements to the Listener

You most likely have been in this position at some time: You made the "best" argument, but the "dummy" you were arguing with rejected your "superior" analysis. Despite our best efforts, we sometimes cannot successfully persuade others to accept our assertions and claims. The reason is simple. Listeners bring their own biases and expectations to any communication environment.

The main job of any arguer is to figure out how to appeal to the audience. Common sense tells you that making assertions and claims without analyzing your audience bodes real danger for your success. Debate constitutes valuable communication training because it emphasizes the key notion that audiences have amazingly different expectations about the nature of good arguments and trains students how to address those diverse audience expectations.

Commitment to Fair Play

Most important, debate relies on participants' accepting principles of fair play. Debate is a game. Debaters agree to conform to the implicit rules of the game, including those of good manners and fairness. The recent episodes of English soccer crowds' disrupting matches by their drunken brawls and unruly behavior constitute good examples of the antithesis of debate. In debate we expect speakers to listen to their opponents, take their turn when it comes, argue passionately for their position, and accept the judge's decision even when they believe the opposing side is mistaken.

Debate, then, is an organized method of arguing. Although there may be many debate formats, the most common are the cross-examination, the Oxford and the Lincoln-Douglas. Regardless of format, a debate consists of equal speaking time, specific speaker responsibilities, a listener orientation, and a commitment to fair play. These characteristics emerged from the growth of debate activity in the United States.

A sample debate is presented in Appendix A at the end of this book. You may want to take some time to read it carefully, to get a sense of how a debate works. To illustrate the debate theories discussed, we will be using examples of this debate throughout the text. The debate, between Florida State University and Macalester College, took place in the championship round of the first National CEDA Tournament, at Wichita State University in 1986. No debate is perfect, but this round is an excellent example of good debate and reveals a number of different techniques that other debaters could emulate profitably.

A BRIEF BACKGROUND OF DEBATE

The History

The roots of academic debate go back to the golden ages of Athens and Rome. Students gave speeches about hypothetical legal, social, and political questions, honing their arguing skills and helping them become societal leaders.[2] Only male aristocrats learned debate skills, because society considered only men as full-fledged citizens. Debate training, with its male and landowner bias, continued during the Renaissance in Western Europe, although less organized than classical training.

Immigrants brought interest in public speaking and debate to the new world. Literary societies emerged in many American small towns, providing citizens the opportunity to debate the issues of the day. These societies gave people an appreciation of the importance of debate and the confidence to participate in public decision-making.

A New England farmer, for example, could attend a political meeting and discuss issues with Daniel Webster or other prominent leaders with ample opportunity for influencing the course of public events. Society encouraged and expected active participation by all citizens.[3]

These literary societies flourished and eventually found their way to college campuses and grammar school rooms. Through classroom speeches and debates, students practiced public-speaking skills and learned about public policy issues. Colleges began debating one another in public events as early as the 1870s.[4] These early debates were public spectacles where everyone on campus observed the combatants. In those times debates were more popular than even football games![5] Gradually, regional and national debate organizations replaced these individual debates, and they sponsored national conventions and tournaments promoting the debate activity. The tournament format, wherein schools and teams gathered at a central location for a series of debates, accompanied universal availability of the automobile in the 1920s and 1930s.[6]

In the early years of debate activity, individual tournament hosts chose a debate topic. Gradually the popularity of the activity came to require a single, national topic. Usually these topics were policy propositions in which debaters researched and debated contemporary public issues and the debate revolved around adopting some new policy proposal. The national college topic for 1928–29, for example, was: Resolved: that a substitute for trial by jury should be adopted. Affirmative teams supported the resolution by arguing that trial by judge was a superior alternative; their opponents defended the benefits of the jury system.

Academic debate in the first half of the twentieth century gradually settled on specific debate formats and agreement on rules. Two-person teams gradually replaced three-, four-, or five-person teams as the dominant model. Other innovations included the use of cross-examination in debate (introduced during the 1920s to high school debate, and later, college debate) and Lincoln-Douglas, or single-person, debate (introduced by R. D. Mahaffey of Linfield College during World War II when there was, naturally, a shortage of people to make up debate teams).

Perhaps the most important development in debate was the heated discussion in the early years of whether it was ethical for students to speak on both sides of the resolution. Opponents of two-sided debate believed that students could be truthful advocates only if they were arguing in favor of the side they believed. Proponents of switching sides claimed that the preparation necessary to argue both sides led students to a more complete understanding of the complex issues the proposition contained. Eventually this issue died out, and students normally prepared on both sides of the resolution.

The debate tournament model has been largely unchanged since the 1930s. Competitive speech and debates often are combined under the term *forensics,*—borrowing from the classical term for legal or judgmental speaking. It has nothing to do with dissecting dead bodies! Debate tournaments typically consist of six or eight debate rounds for each team, with each team expected to debate both sides of the resolution. Forensic tournaments frequently offer competition in public speaking and oral interpretation events in addition to debates. The tournament champion is the team winning the most debates either in the preliminary rounds of the tournament or during a single-elimination-round format for teams that were the most successful in preliminary rounds.

Policy proposition debate was the primary debate format until recent years. Concerns about excesses of policy debate rounds (such as fast delivery and narrow interpretations of resolutions), however, led to creation of the Southwest Cross-Examination Debate Association in 1971.[7] This organization rapidly grew in popularity and is now called the Cross-Examination Debate Association (CEDA). CEDA often debates resolutions in which the focus is on the value-related issues in the resolution rather than on specific policy proposals. For example, a recent resolution was: Resolved: that significantly stronger third-party participation in United States presidential elections would benefit the political process.

Academic Debate Today

Current academic debate in the United States takes three forms: policy debating, sometimes referred to in debate literature as "NDT style";[8] value debating, sometimes called "CEDA style"; and informal, audience debating, which takes place at a few colleges.

Policy debate and non-policy, or value, debate have similarities and differences. They are similar in the sense that they share a common format (such as cross-examination); and they frequently debate policy-oriented resolutions, as the example of the CEDA resolution about third parties and the sample debate (Appendix A) show. It is also not completely out of the ordinary to find debaters arguing about the value implications of a policy resolution or the policy implications of a value resolution.

Policy debating and non-policy debating have some differences, too. First, *policy and value debates consider policy matters in different ways.* To think that value debate discusses abstract or philosophical values is errant. Most value debate resolutions (for better or worse) concern the value implications of a policy problem. For example, a value resolution might be, "Gun control is desirable," whereas a policy resolution might be, "Gun control should be adopted in the United States." This points up the blurry line that sometimes exists between policy and value resolutions. It is certainly the case in real-world decision making, in which decision makers inevitably must consider values and policies together because every policy has an underlying set of values that must be considered.

Second, *policy and value debates analyze different stock issues.* Different kinds of issues are analyzed when debating different kinds of resolutions. The issue of "workability," for example, is an important policy stock issue that is less important in debating a value resolution. Gun control, for example, may be "desirable" even if it never could be implemented. Sometimes value debaters address policy issues such as workability, but they do so only when analyzing the stock issues special to value debate. Chapter 3 introduces those issues.

In summary, academic debate is a twentieth-century extension of a longstanding educational practice. The popularity of debate led to the growth of debate organizations, tournaments, and corresponding changes in debate practices. Academic debate remains popular because it provides valuable career training and life experience.

WHY DEBATE?

Students have many pressures on their time. Classes, part-time jobs, a social life, and outside activities all erode the amount of time students might devote to another activity. Why is debate as valuable or more valuable than other student activities? A person ought to participate in debate for at least four reasons.

1. *Debate is the foundation of a free society.*

Effective government and the smooth operation of society require people who are willing and able to develop and argue their positions in a practical way. The American founders installed institutions, such as Congress, that use debate as a critical method to ensure that decision-makers examine competing positions before reaching a decision. Parliamentary procedure has emerged as a system of rules to promote fair discussion and debate in a forum of any size.

We begin to argue as children. Children quickly learn the importance of argument in settling disputes and in persuading others. As adults we rely on arguments as a crucial alternative to violence or coercion in settling disagreements. These basic, primitive arguments sometimes take the form of debates, in which "sides" divide up and people argue whether the Redskins can beat the Broncos, or if aid to the Nicaraguan Contras is desirable, or even whether a college education is worth the cost. We know, without prompting, that when we debate, we take turns; we give each side equal time; and we have to avoid letting the debate escalate into destructive conflict. Disputes do, of course, sometimes escalate. But in contexts in which people use meaningful, productive, fair debate, we can address and explore problems adequately and competing positions fully before reaching decisions.

2. *Debate is an important career skill.*

Studies on the subject are consistent: Employers are looking for people who are able to articulate ideas both orally and in writing, create arguments that employ sound reasons and evidence, and are able to refute opposing positions that are logically deficient. Among many examples of careers employing debate skills:

- Trial attorneys are debaters arguing the merits of a legal case or the guilt or innocence of a defendant.
- Public relations professionals sometimes debate the perception that their clients are not acting in the public interest.
- Lobbyists advocate adopting a bill or granting a contract by debating their positions with the positions of other lobbyists.

□ Political candidates are routinely expected to debate during the course of a campaign.

Debate also benefits students. Studies show that debate trained individuals are better students; they more efficiently discriminate between good and bad arguments; and they are effective public speakers.[9] These skills are useful not only in class but in a variety of careers as well.

3. *Debate builds courage.*

The fear of public speaking affects a significant number of Americans. When faced with standing up and speaking, many people experience physical symptoms. Some of these symptoms are more than trivial in nature.[10] Countless others are unable to argue confidently in public about issues on which they are knowledgeable.

Debate training is helpful in building courage. Preparing a debate case or position, anticipating opposing viewpoints, and publicly testing those positions in oral competition with another person entails considerable courage. Some people are naturally good at talking, or "b.s.ing." The rest of us must work at these skills. Even if we are confident, we must confront the unknown skills of our opponent and the expectations of the listener. Debate teaches us that we can never anticipate every contingency, and this constant uncertainty is both challenging and exciting. It is exciting in that debate presents an intellectual challenge that has few equals. Debate takes place in a context in which the outcome does not depend on physical skills but, rather, perseverance, preparation, and courage under fire.

4. *Debate is a life-skill.*

According to Alvin Toffler, "future shock" occurs when people confront constantly changing conditions and enormous amounts of information as they struggle to make good decisions. Daily we face so much information that our information-processing capabilities break down and, thus, more information leads to poorer rather than better decisions.[11] The information explosion is apparent in virtually every context including education. So much of the specific information we learn in classes will become quickly outdated. In a world where the amount of information is exploding, the key is probably not *what* a person learns, but whether a person learns *how* to learn.

Debate can help overcome these obstacles. Debate is a form of critical thinking, a way of gathering and interpreting information. A debater learns not to trust assertions. A debater knows how to appreciate and overcome objections to a position and appreciate that problems and issues have more than one side. These are the kinds of skills that are valuable throughout life.

SUMMARY

This chapter introduced the subject of academic debate. It defined the essential characteristics of debate, its background, and why it is a valuable activity. Appendix A, at the end of this book, presents a sample academic debate that will give you a general idea of the debate format and will be used in subsequent chapters to illustrate various concepts.

ENDNOTES

1. During 1988–89 more than 300 colleges and 2,500 college students participated in contests sanctioned by the CEDA Debate Association.
2. George Kennedy, *Classical Rhetoric and Its Christian and Secular Tradition from Ancient to Modern Times* (Chapel Hill: University of North Carolina Press, 1980), p. 38.
3. E. R. Nichols, "A Historical Sketch of Inter-Collegiate Debating: I," *Quarterly Journal of Speech* 22 (April 1936): 213–220.
4. E. R. Nichols traced the history of intercollegiate debate in three articles published in the *Quarterly Journal of Speech:* April 1936, pp. 213–220; December 1936, pp. 591–602; April 1937, pp. 259–278.
5. The popularity of debate compared to football is documented in student newspapers of the period.
6. Nichols.
7. Jack Howe, "CEDA's Objectives: Lest We Forget," in *The Philosophy and Practice of CEDA*, edited by Don Brownlee (Wingate: CEDA Debate Association, 1981), pp. 1–3.

8. NDT refers to the National Debate Tournament, which began in 1947 and is considered the national championship tournament for policy debate.

9. Bill Hill, "Intercollegiate Debate: Why Do Students Bother?" *Southern Speech Communication Journal* 48 (Fall 1982): 77–88; Irene Fraser Rothenberg and Joan Berman, "College Debate and Effective Writing," *Teaching Political Science* 8 (October 1980): 21–39.

10. James McCroskey, "Communication Competence and Performance: A Research and Pedagogical Perspective," *Communication Education* 31 (1982): 1–7.

11. Alvin Toffler, *Future Shock* (New York: Random House, 1971).

2

Speaker Duties, Issues, and Debate Formats

─────────────── **Chapter Objectives** ───────────────

☐ Understand the difference between assertions, issues, and claims.

☐ Know why argument is better understood as a process rather than a product.

☐ Differentiate between constructive, rebuttal, and cross-examination periods.

☐ Conceive the ways in which structural and situational expectations influence the kinds of statements made in debate rounds.

☐ Comprehend the three major and three minor types of debate statements.

☐ Visualize how the eight debate speeches might use different combinations of the major and minor debate statements.

Before you can participate productively in debate, you must understand the nature of the debate process: common formats for debate, kinds of debate statements, and commonly encountered debate terms.

THE DEBATE PROCESS

Academic debate involves more than informal arguments about common interests or problems. We typically disagree with each other about subjects such as sports, politics, and movies. We do not structure these disagreements but instead allow the discussion to take any course it may. This is different from the arguing behavior in academic debate. These debates are structured specifically and apply more settled argument methods. Debates differ from informal arguing in the importance placed in debate on using *claims* and *issues* rather than just relying on *assertions*. The differences between assertions, claims, and issues are important in visualizing how debate is different from the unstructured arguing we do every day.

Aristotle observed that any argument has two parts: making a statement and then proving it.[1] Common sense tells us that making an assertion and making a claim are different. Figure 2.1 identifies the relationship between assertions, claims, and issues.

Assertions

Assertions are statements presented without proof. The statement "The Los Angeles Dodgers are the best team in baseball" is an example of an assertion. Asserting is the least complicated arguing form because arguers do not present proof. Assertions may have underlying proof, but the listener may not understand or appreciate the missing proofs and may not accept the validity of the assertion.

Listeners use a variety of methods to evaluate assertions. They consider, among others, the perceived logic of the assertion, their

Figure 2.1   The Relationship of Assertions, Claims, and Issues

Least Complex ⟵⟶ Most Complex
Assertions > > > > > > > > > >Claims > > > > > > > > > > > > Issues

previous beliefs about the subject of the assertion, or their judgment about the believability of the speaker.[2] Although debaters (or arguers in any context) begin with assertions, debates rarely focus on them because the debate process influences the debater to transform assertions into claims and issues. Our arguing experiences confirm the obvious notion that conversations and arguments stagnate when we answer assertions with other assertions. This is why proof must be offered to turn assertions into claims.

Claims

Claims are statements advanced with proof. "The Los Angeles Dodgers are the best team in baseball because they won the World Series" is an example of a claim. A claim does not necessarily have logical or persuasive evidence; it merely reveals the underlying evidence the arguer uses to support the advocated position. A claim is more complex than an assertion because the listener must evaluate, and possibly disagree with, both the premise and the underlying evidence contained in the claim statement, increasing the potential for rejection or misunderstanding.

Academic debate is a process primarily concerned with presenting and testing claims. Debaters can test and measure the strength of proof through the debate process. As debaters test and create issues, they are also combining those claims into substantial patterns that we identify as issues.

Issues

Issues are general areas of dispute consisting of claims and assertions grouped around a particular theme or idea. An issue might be, as examples, "defense policy" or "the defensibility of legalized abortion." Arguers advance a variety of claims and assertions while discussing any particular issue. When we combine many issues, a debate happens.

The Interconnection

Debate is, of course, more than just a collection of assertions, claims, and issues. It is a *process* involving the testing and comparing of claims and issues by arguers.[3] This process is simultaneously predictable and unpredictable. It is unpredictable in the sense that every debate is unique, because arguers never advance and respond to assertions, issues, and claims in the same way.

On the other hand, the degree of predictability created by the expectations of specific debate speeches gives the debater greater freedom in creating and presenting assertions and claims without having to worry that the other arguer may be using some completely different arguing structure.

To illustrate the definition we have advanced, consider this example. If your friend says that "the Los Angeles Dodgers are the best team in baseball," and you respond, "No, the New York Mets are the best team in baseball," you have traded assertions but have not yet debated. Once you and your friend substantiate the assertions with proof, you are making claims: "The Los Angeles Dodgers are the best team in baseball because they won the World Series" or, "The New York Mets are the best team because they won the most games in the regular season." When you and your friend disagree about the standard that should be used in determining which team is best, you have moved to discussing an issue.

In summary, two types of debate statements—assertions and claims—are used to create issues, or areas of dispute. Assertions are statements without evidence. Claims are assertions backed with proof. Issues are problem areas discussed in a debate and consist of assertions and claims about the problem area. Academic debate tries to teach students how to transform assertions into claims, to identify key issues, and to create criteria that can be used to assess competing claims.

TYPES OF DEBATE SPEECHES

Debate is structured oral argument with specific time limits and audience expectations about the content and form of the speeches. The three types of debate speeches are: constructives, rebuttals, and cross-examination periods. The function of each of these types of speeches is clear from their names. Constructive speeches create issues by introducing assertions and claims. Rebuttal speeches refute or rebut opposing assertions, claims, and issues. Cross-examination periods allow debaters to test the opponents understanding of their positions. Table 2.1 summarizes the relationship of these three speech types.

The theory and practice of debate create certain expectations, or "duties," for each speech. Although the content of the speech depends on the particular claims and issues, the structure of the debate context and the expectations of the listeners lend a certain degree of predictability to the speeches. The order of speeches in debates using the cross-examination format is:

First affirmative constructive
Cross-examination by negative
First negative constructive
Cross-examination by affirmative
Second affirmative constructive
Cross-examination by negative
Second negative constructive
Cross-examination by affirmative
First negative rebuttal
First affirmative rebuttal
Second negative rebuttal
Second affirmative rebuttal

Table 2.1 Three Types of Debate Speeches

Speech	General Purpose in the Debate
Constructives	Used to initiate assertions, claims, and issues; and to begin to refute opposing statements
Rebuttals	Used to refute opposing assertions, claims, and issues; and rebuild statements favorable to arguers' positions
Cross-Examination	Used to clarify ambiguous or misleading statements by opponents; reiterate or clarify arguers' positions; and set up subsequent positions

Constructive Speeches

Constructive speeches introduce the issues the debaters will contest in the debate. Debaters use the constructive speeches to build the affirmative and negative "cases" on the resolution. A case is simply *the position or stance the debater takes in arguing for or against the resolution.* Constructive speeches also occur at the point at which debaters attempt to refute the opposing case.

Debaters introduce assertions, claims, and issues in the constructive speeches. They present claims as support for their positions on the issues. You might refer to the sample debate, Appendix A, for some examples; notice how the debaters use the constructives to set up their case by identifying and justifying issues they believe are important.

Rebuttals

Debaters use rebuttal speeches to attack and defend issues already introduced during the constructive speeches. The function of rebuttal speeches is to narrow and focus the debate on particular issues that might persuade the judge to consider one side's case superior to the opposing case. Rebuttal speeches build upon arguments and issues presented in the constructive speeches, particularly those issues the opponents attack. The speakers seek to rebuild attacked arguments and issues and refute opposing arguments and issues, and to summarize reasons why the judge should accept their position.

After both sides have set up their statements and issues in the constructive speeches, they may not present new issues in rebuttals. The purpose of the rebuttal is to respond to statements the opponent has made and to reinforce statements favorable to the arguers' position.

Cross-Examination

During the four cross-examination periods in the debate round, each participant individually asks and answers questions. There are no limits on the assertions, claims, or issues a questioner may ask about, although traditionally the respondent (the person answering the questions) is expected to respond to issues and claims already presented. Listeners expect both the questioner and the respondent to be concise, friendly, and open during the cross-examination process.

Debate cross-examination is very different from the aggressive behavior found in television trials. Debate cross-examination sets up future positions rather than resolve those issues during the cross-examination period. Positions are set up in the sense that the questioner or the respondent uses the questions and answers to attack or defend issues in future speeches.

Each speaker on a two-person debate team presents a constructive speech, which initiates arguments; gives a rebuttal speech, which refutes opposing arguments and rebuilds initial positions; and asks and answers questions during a cross-examination period. A hypothetical example may help to differentiate these speech types. Let us say we are debating the topic: Resolved: that Saul Bellow is the greatest contemporary novelist. Table 2.2 delineates each of these speech types and functions in relation to this example.

ASSERTIONS AND CLAIMS IN DEBATE ROUNDS

How do you know what kinds of assertions and claims to make in a debate round? That is a complicated question. Unlike a play or a professional wrestling match, debate does not follow a script. Debate is exciting because speakers are free to make whatever assertions and claims they want and debaters cannot anticipate opposing assertions and claims with total confidence. Although the debater does not know what the arguments may be, two guidelines can be used to predict how a debate will unfold: (1) structural limitations, and (2) situational expectations.

Structural Limitations

The structure and organization of a debate play a big part in shaping the issues that can be debated. All debates have time limits and a specific speaking order for the debaters. The debate structure gives

Table 2.2   The Debate Speeches and a Hypothetical Debate

Speech Type	Example	Function
Constructive (presents assertions, claims, and issues related to topic)	"Bellow has an authentic and moving style."	Assertion
	"Bellow has received several prizes for his writing, which show his stature."	Claim
	"Style is the most important determinant of the quality of a novelist."	Issue
Cross-Examination (involves questions and answers seeking to clarify and probe statements presented in the debate)	"What novel shows that Bellow is a great writer?"	Question
	"*Herzog,* for one."	Answer
Rebuttal (refutes opposing positions and rebuilds issues favorable to the debater)	"Bellow is not as popular as Stephen King."	Refutation
	"Popularity is not as good a measure as writing quality."	Rebuilding

each speaker a limited amount of speaking time, which influences the number of claims supported by evidence that the speaker can present. The debate structure, through alternating speeches, creates the expectation that the speaker will attempt to clash or disagree with opposing positions. In debate tournaments a debater alternates debating the affirmative and negative sides, requiring that the speaker prepare for a wide variety of issues and cases potentially to be presented by opposing teams.

Situational Expectations

Situational expectations, on the other hand, are expectations derived from the practice of competitive debate. The debate situation consists of many customs and notions unique to the communicative environment of a competitive debate. One important situational idea in a debate is the use of the legal system as a debate model. Borrowed legal terms, such as presumption and the burden of proof, help arguers determine the nature of the issues in the debate. The idea of stock issues (discussed shortly) is derived from a situational expectation regarding the types of proof a listener relies upon in accepting an assertion or claim.

People sometimes describe debate as a game and, as anyone knows, the rules of any game dictate the appropriate strategy. If you're broke and losing at *Monopoly*, it makes no sense for you to get out of jail until someone lands on your hotel on Illinois Avenue! We will discuss the gaming characteristics of debate in later chapters, so it will suffice to say at this point that the debate context creates a unique and specialized form of communication. Every form of debate has situational constraints that influence the content of the debate. Candidates, for example, negotiate political debate formats to suit media expectations and their campaign goals alike.[4]

Situational expectations are those debate elements that differentiate a given round from other debate rounds. Judges have different perceptions of debate, politics, and so forth. Debaters must adapt their arguments to these different listeners.

Other situational elements that should be considered include the strength of the opposing team, the opponent's responses, and the strategy and tactics used in the round. Figure 2.2 depicts the structural and situational expectations of a debate round.

Figure 2.2   Structural and Situational Expectations of a Debate Round

Structural Expectations	Situational Expectations
· Time Limits	· Listener Expectations
· Alternating Speeches	· Demands of the Topic
· Imposed Speaker Burdens	· Need for Clarity

Assertions, Claims, Issues in the Debate

Structural and situational expectations combine to encourage arguers to employ various kinds of assertions and claims. These assertions and claims create the unique "fingerprint" of academic debate. All debate forums emphasize particular types of statements directed toward particular audiences. Debaters must adapt to the situational and structural expectations of the debate round in the same way that lawyers, public relations officers, and legislators select specific and appropriate assertions and claims for the audiences they wish to persuade. All debate speeches have special responsibilities in meeting both the situational and the structural expectations of the debate.

Academic debaters should use their constructive speeches to build arguments. They should use their rebuttal speeches to defend and extend arguments presented during the constructives. Arguers use the cross-examination periods to clarify and expose weaknesses in arguments. We will show later that listeners expect debaters to conform to a certain manner of presenting negative and affirmative statements. Debaters also must readily adjust to the unique elements of the particular debate round. They should prepare to use a variety of different arguments to respond to opponents and meet the desires of their judges.

Types of Assertions and Claims

Claims and assertions are the essential building blocks of the debate. Debaters weave various assertions and claims together to discover issues that will successfully establish their side of the resolution. Table 2.3 lists the common kinds of debate assertions and claims.

Any debate speech will combine many of these kinds of argument, although some speeches contain more of some and less of others. The three major arguing forms are: initiating, signifying, and refuting. These represent the most common actions of debaters. To supplement these arguing forms, debaters also question, clarify, and refocus arguments. Although commonplace, these latter three arguing forms are less critical to the eventual outcome of the debate.

Table 2.3   Types of Debate Assertions and Claims

Major Types	Examples
Initiating	"US military security is threatened by conflict."[5]
Signifying	"The UN is the best thing that you've got, and it's the only empirical example of solving for peace."[6]
Refuting	"Venting is not the same thing as peacekeeping. So if we win that they contribute to the conflict off of venting, that means that we still win, even if he wins his peacekeeping stuff."[7]

Minor Types	Examples
Questioning	"Why is my author inappropriate when he says the words UN in his piece of evidence and concludes that on balance, it's beneficial to the US?"[8]
Clarifying	"They contradicted this definition. Now that means his definition is different from mine, but I'm arguing that that highlights that there is no definite definition of what is and what is not the UN."[9]
Refocusing	"She grants the criteria of military security, so it is her burden to prove that that evidence addresses that."[10]

Initiating

Initiating means introducing an assertion, claim, or issue into the debate round. This usually takes place during the constructive speeches rather than the rebuttals because structural constraints limit rebuttal speeches to considering issues already presented in the debate: There should be no new issues in rebuttals. The first affirmative, as contrasted with the other constructives, most frequently initiates assertions and claims in the debate.

The initiating statement in Table 2.3, "US military security is threatened by conflict," introduces an issue into the debate. At this point, it is an assertion. Once arguers provide proof or evidence, the initiating statement becomes a claim. Initiating statements that are clearly presented and labeled as such provide the listener with an unambiguous understanding of the issue in question.

Signifying

Signifying means giving importance to an assertion, a claim, or an issue. Debaters and listeners do not view every statement in a debate as equally important. One of the roles of a debater is to tell the listener what statements should be considered important and how those statements compare with the ones the other debaters believe are important. Debaters must signify assertions, claims, and issues so the listener will know how to weigh them when considering all the issues in the debate. A debater may signify an argument as being anywhere from "insignificant" to "absolutely crucial" in the context of the debate. In fact, the signification of an argument may itself become an argument. For example:

Crenshaw: "I would argue first of all, that venting is not the same thing as peacekeeping. So if we win that they contribute to the conflict off of venting, that means that we still win, even if he wins his peacekeeping stuff."[11]

Benson: "She says . . . venting does not equal peacekeeping. Of course, it stops wars, and I indicate that that is good in and of itself. And if . . . their national security criterion is number one, then that would . . . make it relevant to the round."[12]

Arguers present some statements to set up future arguments or to occupy the attention of an opposing arguer. Such statements comprise a strategy that might lead an opponent to spend a disproportionate amount of time on an insignificant issue. Other statements are highly important to a position, and the arguer may spend much energy signifying them in hopes of creating an unassailable position in the debate round.

Refuting

In refuting, the assertions and claims presented are designed to overcome opposing arguments. This is the kind of claim most often associated with debate ("yes it is . . . no it isn't"). The audience expects debaters to refute opposing assertions and claims. Refutation requires the debater to understand opposing assertions and claims and show why they are weak. Refutation can be direct: "My opponent says black; I say white." They also can be indirect: "My opponent says black; I say gray."

Questioning

Questioning involves probing the logic or evidence presented by an opposing arguer. The arguer is playing "devil's advocate" to push the opposing side to more completely defend its position or to present additional support for a claim. Debaters often perceive the need to make the opposing side expose more evidence and positions in order to know what in the opposing position to attack.

Debaters who use questioning as a strategy during a constructive speech may ask for specifics. For example: "My opponent suggests that Republican policies have put more people to work. I would like my opponent to tell us exactly how many people are working because of Republican policies." Such questioning produces more information for the debaters as well as for the judge.

Clarifying

Arguers use clarifying to interpret ambiguous or misunderstood assertions or claims. Because language is inherently imprecise, we cannot always make ourselves completely understandable. In addition, distortions caused by the oral presentation of arguments create the ongoing need to clarify arguments and claims.

Clarification may be needed at several junctions in a debate. Occasionally, global clarifications may be needed: "Our position in today's debate is not, as the affirmative suggests, denigrating working mothers. We are suggesting that latchkey children often are not given the care and attention they deserve." On other occasions, specific clarifications may be needed: "The Brown evidence stated that there are no significant psychological differences between children of homemakers and those of working mothers."

Refocusing

In refocusing, the arguer attempts to shift attention in the debate away from one issue toward another. As noted earlier, not every issue has equal importance in a debate. Debaters face the need to attempt to influence the judge's perception of which issues are important. The debater must attempt to deflect attention away from an issue or claim that would hurt his or her case in the eyes of the judge toward a more favorable issue. This is done through *issue comparison*, in which the debater gives ground on an opponent's position, hoping to make that issue seem less significant compared to a competing position: "Although it is true that the affirmative has shown that individuals lose personal privacy because of drug testing, this is more than outweighed by the lives and productivity society saves with unannounced drug tests."

Types of Claims in the Context of Various Speeches

Which of the kinds of speeches feature which kinds of claims and assertions? We cannot answer that question with complete certainty. As noted before, debates are not entirely predictable. But, the structural and situational expectations of debates do suggest that some speakers are more likely to make certain kinds of claims.

The first affirmative constructive speech primarily *initiates* issues. This is the main function of this speech. The speaker introduces the affirmative's issues into the debate. As a lesser function, the speaker also attempts to *signify* issues by anticipating possible lines of negative attack.

The first affirmative might initiate the following argument: "America has better athletes than the Soviet Union." In a value debate, this affirmative also would have to initiate a definition of terms such as "better," and then provide a set of criteria for measuring athletic quality.

The first negative constructive speech has two primary functions: *refuting* and *initiating*. This speaker begins the process of responding to and tearing down the affirmative issues introduced by the first affirmative. The speaker not only refutes but also initiates arguments that the negative will ultimately rely upon to win the debate. The first negative also *questions* affirmative assertions and claims and begins to *signify* why negative issues are more important than affirmative issues.

The second affirmative constructive primarily *initiates*, *clarifies*, *refutes* and *signifies*, while occasionally *questioning* and *refocusing*. Strategically, the second affirmative is trying to rebuild the affirmative case after the initial attacks of the first negative. The speaker initiates additional affirmative claims, assertions, and evidence and clarifies possible misunderstandings of the affirmative arguments. He or she refutes positions introduced by the first negative and begins to signify the importance of some of the issues in the debate.

The second negative constructive *initiates*, *refocuses*, and *signifies*. Although the speaker may use the other argument types, this speech mainly attempts to initiate issues that will be more important than the affirmative case ("compound attacks") and refocus the debate on those issues and to signify issues that the negative will use to win the debate.

All rebuttals *refute*, *refocus*, *signify*, *clarify*, and *question*. All rebuttals have the same basic purpose: to refute opposing claims, refocus the debate on the issues signified as most favorable to the arguer, and clarify any issues that might be muddled or misunderstood.

The crux of the debate, as you will notice, shifts from mostly initiating claims in the constructives toward refuting and refocusing issues in the rebuttals. The debate funnels down the number of issues initiated in constructives to a smaller number of issues that debaters consider important in rebuttals. Each debate differs in the precise combination of initiating, signifying, refuting, clarifying, questioning, and refocusing.

PRESUMPTION AND THE BURDEN OF PROOF

Stock issues are traditional or expected topics that an audience uses to evaluate arguments.[13] Stock issues are a well-accepted premise of the legal system, dating back to ancient times. In a legal case, a prosecutor or plaintiff must prove certain elements of his or her case, such as whether someone committed a crime, to overcome a presumption of innocence. Presumption is important to debate as the way of visualizing the importance of an audience to the debate process.

Even without defining presumption, most people are familiar with the term. Our legal system presumes that a person is innocent until proven guilty. Our Judeo-Christian tradition presumes that God exists. Presumptions are *preconceived beliefs of an audience*. In the absence of contrary assertions or claims, an audience will likely hold to a presumed belief until an arguer makes a convincing contrary case. All audiences hold presumptions of differing strengths about various ideas. We hold some presumptions very strongly, and these would be difficult to overcome no matter how strong an opposing claim might be. We hold other presumptions more casually; these are easier to overcome.

In formulating assertions and claims, an arguer must consider audience-held presumptions. Although one of the situational constraints of a debate round suggests that a judge should remain neutral on the subject matter of the debate,[14] the judge undoubtedly has presumptions regarding the subject matter as well as the nature of debate itself, which the debater must consider in formulating a winning strategy.

SUMMARY

In this chapter we differentiated the three kinds of debate statements—assertions, claims, and issues—noting that assertions are common to arguing, and the debate process emphasizes the importance of claims and issues. Situational and structural factors influence which kinds of debate statements are selected. The six kinds of debate statements common to value debate are initiating, signifying, refuting, questioning, clarifying, and refocusing. Finally we introduced the important concepts of stock issues—presumption and the burden of proof.

ENDNOTES

1. See Aristotle, *Rhetoric*, translated by W. Rhys Roberts (New York: Modern Library, 1954). See also Aristotle, *"Topics,"* translated by W. A. Picard Cambridge and edited by W. D. Ross, in *The Works of Aristotle Translated into English* (Oxford: Clarendon Press, 1924).

2. This is, of course, similar to Aristotle's three forms of proof: ethos, pathos, and logos.

3. See Douglas Ehninger and Wayne Brockriede, *Decision by Debate* (New York: Harper and Row, 1978); Daniel J. O'Keefe, "Two Concepts of Argument," *Journal of the American Forensic Assocation* 13 (1976): 121–128; and Wayne Brockriede, "Characteristics of Arguments and Arguing, *Journal of the American Forensic Association* 13 (1976): 129–132.

4. See Kathleen Jamieson, *Eloquence in an Electronic Age* (New York: Oxford, 1988) and *Packaging the Presidency* (New York: Oxford, 1984).

5. Appendix A, Crenshaw, p. 200.

6. Appendix A, Benson, p. 215.

7. Appendix A, Crenshaw, p. 224.

8. Appendix A, McGinnis, p. 221.

9. Appendix A, McGinnis, p. 221.

10. Appendix A, Crenshaw, p. 224.

11. Appendix A, Crenshaw, p. 224.

12. Appendix A, Benson, p. 226.

13. See the discussion of stock issues in the next chapter.

14. Walter Ulrich, "Debate as Dialectic: A Defense of the Tabula Rasa Approach to Judging," *Journal of the American Forensic Association* 26 (1984): 89–93.

3

Values, Propositions, and Stock Issues

Chapter Objectives

☐ Gain an understanding of the role that values play in argument.

☐ Learn about debate propositions.

☐ Learn to identify the stock issues in value debate.

☐ Develop the ability to apply stock issues in a debate round.

At this point in our discussion of debate, you might begin to compare debate to building a house. The previous chapters have provided you with a basic understanding of the architecture of debate and with some of the tools needed to present debate assertions and claims. In this chapter we describe how you can use the architecture and the tools of debate to argue about values in academic debate.

THE ROLE OF VALUES IN ARGUMENTATION AND DEBATE

Debates should not consist of random statements bandied back and forth. Rather, debate should exhibit a clash of well-developed issues that the arguers hope will be persuasive to the listener. To persuade an audience of listeners, the arguer will have to gain an understanding of how the audience views and perceives the world. Many successful arguers attempt to discover their audience's preferences before they construct their messages. For example, politicians often alter their speeches to better conform to the beliefs and expectations of their particular audiences; lawyers assess the backgrounds of juries before they present their cases; advertisers determine consumer desires and wants before they construct commercials; job applicants attempt to discover the backgrounds and beliefs of employment interviewers.

What Is a Value?

As a debater, you share the situational expectations faced by politicians, lawyers, advertisers, and job applicants. You will have to adjust your assertions and claims to the perceptions and preferences of your particular audience. These perceptions and preferences constitute the values about which humans argue. Milton Rokeach, a well-known value theorist, has defined values as the "core conceptions of the desirable within every individual and society. They serve as standards or criteria to guide not only action but also judgment, choice, attitude, evaluation, argument, exhortation, rationalization, and one might add, attribution of causality."[1] Individuals' core conceptions of the desirable include preferences for money, success, happiness, freedom, fair play, baseball, families, and so on.

We value some things more than others, and often our values conflict. You may value an education but are tired of poverty and consider leaving school for a year to earn money. Or you and a friend are tempted to see a movie on Tuesday night rather than prepare for a mid-term. You can't attend the movie and also study. You can't finish your degree and also work full time.

When you talk and argue with others about problems like these, you are arguing about values. When values conflict, debate is often necessary to order our core conceptions of the desirable. Often the question becomes: Which value (education or money) is more important now? Or: Is the risk of a lower grade worth an evening of relaxation?

Rokeach has provided an extensive and a well-developed classification of values that humans hold. He has discovered that humans have value preferences that tend to cluster into two categories: terminal and instrumental. "Terminal values are those values which refer to end-states or the goals of human existence."[2] According to Rokeach, Americans report world peace, comfort, and happiness as examples of terminal values. Values such as these are important in themselves. In the debate between Macalester and Florida State (see Appendix A), national security was the terminal value supported by Florida State. In addition, both teams accepted the terminal values of peace and conflict reduction.

"Instrumental values," according to Rokeach, "are the preferred modes of behavior or action which are necessary to achieve terminal values."[3] Instrumental values are important because they help humans achieve terminal values. Rokeach has found that Americans report courage, helpfulness, and self-control among the many instrumental values they prefer. In the sample debate, the debaters asked the judges to assess the worth of the United Nations as a peacemaking organization. The debaters treated the United Nations as an instrumental value, or as a method of achieving the terminal values of world peace and conflict reduction.

Value debate, and ultimately all debate, concerns core conceptions of what is desirable. Debate occurs when people perceive differences in values. In informal argument we often agree on what ideas or things are desirable but we disagree about their order of preference or definition. All responsible people highly value life but may have radically different perceptions about when life begins or about the value of abortion. Such disagreement provokes discussion and exhortation.

As we mentioned in chapter 1, informal discussions and arguments are rarely structured or confined by time limits. Academic debate is structured to accentuate and provoke clash between and among values. One team must support the debate, and the other must attack the propositions.

In our experience, however, few academic debates focus on the desirability of terminal values; rather, academic debates tend to feature arguing about instrumental values. In the Macalester-Florida State debate, the terminal value of world peace was not in question. Both teams agreed that world peace was an important terminal value. The question raised in the debate concerned the ability of the United Nations to achieve, and to be a vehicle for, peace. In many, if not most, of your debates, you will not debate about the desirability of terminal values. Instead, you will find that you will debate about the means to achieve terminal values, or the prioritization of terminal values in a particular circumstance.

How Do We Define Values That We Debate?

Scholars who have studied values and argumentation have discovered that terminal or core values are highly resistant to change. As Matlon has noted, "Core values do not readily change," core values can be shifted and moved "in positions of dominance along a value hierarchy."[4] Accordingly, a value hierarchy is an organization of "values enabling us to choose between alternative goals and actions, and enabling us to resolve conflict."[5]

There are both individual and group hierarchies. You may choose to postpone your quest for wealth in order to acquire a good education. You still may hold a terminal value favoring comfort and wealth, but your belief in the value of an education may be more important and significant for the next four years. There are also societal value hierarchies. We may choose to spend more money on defense than on education. We may believe in both as important values, but because we must operate with a limited budget, we must choose to emphasize one at the expense of the other. Argumentation and debate serve the function of changing, modifying, or reinforcing the audience's value hierarchy. For example, consider the following terminal values:

freedom—equality

peace—national security

pleasure—mature love

sense of accomplishment—family security

wisdom—an exciting life

As you consider these pairs of terminal values, you can see that in given situations they may be mutually exclusive. Debate propositions often illustrate clashes between terminal values. In the past three years, CEDA resolutions have structured clash around the following terminal values: Should we mandate drug tests (to guarantee public safety), or should we disallow drug testing (to prevent violations of privacy)? Should we aid the Contras to preserve national security from the threat of Marxism, or should we withdraw support and recognize the choice made by the citizens of Nicaragua?

Value hierarchies then become the focus of discussion and debate. Advocates attempt to persuade an audience to adopt the advocate's hierarchy of values. Advocates can present many assertions and claims to achieve such a persuasive effect. For example, an advocate may agree that environmental protection is an important terminal value but might suggest that, given high unemployment rates, economic development (as a terminal value) is a more important consideration in the present circumstance. Or an advocate may agree that equality is a valid terminal value but may argue that because blacks have experienced two centuries of discrimination, they should receive preferred treatment in the job market. As another example, an advocate might agree that preservation of life is important and that abortion is wrong but might argue that, given limited resources, policy-makers should focus money, energy, and efforts on sex education rather than on creating legal restrictions on abortion. In each of the cases discussed, the advocate may agree with both of the terminal values in question but might rank one higher, given the circumstances.

What Assertions and Claims Support a Value Hierarchy?

In most debates the advocates present a preferred value hierarchy, compare it to the existing state of affairs, and then attack the value hierarchy of an opponent. Examination of the sample debate and other controversies reveals that debaters can use many assertions and claims to defend preferred value hierarchies. The examination also might show that most argument revolves around instrumental rather than terminal values. Table 3.1 illustrates some of the values in conflict in the Florida State-Macalester debate. As you can tell, neither team questioned the desirability of the terminal values of peace and national security but chose to disagree about the capacity of the United Nations to achieve both peace and national security.

Debaters use some recurring issues to evaluate where values fit on hierarchies. Among the most important are claims using significance, cause-effect, utility, and principle.

1. *Significance.*

An advocate may attempt to argue that there is a compelling need to adopt the advocate's value hierarchy. Florida State—the affirmative in the sample debate—claimed that the United Nations had failed to solve many of the conflicts in the world. Given that both teams and the audience apparently agreed that resolution of conflict is a desirable goal, this claim helped to validate the importance of the affirmative's value hierarchy.

2. *Cause-effect.*

On occasion an advocate may make use of cause-effect argumentation to gain acceptance of a preferred value hierarchy. Cause-effect claims identify the reason for a given effect. For example, an advocate might identify poverty as a cause of crime. If this position is accepted, the advocate might suggest that poverty reduction programs could be the most effective means (or terminal value) of

Table 3.1   Value Hierarchies of Florida State and Macalester in Sample Debate

Florida State	Macalester
Terminal values	Terminal values
1. Peace	1. Peace
2. National security	2. World peace
Instrumental values	Instrumental values
1. Unilateral action by United States	1. United Nations

reducing crime. In the sample debate, the affirmative claimed that the United Nations had actually caused conflict in the world. In response, the negative claimed that the United Nations had served to contain and reduce violence in the world. If a critic were to accept the negative's position on causality, the United Nations would be placed high on the agenda of effective peacekeeping institutions. If, on the other hand, the critic were to accept the affirmative's claim of causality, the United Nations would be removed from an agenda of effective peacekeeping institutions.

3. *Utility.*

An advocate might assert that an issue should be evaluated on the basis of a cost-benefit analysis. The advocate might simply assess the financial consequences of a given policy or value. An advocate might agree that poverty is an important cause of crime but disagree that poverty programs work to reduce crimes. This advocate might assert that severe criminal penalties appear to reduce the crime rate and that, until poverty programs are improved, imposition of severe criminal penalties should be at the top of a value hierarchy of crime prevention and reduction.

In the debate between Florida State and Macalester, the advocates did assess the effectiveness of the United Nations as a peacekeeping institution. The advocates debated the question: Has the United Nations served the cause of peace? After hearing the negative and the affirmative assertions and claims on the issue, the judges had to answer this question based upon the criterion of utility.

4. *Principle.*

An advocate might claim that we should hold to a certain value or policy because "it is right." That is, an advocate might assert that society should endure some costs to guarantee certain principles. An advocate could claim that some guilty criminals are released because police are forced to acquire search warrants, read potential defendants their rights, and so forth, and suggest that society should bear this cost because even guilty individuals have rights. Such a claim places the defendant's rights at the top of a value hierarchy even though some guilty criminals might be released.

In the debate between Florida State and Macalester, the negative asked that the judges assess the United Nations on the basis of realistic criteria. By rereading the second negative issues and claims, you will see that he urged the judges not to expect the United Nations to solve all the conflicts in the world. As such, the principle of the United Nations was argued to be important in its own right.

These and other arguments can help an advocate persuade an audience to accept a preferred value hierarchy. Thus, one of the first steps you will want to take, when faced with a debate resolution, is to identify the terminal values in question and then to create issues, assertions, and claims that will help you construct a preferred value hierarchy.

To recap—we have defined values as "core conceptions of the desirable." We have adopted Rokeach's classification of values into terminal (end-goals) and instrumental (the means to achieve an end-goal). We have seen that most debate tends to focus on the organization of values along a hierarchy and that an arguer can present certain issues, assertions, and claims to help persuade an audience to prefer the arguer's value hierarchy.

DEBATE PROPOSITIONS

As discussed in chapters 1 and 2, modern academic debate is much more structured than informal argument. The debate proposition, or the debate resolution, defines the ground of the debate. In informal argument, an advocate may choose to avoid issues or follow tangents; in academic debate, the debate proposition limits such choices. The debate proposition serves to define the nature and the course of a debate.

Several kinds of propositions lead debaters to present and develop various kinds of issues. Some propositions lead advocates to discuss questions of utility; others prompt discussion of cause-effect; still others evoke statements about principle. In the end, all debate propositions and all issues, claims, and assertions potentially or actually concern values.[6] The debater's goal is to transform the debate proposition into a preferred value hierarchy and then to persuade a judge to accept that hierarchy.

A debate proposition is a statement that an advocate must either defend, if on the affirmative, or reject, if on the negative. Framers word debate propositions to provoke disagreement and debate. In the debate tradition, debaters have encountered three general types of resolutions: those of fact, policy (action), and value. We believe that all debate is ultimately about values and that debaters might consider questions of fact, value, and policy in almost any debate context. Debate propositions attempt to structurally define the nature of a debate round. But, given the nature of modern debate and debate propositions, the traditional distinctions between propositions of fact, policy, and value have virtually disappeared. We discuss the three kinds of debate resolutions here to highlight how they feature different questions, problems, and statements.

1. *Propositions of fact call for debaters to argue about the nature of reality.*

In the sample debate, the debaters discussed several questions of fact. For example, the affirmative argued that the UN fueled conflict in the Middle East; the negative disagreed. The debaters considered many other issues, but questions of fact were significant in the debate outcome.

Even when considering resolutions of fact, advocates cannot avoid questions of value. We answer questions of fact with standards derived from our values. Recall that Macalester argued that we should not expect the United Nations to solve all the problems of the world. As such, this value criterion helped the judges to assess the effectiveness of the United Nations as a peacekeeping organization. We often debate other propositions of fact. As examples:

Resolved: that racism has increased in the last twenty years.

Resolved: that the University of Southern California has won more Rose Bowls than the University of California at Los Angeles.

Resolved: that Mike does and David does not read the *Sporting News*.

Propositions of facts are limited to issues and questions about the nature of reality. Advocates are not required to defend a policy or an action. Even if racism is proven to have increased, the affirmative would not have to defend a policy (such as affirmative action) to deal with racism. Even if it is proven that USC has won more Rose Bowls than UCLA, the affirmative would not have to defend a policy (such as having UCLA drop out of the PAC 10). Even if the affirmative proves that David does not read the *Sporting News*, the affirmative is not obligated to argue that David should read the *Sporting News*.

2.   *Propositions of policy call for specific courses of action or policy.*

The resolution debated by Macalester and Florida State was also a policy resolution. The resolution called for the affirmative to defend US withdrawal from the United Nations. Such an action obviously would be a policy. Before such an action could be taken, advocates would have to prove that membership in the United Nations has failed to serve the interests of the United States or the world. The affirmative argued that membership in the United Nations had failed to serve the interests of the United States because the United Nations had not produced peace. This was a factual claim that led the debaters to debate about the UN's effectiveness in reducing tension. Policy resolutions often lead to disagreements about facts and values.

Some other examples might help to illustrate policy resolutions:

Resolved: that the federal government should enact significant affirmative action programs to reduce racism in America.

Resolved: that UCLA should hire a new football coach.

Resolved: that David should subscribe to and read the *Sporting News*.

Unlike resolutions of fact, policy resolutions do provide for the affirmative to defend a specific course of action. Policy resolutions contain the word "should" and also tend to identify an agent of action. Questions of value and fact come into play during debates about policy, but the negative might choose to argue only about the affirmative's plan of action.

3.   *Propositions of value assess the nature of the world, a proposed policy, or any other event or object of human concern.*

As we have mentioned several times, all debate in some way is about values. Sometimes a proposition focuses debate on a plan of action. Other propositions feature questions about the nature of facts. Finally, in the case of value propositions, some propositions feature assessments of worth. Value propositions call for explicit and direct testing of core preferences and beliefs.

The debate between Macalester and Florida State tested a belief that the United Nations is a worthwhile peacekeeping body. The debaters used some "value standards" to assess the United Nations' worth. The advocates, in the criteria section of the first affirmative and in the observation section of the second negative, offered criteria that the critics could use to make that judgment.

Consider some other examples of value resolutions:

Resolved: that America has failed to provide meaningful opportunities for equal rights for racial minorities.

Resolved: that USC has a better football team than UCLA.

Resolved: that baseball is superior to football as a sport.

Value resolutions tend to feature evaluative terms. Note the words "better" and "stronger" in the resolutions above. Unlike policies of fact and policy, resolutions of value demand that the advocates debate questions of worth and judgment. Again, debaters cannot avoid questions of fact and policy. An advocate supporting a proposition saying that America has failed to guarantee civil rights for blacks would have to show the specific areas in which America has failed to provide civil rights. In addition, the negative might demand that the affirmative show that, given the current climate of opinion, it is possible to better guarantee civil rights for blacks.

In summary, then, debate propositions shape the direction and focus of a debate. The three traditional kinds of propositions are those of fact, policy, and value. Each proposition tends to direct debaters to consider different dimensions of a value problem. Regardless of the proposition, all debate concerns values.

THE ROLE OF STOCK ISSUES

Ancient Greek and Roman rhetoricians first identified the concept of stock issues. As they argued in court and in legislative assemblies, they noticed that many disputes raised the same questions or issues regardless of the facts. These rhetoricians recognized that the context determined the kinds of issues that advocates had to address. Before the factual questions could be answered, the arguers had to agree on the "status" or nature of the dispute so they would consider the appropriate issues to settle the dispute.

Using the example of a murder case as a capital crime, the accusers and defenders knew that they had to address four stock issues in either convicting or vindicating the accused. First, the defendant might object to the proceedings, arguing that the court had no jurisdiction over the crime. Second, the defendant could argue that the act was done in self-defense and therefore was not murder (here, the court considered the question of definition of the crime of murder). Third, advocates could consider the quality of the charge; the defendant might plead guilty to manslaughter. Finally, the advocates might suggest that the defendant did not have a motive to murder.

These stock issues provided the litigants a clear understanding of the elements of the dispute that would ultimately determine its outcome. If the prosecutor was unsuccessful in proving each of these issues, the accused likely would be released. This burden of proof, as noted in chapter 2, became a formal part of our legal system.[7]

Ancient Greek and Roman arguers often based their claims on the issues of procedural objections, definitions, quality, and motive. These stock issues are still commonly used in legal disputes. Student debaters adopted the legal notion of stock issues in the twentieth century when arguing policy and value propositions. Table 3.2 points

Table 3.2 Stock Issues in Policy Debate

Stock Issue	Question Defining Stock Issue
Topicality	Did the debater interpret the debate resolution in a reasonable manner?
Significance	Did the debater present a claim important enought to warrant the audience's attention?
Inherency	Did the debater describe why the present system is unwilling or unable to deal with the significant problem?
Solvency	Did the debater deal with a problem that could be solved with the affirmative plan?
Disadvantages	Would the plan create more problems than it would solve?

up the similarities between stock issues for policy debate and those used by classical arguers.[8]

Debaters who argue policy issues often center their assertions and claims on one or more of the five issues presented in Table 3.2. Stock issues help debaters and judges determine who won the debate. Debaters do not necessarily discuss all stock issues in all debate rounds. Structural and situational constraints affect a debater's development of the stock issues.

STOCK ISSUES IN VALUE DEBATE

Perspectives on stock issues other than those presented in this text are given in the bibliography at the end of this chapter. The stock issues identified here do overlap with those discussed by other authors. Each debate proposition tends to emphasize different stock issues. Ultimately, you will have to examine the debate proposition first and then identify the stock issues that appear to best fit the proposition. You will need to know some structural expectations regarding stock issues. The stock issues of value debates are:

1. The issue of definition: How are the issues and values implied in the resolution defined?

2. The issue of criteria: What assumptions can be made about members of the audience and their value system?

3. The issue of significance: Is the problem serious enough to affect members of this audience and their relevant value hierarchies?

4. The issue of comparison: Is this problem more worthy of audience attention than competing problems?[9]

Stock Issue of Definition

The first step in any value debate is to define the important ideas the debaters will discuss. In the debate tradition, arguers are always advised to "define your terms." This admonition is important because debaters often fail to achieve a common understanding of the key terms. If opposing debaters are using different definitions of the key terms, there may be no clash in the debate. In many debates the first affirmative defines the key value terms of the resolution or may define a term that may be controversial. As in other dimensions of debate, the issue of definition is open to dispute.

Definitions are important in the debate round because they allow the advocates to claim the argumentative ground by restricting or expanding the meanings of key terms or words. If an advocate is able to persuade the opponent and the judge to accept a particular definition, the advocate's case might be easier to make. In the ongoing debate about the value of freedom of choice for women to have abortions, a big part of the debate relates to the definitions of "murder" and "life." Arguers debate whether a fetus is a "person" in the common-sense use of the term and whether, therefore, the abortion is properly defined as "murder." In the debate about abortion and in debates about other important issues, the definition of key terms may constitute the focus of argument.

The affirmative is given the right to define the terms of the debate proposition because that side initiates the claims and issues in the debate. Judges and opponents expect the affirmative to provide reasonable definitions facilitating appropriate clash over the issues the affirmative introduces. The negative has the right to question the reasonability of the affirmative's definitions if the negative believes that the affirmative has inappropriately defined its terms. In the sample debate, the first affirmative provides us with a good example of how the affirmative introduces definitions:

> (A) subpoint, definitions. Initially we'd like to note that the affirmative has the right to reasonably define terms because otherwise the negative could always define the affirmative as falling outside the scope of the resolution. . . . The term United Nations implies only the General Assembly, the Security Council, and the Secretariat.[10]

At this juncture, the first affirmative quoted Thomas Franck (the prominent United Nations scholar) in support of this United Nations definition.

This is an important moment in the debate, for if the affirmative can prove that this definition is strong, it can claim that many of the benefits provided by the United Nations can be achieved by agencies other than the United Nations. The first negative, in her speech, responded in this manner:

> I'm on their observation one now. [In the] (A) subpoint [the affirmative presents] definitions, that they have the right to be reasonable. First argument here is we will argue that they need to realistically define. . . . They argue [that the UN is only the] General Assembly. First argument is parallel to Congress. Now when Congress debates and decides that something needs to be done, they delegate that to an agency which they set up, or a commission which they set up, and that's a delegation of responsibility. And we argue that there's the same delegation within the United Nations.[11]

Here, the first negative is attempting to use an argument based on an analogy in an attempt to suggest that the affirmative's definition is not reasonable.

The issue of definition is of great consequence in this particular debate and in many other debates. Debaters' selection of definitions may be of critical importance. Some rules should guide the selection of appropriate definitions. If the debater considers these rules, or suggestions, strong definitions may result. The rules are drawn from Aristotle's works and from a logical tradition standing the test of time. Many writers now urge those who define to take a contextual view of the meanings of terms—that is, definitions serve a specific purpose at a specific time.[12]

> *Rule one: Good definitions specify the context in which, and the purpose for which, a definition is needed.*

Debaters have to find field-specific definitions. A field-specific definition comes from an expert who has acknowledged competence in a given subject area. For example, although it may be tempting to turn to *Webster's Dictionary* for definitions of the key terms of a resolution, stronger definitions will come from authors who have spent time and effort attempting to understand the area under discussion. Thus, the first affirmative in the sample debate made an appropriate choice in using Thomas Franck's definition of the United Nations. Franck, one of the acknowledged experts in the field, has studied the United Nations and has earned the right to offer useful definitions.

> *Rule two: Good definitions should give the nature of the object defined.*

A good definition provides the debater with the essence of the thing defined. In the sample debate, the debaters argued about what makes up the essence of the United Nations. The affirmative suggested that the United Nations consists of the Security Council, the Secretariat, and the General Assembly. The negative responded by arguing that the United Nations consists of more than the three bodies identified by the affirmative. The negative claimed that an adequate definition of the UN would include its operating agencies such as the World Bank, the World Health Organization, and so forth.

Rule three: Good definitions provide for careful distinctions and reasonable clarity.

Definitions permit debaters to focus on the important issues of the debate. A good definition allows an advocate to draw important distinctions between concepts. In addition, a good definition should promote clarity, not confusion.

In the sample debate, the first negative challenged the definition of the United Nations in this manner: "Why is the affirmative definition [from Franck] distinct? Why is that the only definition [of the UN that can be accepted]?"[13] The claim here was that the Franck definition did not provide useful distinctions and clarity.

The second affirmative defended the distinctiveness and the clarity of the definition of the United Nations provided in the first affirmative. He argued that it is empirically true that a nation can belong to one of the UN subsidiary agencies and not belong to the UN. Here, the second affirmative claimed that Switzerland belongs to a lot of these specialized agencies and it is not a member of the United Nations. This is a good attempt, for when a debater can point to empirical reality in support of a definition, the definition may take on additional strength.

Rule four: Good definitions tend not to be idiosyncratic or unusual.

On occasion, a debater may pluck a definition out of context and use it to support an unusual interpretation of the debate resolution. This use of definitions merits close scrutiny, as it may reveal that most experts in the field disagree with the idiosyncratic interpretation. Although such a consensus does not necessarily mean that the definition is wrong or weak, it does mean that most of those who have written on the subject area do not believe that the idiosyncratic definition helps the discussion. As noted previously, if experts in the field all were used to their own definitions of key terms, useful discussion may not occur.

Questions of definition constitute the first stock issue in a value debate. Advocates offer definitions to provide the judge with an understanding of the meaning of certain terms. As we have suggested here, definitions are open to debate, and certain rules may be used in selecting and testing definitions.

Stock Issue of Criteria

After a first affirmative has offered definitions of important terms in the resolution, criteria is introduced next. These are used to measure and assess the issues in question.

If a friend says, "Professor X is a much better teacher than Professor Y," and you respond, "No, Professor Y is a better teacher than Professor X," you may be asked to provide a reason supporting this belief. You might respond that Professor Y tells hysterically funny jokes. Your friend might agree but say that Professor X's puns provoke more laughter than Professor Y's jokes. If you reflect on this statement, you will note that humor has become the standard or measurement of good teaching in this instance. Both arguers agree that good teachers are funny. The argument then revolves around which professor the arguers perceive to be the most humorous.

How is humor measured? Your friend suggests that the volume of laughter provoked by a professor is the best measure. This becomes the criterion or the measurement of good teaching. In the same way, debaters offer criteria to measure the strength of issues, claims, and assertions. Criteria are "measuring sticks" that can be used to gauge the desirability of a value. Every value-oriented controversy must include some attempt to tell listeners how they ought to measure values in that context. If, for example, you try to persuade us that Professor X is a "good" teacher, you also need to tell us the criteria you are using to make that value judgment.

The selection and use of criteria in debate rounds have rules. Some debate theorists do not believe that affirmative speakers are obligated to include criteria for the evaluation of arguments. As such, these theorists do not believe that the issue of criteria is a stock issue. We believe there are sound reasons for considering criteria as a stock issue. Most first affirmative speakers in CEDA debates do include criteria in their analysis of the resolution. In addition, value terms cannot be debated or assessed without a method to measure or weigh the arguments that might revolve around the value terms. Regardless, criteria arguments are encountered in almost all CEDA debates.

> *Rule one: Criteria in use should be contextually designed and the best available.*

Selecting appropriate criteria may be difficult. In many debates, arguers agree on the criteria in use. On occasion, they disagree. Recall, for example, the disagreement between the two students about the teaching abilities of Professor X and Professor Y. An observer or a critic of this claim might question the relevance of humor as a standard to assess teaching. The educational research has revealed mixed results regarding the relationship between use of humor by a teacher and a student's education. One might question using the volume of laughter as an effective teaching measurement.

A critic of the argument might suggest an alternative standard or set of criteria for measuring effective teaching, arguing that teachers should be evaluated by how well they educate rather than how well they entertain. Humor may be more an index of entertainment than of education. Some standards that arguers might use include: How much did the students of Professor X and Professor Y learn about the subject area? How well did the students of X and Y perform on standardized tests in the subject matter? How do the peers of Professors X and Y perceive their teaching? The arguer attempts to convince the listener that there are a host of standards for assessing teaching that are more appropriate than the criterion of laughter.

Arguers should base the selection of criteria on contextually and field-related grounds. Again, the standards selected should "fit" the field in question. Experts in the field often offer this type of criteria, and the debater would be wise to use them. In addition, negative debaters should be ready to offer counter-criteria to respond to those offered by the affirmative—a strategy the negative used in the sample debate. As opposed to the criteria the first affirmative offered, the first negative urged the critics to judge the United Nations on an on-balance basis and to reject unrealistic standards in their assessment. This allowed the negative to focus the debate on plausible rather than utopian grounds of assessment. Criteria based on plausible grounds lead both the negative and the affirmative arguers to compare and to assess our common existence and the associated problem.

Rule two: Criteria should provide a level of measurement.

If disagreeing arguers are to compare their claims, they will have to make use of a standard of measurement. In the absence of a standard, no true argument is possible. For example, I might say that country music is better than classical music. I might provide proof for this statement by saying that more people buy country music albums than classical music albums. The standard of measurement I have offered is the number of record albums purchased.

This standard is clearcut and precise. Other standards of measurement are in common use. If you plan to buy a new or used car and you wish to determine a fair price, you would want to examine the "Blue Book." Many careful consumers consult *Consumer Reports* before they purchase a major item. *Consumer Reports* sets up a series of standards and then tests products, making use of these standards. A good set of criteria provides arguers with yardsticks that can be used to determine the worth of a given value.

In the sample debate, a major issue revolved around determining appropriate public expectations of the United Nations. The first negative offered a criterion to help in developing these expectations. She argued that the affirmative "suffer(ed) from lofty expectations" about the United Nations. She suggested that the affirmative "expected too much out of the peacekeeping forces" and that "it's not surprising that they conclude that they [the UN] fail[s]."[14] The first negative attempted here to establish a standard of measurement that could be used to assess the desirability of the UN. In framing the issue in this way, the negative persuaded the judges by the end of the debate that they should not evaluate the success of the United Nations in absolute terms.[15]

The affirmative implicitly agreed with this standard of measurement but added that "certainly we can't expect [the UN] to stop every conflict, but you don't want them to create any of them."[16] The affirmative attempted here to suggest that the United Nations actually caused conflict.

Rule three: Criteria should provide for realistic comparisons.

A good set of criteria will set levels of measurement. In addition, a good set of criteria will allow the advocates and judges to compare states of existence and to make tenable comparisons. Such comparisons allow for judgments based upon the human condition. Again, the negative position on appropriate public expectations about the United Nations is useful. If an affirmative had claimed that the United Nations failed to create peace on earth, a reasonable response would be that creation of peace on earth is an unrealistic expectation. Rather, the United Nations should be assessed as a human organization and we should use relative as opposed to absolute standards of measurement.

In value debate, a good set of criteria allows for comparison in four directions. First, the affirmative can use the criteria to compare the performance of the present system with desired values. Second, the affirmative can use the criteria to compare the present system with a preferred, but attainable, system. Third, the negative can use the criteria to suggest that the present system has met the desired values. Fourth, the negative can use the criteria to suggest that the implications of the affirmative's analysis would be undesirable.

Again, criteria are standards and yardsticks that can be used to measure the quality or quantity of a value. For a value debate to occur, contextually designed criteria provide for determining appropriate levels of measurement and allow comparisons to be made. In value debate it has become a tradition for speakers to present definitions and criteria statements and to debate these statements.

Stock Issue of Significance

Arguers have always analyzed the issue of significance. We define significance as the *perceived importance of the problem area.* An affirmative speaker has to show to the satisfaction of the judge that there is a problem deserving our attention. Negative speakers may choose to argue that the problem is not important or that it is over-dramatized. The following guidelines expedite analyzing the issue of significance.

> *Rule one: To be significant, an issue, claim, or assertion must be connected to an audience's values.*

An audience will perceive a problem to be important if an advocate is able to show that the problem affects the value hierarchies of the audience. The debater should attempt to discover reasons why the audience should be concerned. In the sample debate, all advocates discussed issues of great importance: regional war, nuclear war, and the like. Without doubt, most audiences would consider these to be problems of serious magnitude.

Rule two: Issues of significance do not have to be quantified and should be problems with identifiable and arguable solutions.

Some issues should be of serious concern but are not amenable to quantification. Advocates in the public forum often discuss problems that cannot be translated into numbers. In value debate, advocates may choose to provide quantification for their claims of significance, or they may not. The loss of liberty or justice may not have a numerical value, although such losses should concern most audiences. Even though statements may be beyond quantification, they are still open to debate. We use the debate process to determine what should be done, if anything, to deal with the problems.

In addition, advocates should deal with problems that have plausible solutions. Issues without solution may be beyond the realm of true or interesting debate since there would be no way for an outcome.

Rule three: A criterion for significance should be apparent.

Arguers cannot separate issues of significance from those of definition and of criteria. The problems of poverty and unemployment can be quantified. The significance of poverty and unemployment are determined by applying sets of criteria to these problem areas. The Brookings Institute and the Urban League may use different sets of criteria than the Heritage Foundation and the federal government use to measure poverty and unemployment. As a result, they may reach widely disparate conclusions about the significance of the problem areas. Ultimately, issues of significance may involve disagreement about the selection of criteria.

Stock Issue of Comparison

When the advocate considers the issue of comparison, he or she considers the question: Is this problem more worthy of audience attention than competing problems? It is here that the advocate would place the debated problem area in the context of current political, economic, and social reality. For example, when advocates for the

Star Wars program suggest that the United States should deploy the system to prevent nuclear war, opponents suggest that we cannot afford, given the other national concerns that must be addressed, to spend billions of dollars on this system of defense.

The stock issue of comparison asks the advocates to compare issues of concern in an attempt to order them on personal and social agendas. Negative teams structure their claims on this stock issue in the form of *value objections* (discussed in chapter 7). We suggest three rules for issue comparison.

> *Rule one: Issue comparison should be made using a criterion based upon contemporary experience.*

Debates often become polarized. Polarization occurs because debaters assume that a value is either good or bad. The stock issue of comparison should lead the debater to consider values in their context. Values that are in conflict may never exist in harmony because they naturally compete. A comparative stance on issues encourages debaters to consider which value is most important in a given context and a given time.

> *Rule two: Values that emerge from an argument as most important deserve a higher status on the audience's value hierarchy.*

Debate should produce an ordering of values on both personal and societal agendas. Agendas of this nature are in constant flux. Debate allows us to test these agendas. Some debate resolutions may ask for a comparison of two terminal values. For example, you might debate the resolution, "Economic development is more important than environmental protection." Most audiences accept both economic development and environmental protection as important values. If a negative could successfully argue that greater economic development would harm the environment and human health, the audience might place economic development below environmental protection on its value hierarchy.

> *Rule three: Values that can be remedied deserve higher status than those without solution.*

We noted earlier that "solvency" is an issue intrinsic to policy propositions. Although value debates usually would not reject a value solely because the problem does not have a workable solution, the issue of comparison suggests that when decision-makers compare two values, the value that can be addressed or solved would take precedence over the one that is not capable of solution. Most decision-makers prefer to address values and policies in which they can see measurable improvement through their actions. Dieters, for example, constantly look for diets that will make them look better immediately rather than to follow weight reduction principles that have long-range benefits but fewer immediate reinforcements.

SUMMARY

Values are an integral part of our functioning as human beings. They express our commitments to objects, ideas, and courses of action. Values can be differentiated as terminal or as instrumental. Values are often discussed in the context of the propositions debated. Propositions are divided into questions of fact, policy, and value.

Stock issues are found in every debate round. They allow debaters to formulate positions before and during a debate. In this chapter we have discussed the history and the evolution of stock issues, defined and illustrated the five stock issues in value debate, considered some examples of how debaters make use of stock issues, and discussed how arguers develop and test stock issues.

——————— ENDNOTES ———————

1. Milton Rokeach, *Understanding Human Values* (London: Free Press, 1979), p. 16.
2. Rokeach, *The Nature of Human Values* (London, Free Press, 1981), pp. 11–14.
3. Rokeach, *The Nature of Human Values*, pp. 11–14.
4. Ronald J. Matlon, "Debating Propositions of Value," *Journal of the American Forensic Association* 14 (1978): 194–204.
5. Rokeach, *Understanding Human Values*, p. 49.

6. Chaim Perelman and L. Obrechts-Tyteca, *The New Rhetoric* (Notre Dame: University of Notre Dame Press, 1969); Matlon, pp. 194–204.

7. Ray Nadeau, "Hermongenes' On Stases: A Translation with an Introduction," *Speech Monographs* 31 (1964): 361–424.

8. Among many good texts on policy debate and argument are George W. Ziegelmueller and Charles Dause, *Argumentation: Inquiry and Advocacy* (Englewood Cliffs, NJ: Prentice-Hall, 1975); Richard D. Rieke and Malcom D. Sillars, *Argumentation and the Decision Making Process* (Dallas: Scott Foresman, 1984).

9. Michael D. Bartanen and David A. Frank, "The Issues-Agenda Model," in *Advanced Debate*, edited by David A. Thomas and Jack Hart (Lincoln, NE: National Textbook Company, 1987), pp. 408–416.

10. Appendix A, Crenshaw, p. 199.

11. Appendix A, McGinnis, p. 206.

12. For further reading, see Raziel Abelson, "Definition," in *Encyclopedia of Philosophy* (Vol. 1), edited by Paul Edwards (New York: Macmillan, 1967).

13. Appendix A, McGinnis, p. 206.

14. Appendix A, McGinnis, p. 204.

15. See the judges' written decisions in John Boaz and James Brey, editors, *1986 Championship Debates and Speeches* (Normal: Illinois Press, 1986), pp. 100–101.

16. Appendix A, Delao, p. 210.

———— Appendix to Chapter 3 ————
Select Bibliography: Scholarly Materials on Value Theory and Value Argument

General

Advanced Debate.
> Edited by David A. Thomas and Jack Hart (Lincoln: National Textbook Company, 1987), contains thirteen articles on value debate.

Alta Summer Conferences on Argumentation: Proceedings.
> Papers on topics related to argumentation, gathered each summer by experts in the field of argumentation. Most academic libraries carry these proceedings.

Argumentation and Advocacy: the Journal of the American Forensic Association.
> Key articles on value debate and argumentation. Most academic libraries carry this journal.

CEDA Yearbook.
> Published annually by Cross Examination Debate Association; contains articles devoted to the theory and practice of value debate.

Championship Debates and Speeches.
> An annual publication providing the reader with final-round transcripts of debate and individual event competitions; published jointly by Speech Communication Association and American Forensic Association.

Issues Related to Value Argumentation and Debate

Ethics
Journal of Value Theory
Philosophy and Public Affairs
Philosophy and Rhetoric

Value Theory

Fisher, Walter R. "Toward a Logic of Good Reasons." *Quarterly Journal of Speech* 64 (1978), 376–384.

Johnson, Allison H. *Modes of Value*. New York: Philosophical Library, 1978.

Kohlberg, Lawrence, Charles Levine, and Alexandra Hewer. *Moral Stages: A Current Formulation and a Response to Critics*. New York: Darger, 1983.

Perelman, Chaim H., and L. Olbrechts-Tyteca. *The New Rhetoric: A Treatise on Argumentation*. Notre Dame, IN: University of Notre Dame Press, 1969.

Rawls, John. *A Theory of Justice*. Cambridge: Belknap Press, 1971.

Rescher, Nicholas. "The Study of Value Change." *Value Theory and Social Sciences*, edited by Ervin Laszlo and James B. Wilbur. New York: Gordon and Breach, 1973.

Rescher, Nicholas. *Introduction to Value Theory*. Englewood Cliffs, NJ: Prentice Hall, 1982.

Rokeach, Milton. *Beliefs, Attitudes and Values*. San Francisco: Jossey-Bass, 1968.

Rokeach, Milton. *Understanding Human Values* London: Free Press, 1979.

Rokeach, Milton. *The Nature of Human Values* London: Free Press, 1981.

Steele, Edward D., and Charles W. Redding "The American Value System: Premises for Persuasion." *Western Speech* 26 (1962), 83–91.

Werkmeister, William H. *Historical Spectrum of Value Theories*. Lincoln, NE: Johnsen Publishing, 1973.

Value Argument

Bartanen, Kristine M. "Application of the Narrative Paradigm in CEDA Debate." In *Advanced Debate*, edited by David A. Thomas and Jack Hart. Lincoln, NE: National Textbook Company, 1987, pp. 417–428.

Bartanen, Michael D., and David A. Frank. "The Issue-Agenda Model." In *Advanced Debate*, edited by David A. Thomas and Jack Hart. Lincoln, NE: National Textbook Company, 1987, pp. 408–416.

Bartanen, Michael D. "The Role of Values in Policy Controversies." *CEDA Yearbook*. Northridge, CA: CEDA, 1982, pp. 19–24, 31.

Church, Russell T., and David C. Buckley. "Argumentation and Debating Propositions of Value: A Bibliography." *Journal of the American Forensic Association* 19 (1983): 239–250.

Fisher, Walter R. "Debating Value Propositions: A Game for Dialecticians." In *Dimensions of Argument: Proceedings of the Second Summer Conference on Argumentation*, edited by George Ziegelmueller et al. Annandale, VA: Speech Communication Association and American Forensic Association, 1981, pp. 1014–1030.

Matlon, Ronald J., "Debating Propositions of Value." *Journal of the American Forensic Association* 14 (1978): 194–204.

Rowland, Robert. "The Philosophical Presuppositions of Value Debate." In *Argument in Transition: Proceedings of the Third Summer Conference on Argumentation*, edited by David Zarefsky et al. Annandale, VA: Speech Communication Association and American Forensic Association, 1983, pp. 822–836.

Sillars, Malcom O., and Patricia Ganer. "Values and Beliefs: A Systematic Basis for Argumentation." In *Advances in Argumentation Theory and Research*, edited by J. Robert Cox and Charles Arthur Willard. Carbondale: Southern Illinois University Press, 1982, pp. 184–201.

Toulmin, Stephen. *An Examination of the Place of Reason in Ethics*. Cambridge, MA: Cambridge University Press, 1950.

Tuman, Joseph S. "Getting to First Base: Prima Facie Arguments for Propositions of Value." *Journal of the American Forensic Association* 14 (1987), 84–97.

Warnick, Barbara. "Arguing Value Propositions." *Journal of the American Forensic Association* 18 (Fall 1981), 109–119.

Wenzel, Joseph P. "Toward a Rationale for a Value-Centered Argument." *Journal of the American Forensic Association* 13 (1977), 150–158.

4

Proof in
Academic Debate

- ☐ Understand the theoretical importance of proof in debate.
- ☐ Be able to define proof in a debating context.
- ☐ Identify the situational and structural factors influencing an audience's acceptance of proof.
- ☐ Differentiate various kinds of proof used in debate rounds.
- ☐ Understand where and how to find evidence to use in a debate round.

We agree with philosopher Chaim Perelman that an argument is much like a rope: There are many strings and strands making up the rope, and there are a host of proofs involved in presenting an argument.[1]

THE ROLE OF PROOF
IN THE DEBATE PROCESS

You recall the illustration in chapter 2, differentiating assertions, claims, and issues (Figure 2.1). Proof is what makes claims and issues more complex than assertions. Proof is *any tangible and material support used to justify accepting a statement as true or valid.* Proofs are both *substantive* and *motivational.* Substantive proofs are quotations or facts that a debater intentionally invokes. We refer to these as claims and evidence. Motivational proofs are judgments the listener makes about the debater or the claim that influence them to accept statements. Both are equally important to the debate process.

Substantive Proofs — The quality of the debater's external support (evidence).

— The strength of the debater's reasoning.

Motivational Proofs — The listener's perception of the debater's credibility.

— The adaptation of the evidence to the audience.

To illustrate these aspects of proof, consider the following example:

Mike: "Los Angeles is the best team in baseball because they won the World Series."

Dave: "No, Oakland is the best team in baseball because they won more games in the regular season."

The proofs used in this exchange include the support the arguers use (winning the World Series and having the best record in the regular season), and any perceptions a listener has about how well Mike and Dave argue about these competing claims. Evaluating which evidence is superior in this example is not an empirical question. Thus, there is uncertainty about which arguer has introduced the superior proofs. That standards of evidence and proof are arguable is what energizes the debate process. In review, we define proofs as all external and internal items a speaker uses in attempting to convince a listener to accept the truth or validity of a statement.

THE ROLE OF PROOF
IN ACCEPTING CLAIMS

Why do arguers use claims rather than assertions, and why do audiences prefer evidenced claims to unevidenced assertions? We suspect that listeners instinctively prefer claims to assertions, wanting to know what (if anything) is behind an assertion. Consider another hypothetical conversation:

> Dave: "Spike Owen is the preeminent shortstop in the major leagues!"
>
> Mike: "You must be kidding. Why would you think that?"
>
> Dave: "Well, first of all he . . . ."

This conversation is probably similar to those you have every day. Someone makes an assertion. Someone else asks the simple question "why?" This conversational logic is an important part of our personal decision-making behavior. Philosopher Stephen Toulmin characterized argument using his familiar model:

Simplified Toulmin Model

Warrant

Grounds ——————————————— Claim

Toulmin devised an elaborate model of argument based upon the idea that receivers expect people who initiate statements to provide "grounds" or evidence that will make sense (be "warrantable") to the listener.[3] Communication scholars since the time of Aristotle have consistently documented the importance of evidence to listeners.[4] This is not to say that listeners necessarily prefer "sound" evidence to "fallacious" evidence, as even the most casual watcher of television commercials knows that the quality of evidence used to justify spending our hard-earned money can be very weak![5]

Again, proof is a key element of debate, transforming assertions into claims. Proof is the support that an arguer uses to justify a listener accepting a statement. Proof is important to debate because listeners expect people who initiate claims to be able to support them. This places the burden on the arguer to present proof. Unfortunately, the debater may not be confident about the quality and quantity of proof that have to be provided.

TYPES AND STANDARDS OF PROOF

In academic debate, the listener is always the arbiter of whether both *sufficient* and *persuasive* proof exists to back up a claim or an issue. Discovering and presenting proof is a continuous debate process, as the sample debate illustrates.

Both Macalester and Florida State presented many claims in defense of their positions. The advocates presented numerous pieces of evidence in the form of expert opinion on the relative efficacy of the United Nations as a peacekeeping union. Use of this evidence created many interesting, competing issues in the debate and was crucial to the listeners' judgment that these debaters were knowledgeable and credible.

Ideally, debate revolves around the testing of evidence (substantive proofs) because evidence plays such a prominent role in the debate process. Different forms of evidence have disparate levels of persuasive strength. The debaters test the evidence introduced in the debate by clashing with the claims presented by their opponents. The debaters present alternative evidence and criticisms of opposing evidence. This testing should allow the listener to determine who has presented the strongest evidence.

TYPES OF DEBATE EVIDENCE

The first step in testing evidence is to understand the types of debate evidence special to value debates. These include expert opinion, socially accepted facts, and tradition or precedent:

Expert opinion   Statements by qualified persons
                            about a subject in question.

| Facts | Perceptions of reality that may have social consensus. |
| Precedent and tradition | Consensually shared social behaviors and standards. |

These types of evidence are different from evidence used in other arguing and debating contexts such as academic policy debates, legislative debates, and legal trials. This reflects both *situational* and *structural* expectations that govern how debate occurs in any context. The debate structure, in which the topic debated is, by design, one that requires library research, inspires the prevalence of expert opinion and factual evidence. These are the most concrete forms of evidence available in discussing the public policy issues most often used in debate. The situational expectations of value debate create the need to consider precedent and tradition because precedent and tradition are crucial to considering value claims.

1. *Expert Opinion.*

Certain people have earned the right or have the power to influence the way we think and behave. Experts may help us understand complex issues and may highlight values that may be used to make difficult decisions. When experts disagree, the expertise and qualifications of each expert may become the focus of the evidence testing in the debate. Notice how often the debaters in the sample debate called upon expert opinion and took the time to qualify the experts they were quoting.

The first negative did a particularly good job in providing qualifications for her sources. She quoted Richard Gardner, professor of law at Columbia; Thomas Franck, author of the classic text on the UN; Alan James, professor of international relations; and so on. By qualifying her sources, she gave additional strength to her claims. We tend to vest greater trust in those who have established a record of expertise and careful thought in a given area. When experts disagree, the task of making a judgment becomes quite difficult. When they do disagree, as they often do, listeners need standards and sets of criteria to determine which expert has a stronger perspective.

2. *Facts.*

Facts are perceptions of reality. We may or may not consider facts as "true" statements (e.g., "The earth is round"). Some facts are perceptions of reality achieving social consensus, such as a statement that "America is a powerful nation." Some perceptions may not be in question; others may be the focus of much disagreement. Debates about social issues might center on questions such as: What is the level of unemployment? How many people are harmed by ingesting drugs? How has the fiscal policy of the current administration affected the well-being of the American family? Answers to questions like these require careful surveys, interviews, and a host of social-scientific methods of gathering information. A critical issue in a value debate may revolve around disagreement over the accuracy and acceptability of facts.[6]

In the debate between Macalester and Florida State, there was an argument about how well the United Nations had kept peace in past conflicts. The debaters presented specific instances as examples to support a generalizable claim that the United Nations had failed or had succeeded in this function. Evidence offered by the advocates tended to come from expert sources who had reached conclusions regarding these historical examples. In addition, the debaters made various claims about the current capacities of the United Nations. Factual claims about UN success in peacekeeping played a major role in the debate.

3. *Precedent and tradition.*

Precedents and traditions are previously held beliefs about appropriate actions and behaviors. We give strong presumption to precedent and tradition as guidelines for appropriate action. Precedent and tradition may serve to shape perceptions of reality. As such, they may not be the center of the discussion, although they influence the course of debates. In debate, arguers often use precedents and tradition as starting points for their arguing. For example, an advocate might assume that the right of free speech should be maintained because it works to provide a free society, is part of the American tradition, and has a firm precedent in American law.

Precedent and tradition are often cited in the form of criteria arguments. As noted in the previous chapter, criteria arguments are an important element of value debate because these arguments provide the means for determining the relative importance of competing values.

Traditions and precedents often, for good reason, have a powerful argumentative force behind them; many audiences accept them at face value. But traditions and precedents may be challenged and are open to argument.[7] For example, the Supreme Court in *Plessy v. Ferguson* (1893) sanctioned racial discrimination. This case served as precedent until the famous 1954 *Brown v. the Board of Education* case. In the intervening years a series of changes occurred to alter how society viewed the issue of race relations. This shows that precedents may be overturned and traditions altered and abandoned. Change may come about gradually or through a series of "revolutions."[8]

In review, expert opinion, facts, and precedents and traditions are the most common types of evidence used in value debate rounds. Such evidence is the primary component of an argument. Debate is, in part, a process of testing the proof.

EVALUATING EVIDENCE

Evidence is evaluated on a continuum in which the judge and the advocates consider the relative strength and weakness of the evidence in question. Certain standards and criteria have evolved to help in that evaluation. Although there are particular means of evaluating the appropriateness of each the three types of evidence, two criteria apply to all evidence introduced in a debate: sufficiency and propriety.

Sufficiency

The first general question asked about any evidence is simply, "Is there enough?" Unfortunately, no tangible method is available to measure how much evidence is "enough" in any context. Unlike the legal system, in which measures such as the "preponderance of evidence" and the "clear and convincing" standard of evidence have evolved to help decision-makers evaluate whether sufficient evidence exists in a controversy, academic debate has no agreed-upon measure of sufficiency.

In the Macalester-Florida State debate, both teams introduced a significant quantity of evidence. The amount of evidence introduced in this debate is typical of many CEDA debates, although it is far less than the amount found in NDT debates.[9] The primary reason for introducing so much evidence was the debaters' perception that the judges in the debate round expected them to present a lot of evidence. The judges of that debate were all experienced debate teachers of teams that also presented a lot of evidence in their debates. If Macalester and Florida State were to face a different audience (perhaps a class of fourth graders or a group of professors with expertise on the United Nations), they likely would present a different amount of evidence. *Audience expectations determine how much evidence will be sufficient in the debate.*

Propriety

Is the evidence appropriate for proving the point it is asserted to prove? Standards regarding the propriety of evidence are different for each of the types of evidence we have introduced.

Standards for Evaluating the Testimony of Experts

Experts present opinions, ostensibly in their areas of expertise, which guide listeners in wisely choosing between various values and courses of action. Many standards and sets of criteria can be used to test the relative quality of expert opinion:

1. *Is there any reason to doubt the neutrality or impartiality of the expert?*

On occasion, an expert may be "bought off" (co-opted by groups he or she criticizes) or may advocate a partisan position rather than acting as an impartial observer. Debaters should be aware of those who may personally profit from an opinion or, because of rigid ideological blinders, cannot provide a fair interpretation of the data or information in question.

An example of this evidence test is found in the sample debate. Note how the first negative questioned the quality and strength of the Heritage Foundation evidence. The affirmative used the Foundation's conclusion that the United Nations had not succeeded in its peacekeeping efforts. The first negative quoted a Heritage Foundation source (Berton Pines) who observed that the Foundation's role was not "to be some kind of Ph.D. committee giving equal time. . . . Our role is to provide conservative public policymakers with arguments to bolster our side."[10] The second affirmative defended the Foundation and its conclusion.[11] This argument about the qualification of the Heritage Foundation provides us a clear example of how debaters can question the intent or an opinion of an expert.

2. *Is the expert qualified to issue judgments about the issue in question?*

Some experts provide opinions on subjects outside of their areas of expertise. These opinions may not deserve special status. For example, when discussing foreign affairs, debaters sometimes quote linguist Noam Chomsky, who trained and earned his fame for his work in linguistics. Although Chomsky's work in linguistics is justifiably famous, some of his writing in foreign affairs smacks more of advocacy than of scholarship and may not reflect a careful and neutral assessment of the various topics he addressed. Of course, in the spirit of debate, some people defend Chomsky's opinions on foreign affairs.[12]

In a sense, the second affirmative implicitly employed this standard while observing that "She says [that the] Heritage Foundation [is a bad source] . . . [W]ho the heck is the *Atlantic Monthly*? How come that beats [is better than] the Heritage Foundation?"[13] This claim illustrates how a debater can question the qualification of a source or opinion.

3. *Does the expert have a good track record, and does the expert's opinion reflect or deviate from the consensus of the experts?*

Debaters also test the opinion of an expert by considering the expert's record. The advocate would do well to know how successfully the expert acted in past situations involving questions in the expert's field. Has the expert made predictions or judgments validated by later events? Does the expert reflect positions consistent with other experts in the field? This question evokes the possibility that the expert may present an idiosyncratic interpretation while analyzing a question. Certainly an expert has the right to present such an interpretation, but in a sense the burden of proof is on the expert who presents an opinion that runs counter to a consensus of the best scholarship in a field.

Standards for Evaluating Factual Claims

Assertions of fact are not considered independently of our evaluation of the person making the assertion. The distinction between expert opinions and factual assertions as types of evidence is not absolute. The debater can, and often does, use the tests of expert opinion as a way of testing assertions of fact.

In the sample debate, Florida State initiated a claim that the United Nations had failed to keep the peace. The first affirmative quoted Tugwell, Kirkpatrick, Yeselson, and Gaglione to support the claim that the United Nations actually had exacerbated world tensions. These sources also suggested that the UN had not effectively controlled the conflict in the Middle East.[14] The negative responded that the United Nations is generally effective and cited Gardner, Franck, and others supporting this claim.[15] The second negative also offered specific examples to support his claim and the negative's generalization. Given this clash of opinion, debaters and judges need standards to assess the relative strengths and weaknesses of factual assertions such as this. Familiar standards of scientific measurement can help in this determination.

Because debate resolutions tend to focus on broad questions of social policy, debaters often must determine the nature of our empirical reality. For example, debaters may need to know the number of drug addicts in America or how many people own guns. Empirical questions are often answered by using the *scientific method*. The scientific method attempts to make accurate reports of empirical reality through a variety of techniques, which have strengths and weaknesses.

The scientific method often yields generalizations based on carefully gathered and interpreted information. In debate, answers to the various issues frequently depend on generalizations. These generalizations often take the form of statistics. Whether based on statistics or on other information, generalizations do not automatically deserve an audience's acceptance, because the evidence may also be weak or flawed. Before examining the evidence, the debater will want to pose questions about the expertise of those who authored the studies. Empirical studies often have critics. If you have read studies about the harms of cigarette smoking published by pro-smoking and anti-smoking advocates, you probably can visualize how empirical studies may be controversial.[16]

Debaters should try to find books and articles written by critics of particular empirical studies to provide the debater with specific criticisms of the studies in question. In the sample debate, no social-scientific studies were introduced. We will illustrate how studies such as this can be the focus of debate by considering the following claim: Based on the conclusion of the Congressional Budget Office, United States unemployment is decreasing.

The first step in evaluating this claim is to consider the *status of the source* linked to the evidence. In this case, the Congressional Budget Office has an excellent track record, is nonpartisan (so it does not have an ideological bent), and makes use of experts in the given field. But being a strong source is not enough; it may fail to meet some basic questions necessary to assessing the status of a factual claim issued by an expert.

1. *Is the sample representative?*

If the Congressional Budget Office surveyed one district in Massachusetts and found that very few people were unemployed in that district, the sample used for the conclusion might not be *representative* of all congressional districts. If the CBO then had used this finding to build the claim that unemployment in the United States has decreased, the proof would be weak. Massachusetts may not be representative of the nation as a whole; it is located in the Northeast; it has many more colleges and universities than, say, southeastern Texas; and it has a different industrial and economic foundation than the South or the Pacific Northwest.

If, however, the CBO study had sampled different parts of the nation and reflected a representative sample of unemployed workers in America, a claim suggesting that unemployment has decreased may be warranted. Again, the claim is strong because the factual assertion is based on a study by a qualified source that drew conclusions from a representative sample.

2. *Did the researchers use an appropriate measure?*

To accurately perceive reality and create strong factual claims, researchers use research measures they hope are both *valid* and *reliable.* The methods must measure what the researchers design them to measure and must be accurate in measuring a particular phenomenon. For example, if the CBO's measure had placed part-time or underemployed workers in the category of being employed, the results may not be accurate because many experts would not consider these workers truly employed.

Although no empirical studies were cited in the Macalester-Florida State debate round, Macalester did offer a validity standard for measuring the peacekeeping efficacy of the United States. Macalester suggested that the judges should not have overly high expectations for the United Nations in peacekeeping.[17] If the debate judges were to adopt this standard, they would not evaluate United Nations successes and failures in absolute terms.

The reliability of a measure also can be determined by examining its consistency. For example, if the Congressional Budget Office had measured the unemployment rate on Monday and Tuesday in the same area and if the unemployment rates on these two days had been radically different for no apparent reason, the measure of unemployment may be weak. A measure is consistent if it reveals consistent results over time.

Standards for Evaluating Traditions and Precedents

Precedents and traditions can be challenged if the advocate is able to persuade a judge that the tradition in question no longer serves a useful function or does not apply in a given case. When testing the strength of a given precedent or tradition, the following standards apply:

1. *Is the tradition or precedent used by experts in the field?*

Those who spend time reflecting upon issues in a given area often come to a consensus regarding what measure should be used to guide judgment. In the debate between Macalester and Florida State, the debaters utilized the "lofty expectations" standard introduced by experts in the field for evaluating UN actions.[18] Although this standard was appropriate here, other debaters could debate other traditions and precedents.

2. *Do contemporary factual assessments justify the precedents or traditions?*

Times change, and changing perceptions may make traditions or precedents invalid. For example, people once believed that women were unfit for leadership positions. They based those assumptions, in part, on studies purportedly showing that women were inferior to men in leadership. In the last twenty years further research findings rendered this conclusion invalid. Discrimination against women is an assumption that our society no longer accepts, making it unreliable as a tradition.

3.   *Does the specific case fit the precedent or tradition?*

A tradition may apply in some situations, to some people, or to some time periods. A standard or precedent may apply to a given case but not be appropriate for another case. For example, government often limits the well-accepted tradition of free speech during wartime.

In most debates the strength of a claim bears a close relationship to the strength of the proof. Many forms of proof and various ways to test the strength of proof are available. Skilled debaters learn to offer various proofs supporting their positions and use the different tests of proof in examining their opponents' evidence.

THE DISCOVERY AND PRESENTATION OF PROOF

The debater must find and process the evidence to use in the debate round. As evidence sources, debaters usually use books, magazines, and scholarly journals. Debate research is like any other library research: The researcher must analyze the issues of the topic, find the critical sources, and then synthesize and present the information in ways that are meaningful to the audience.

You will want to develop some useful research habits. You will want to use the library efficiently. Debate should teach you how to enter a library with a *research plan* and then to exit with evidence you can use in debate rounds. A research plan should help you discover the best sources on the debate topic. Before you construct a research plan, you should establish some goals. When the debate season begins, the research plan will be relatively general. As the season progresses, your plans will become much more directed and precise.

Discovering Proof

To discover evidence, you will want to consult several sources. Table 4.1 presents the six types of sources upon which you will want to draw for evidence, and specific examples for each. All these sources are indexed. Indexes should save you much time. And many libraries now have computers that can provide you with a list of sources to use in gathering your evidence. The steps you should take next are:

1. *Locate classic books and recent articles.*

When faced with a debate resolution, a first step is to find the classic books and articles in the field of the resolution. The debater should develop an understanding of the debate resolution based upon the most recent and best sources. These can be identified and located through source indexes. Understanding the history of the resolution and those aspects contributing to the current state of affairs helps the debater argue successfully. The Macalester and Florida State debaters show such an understanding of the foundations and operating principles of the United Nations. In addition, both teams appeared to have read classic texts in the field, such as Thomas Franck's *The United Nations*. Locating the appropriate texts and articles is essential to making use of the conclusions as a basis for claims, or at least preparing for other debaters' drawing upon the same sources.

2. *Expand the Sources.*

After locating the important sources, the researcher gradually expands his or her information to include as much evidence as possible on all issues that might be debated. Debaters can discover useful information in footnotes. The debater also may want to talk with professors or others who may be experts in the area of the debate resolution.

3. *Conduct research continually.*

Successful debaters develop a habit of researching on a continuous basis. They read a national paper daily, and they are constantly searching for the best and most recent evidence.

4. *"Cut" the evidence.*

After locating and using some of the indexes, key books, and articles on the debate resolution, some of that information should be recorded as evidence. All debaters must learn the art of "cutting" or selecting evidence. This art has some guidelines.

Table 4.1   Sources of Evidence for Academic Debate

1. Newspapers	2. News magazines
Indexes of newspapers	Indexes of news magazines
New York Times	*Time*
Christian Science Monitor	*Newsweek*
Wall Street Journal	*U.S. News and World Report*
USA Today	*Business Week*
Other international, national and regional newspapers	Other national news magazines

3. General magazines	4. Professional journals
Indexes of general magazines	Indexes of professional journals
New Republic	Example: *Foreign Affairs*
Commonwealth	Example: *Federal Probation*
Harper's	Example: *Harvard Law Review*
National Review	
Fortune	
Other general magazines	

5. Government documents	6. Books
Indexes of government documents	Indexes of books
Congressional Record	Example: Thomas Franck, *The United Nations*
Hearings before committees of the House of Representatives	Other books
Hearings before Senate Committees	
Executive documents	
Other government documents	

First, the evidence should come from a qualified source (using the tests of source quality developed above). Then, you should cut the recent evidence. You will want evidence that reports the present, not the past. Evidence discovered in the morning paper might go into the first affirmative or into the negative evidence briefs.

The evidence should contain the reasons why the source you quote has reached a particular conclusion. New debaters and advanced debaters who should know better often present "blurb" pieces of evidence. For example, if someone argues that "According to Professor Smith, there is no correlation between oat bran and heart conditions," and does not give the reasons upon which Professor Smith based this conclusion, the evidence is "blurby." The advocate must study the reasons the professor used to reach the conclusion: "Professor Smith conducted two carefully conducted studies in which she compared the rate of heart disease of those who consumed oat bran and those who did not. She found that those who consumed oat bran had far fewer heart problems than those who did not." This latter evidence provides the judges and the audience with the reasons for the conclusion.

On occasion, debaters will read conclusionary evidence. For example, the affirmative in the sample debate might have quoted Dr. Tugwell's testimony in a different manner: "Contention two: The UN heightens conflict. Mr. Tugwell stated that the UN is essentially useless in controlling conflicts. Move now to contention three. . . ." Contentions with supporting evidence and reasons are almost always stronger than those lacking such evidence and reasons.

The debater uses evidence to turn assertions into claims, and this requires that the evidence be both accurate and trustworthy. Perhaps the most important principle of cutting evidence is that the debater should not omit information that would change the author's meaning, or alter or omit information that explains any conclusions the author has drawn. The temptation may always exist to alter the intended meaning of a piece of evidence, but the temptation should be resisted. As a matter of ethics, it is wrong to distort or shape evidence to serve an argument that the author of the evidence may not support. Further, as a matter of practicality, if a debater is caught distorting evidence, the penalties range from the judge's lowering the speaker's points to the possible loss of a college education!

Organizing and Presenting the Evidence

Having all the evidence in the world will not be of much use unless it exists in a form that can be employed effectively and presented in a debate round. Evidence should be adjusted to the audience, and the audience should be adjusted to the evidence. The method of delivering a message and the organization of a claim may greatly influence how the audience perceives the evidence. Unfortunately, many debaters neglect delivery as an essential part of the debate process. Evidence delivered in an uninspired or garbled manner may lack the power it deserves. Similarly, an audience may completely ignore poorly organized evidence.

Contemporary debaters use two methods of recording and organizing evidence: evidence cards and briefs. While in the modern era, the brief has become the predominant method of organizing evidence, in order to be flexible, you may want to make use of both systems.

1. *Evidence cards.*

Debaters often record, file, and use evidence in the form of evidence cards, or quotations. A sample evidence card looks like this:

> Prof. Donald Puchala, University of South Carolina, *US, UN, and Management of Global Change*, 1983, pp. 351-2.
> "American support of UN peacekeeping, on the other hand, has enabled the United States to participate in the diplomacy of concilliation that both preceded and followed peacekeeping episodes. This has been especially important for American foreign policy in the Middle East."

The idea behind recording debate evidence in this manner is to give the debater easy access to the information in a way that is most usable in the debate round. An evidence card usually consists of *one idea* in the form of an *exact quotation* that includes all necessary *bibliographic information.*

Each evidence card should contain only one idea. This makes the evidence easier to introduce in the debate and makes the evidence easier for the judge to understand. The need for an exact quotation should be apparent. Debaters provide bibliographic information for debaters or judges to verify the existence and content of the evidence, if needed. The process is the same as in creating footnotes and bibliographies for research assignments or term papers. Bibliographic information should include the author, the author's position or qualifications, the source or location of the information, date of publication (or of your personal communication), and page numbers, so others can locate the information.

Some debaters use a color-coded system to help them organize and categorize their evidence. Others create an elaborate system of files that they use for constructive and rebuttal speeches. Still other debaters organize their evidence according to topics, stock issues, or other categories. Ultimately, each debater should create a system that best meets his or her needs and those of the partner.

   2.   *Briefs.*

Experienced debaters soon learn that certain issues require several evidenced responses organized around central themes. The debaters organize these responses on briefs, or sheets of paper containing several responses to a given issue. If, for example, you are debating a resolution that membership in the United Nations is no longer beneficial to the United States, you want to find evidence that membership in the United Nations has been beneficial to the United States. The second negative in the sample debate created and read a brief that reported the benefits that membership in the United Nations has provided the United States. We reconstructed two briefs that the debaters might have used in the sample debate, and these are found in the appendix to this chapter. You might compare these briefs to the evidence as it appeared in the debate.

As you examine the two briefs in the appendix, you will note that we list the titles of the claims above the pieces of evidence. These titles are called "evidence slugs." Evidence slugs tell the debater the claim that the evidence supports on the brief.

The two briefs are slugged "Past examples of UN peacekeeping success" and "Current examples of UN peacekeeping success." The slugs allow the debater to quickly locate the brief in a filing system. In modern debate, most debaters now place their briefs into folders. They name the various folders according to the major issues. For example, the Macalester second negative probably had a file titled "UN is an effective peacemaker." Debaters usually organize these files by issue and place them in evidence "oxboxes" or other containers. Advanced debaters have developed rather sophisticated organizational systems for evidence files.

The two briefs illustrate how contemporary debaters organize their evidence. Much work went into finding, cutting, and arranging the evidence. As such, these two model briefs might guide you in constructing your briefs. Note how the two briefs work together. One brief provides examples from the past. Anticipating a response that such examples are dated, the negative has a second brief to provide the judges with current examples of UN peacekeeping.

SUMMARY

Proof is a cog in the arguing process because of its intrinsic importance to the arguing process. People expect debaters to support their claims and apply standards of sufficiency and propriety to the proof they confront. Proof is both substantive and motivational and substantive proof in the form of evidence contributes to creating motivational proof. Value debates rely on three major evidence forms: expert testimony, factual assertions, and precedent and tradition. Judges and debaters apply certain tests to each of these forms of evidence to determine whether the evidence is sufficient and persuasive.

Debaters also must discover proof. They have to find many pieces of evidence. To find evidence, a debater needs a research plan to enable wise and efficient use of time. Once debaters discover evidence, they have to organize and arrange it. In contemporary debate, most debaters use briefs. Briefs provide organized and documented responses to issues that debaters expect to encounter.

ENDNOTES

1. See Chaim Perelman (trans. John Petrie), *The Idea of Justice and the Problem of Argument* (New York: Humanities, 1963).
2. Stephen Toulmin, *The Uses of Argument* (Cambridge, MA: Cambridge University Press, 1958).

3. Toulmin.

4. See Mary John Smith, *Persuasion and Human Action* (Belmont, CA: Wadsworth, 1982).

5. Michael Schudson, *Advertising, The Uneasy Persuasion* (New York: Basic Books, 1984).

6. Gary Iseminger, "Successful Argument and Rational Belief," *Philosophy and Rhetoric* 7 (1974): 47–57.

7. Albert Jenson and Stephen Toulmin, *The Abuse of Causistry* (Berkeley: University of California Press, 1988).

8. Thomas Kuhn, *The Structure of Scientific Revolutions* (Chicago: University of Chicago Press, 1970).

9. In fact, according to many observers, the quantity of evidence in the debate is one of the clearest differences between CEDA and NDT debate styles.

10. Appendix A, McGinnis, pp. 207.

11. Appendix A, Delao, pp. 212.

12. Ellie Kirzner, "Still Chomsky after all these years: The life of America's leading dissident," *NOW: Toronto's Alternative Weekly*, Oct. 22, 1987, excerpted in *UTNE Reader* 29 (1988), 82.

13. Appendix A, Delao, p. 212.

14. Appendix A, Crenshaw, pp. 199-202.

15. Appendix A, McGinnis, pp. 204-208.

16. Because many debate critics have had training in the communication sciences, some of the texts in that field may be useful. See, for example, James Anderson, *Communication Research* (New York: McGraw-Hill, 1987).

17. Appendix A, Benson, pp. 215-216.

18. Appendix A, Benson, pp. 215-216.

——— Appendix to Chapter 4 ———
Sample Briefs

PAST EXAMPLES OF UN
PEACEKEEPING SUCCESS

Thesis: The United Nations has kept the peace around the world.

1. Congo

Indar Rikhye, *The Theory and Practice of Peacekeeping* (New York: St. Martins Press, 1984), p. 89.

"International peacekeeping not only survived the challenge but established beyond any doubt that, without its involvement, the Congo would have ceased to survive as a unified nation and could easily become a battle ground of economic warfare."

UN played a crucial role in the Congo.

Indar Rikhye, Michael Harbottle, and Bjorn Egge, *The Thin Blue Line* (New Haven: Yate University Press, 1974), p. 91.

"The part that ONCU (United Nation's Congo Operation) played in this deserves its rightful recognition — and can clearly be regarded as a justification for the United Nations' overall conflict control policy of combining military operations with political and conciliatory efforts."

2. Cuban Missile Crisis

Connor O'Brian, "U. N. Theater," *The New Republic* 4 (Nov. 1985), p.18.

"More than any other episode in the UN's history, the Cuban missile crisis suggests that the world might have been more unsafe if it weren't for the UN's unimpressive repertoire of tricks."

Brian Urquhard, "International Peace and Security," *Foreign Affairs* (Fall, 1981), p. 9.

"The United Nations played an essential role in the Cuban Missile Crisis in 1962, not only providing a forum where both sides could expound their positions publicly, but also in suggesting, through letters from Secretary-General U. Thant to Chairman Krushchev and President Kennedy, steps that might be taken simultaneously by both sides to de-escalate the crisis."

3.   Yom Kippur War

Anthony Parson, "The United Nations and International Security in the 1980's," *Millennium: Journal of International Studies,* pp.106–107.

"At the end of the Yom Kippur War of October 1973, there was a situation of the most appaling danger to global peace . . . . The world came close to a naked confrontation between the superpowers on a battlefield. Neither side could find a way to climb down. At the last moment, they used the Security Council of the United Nations as a ladder from which to dismount their high horses."

CURRENT EXAMPLES OF EFFECTIVE UN PEACEKEEPING SUCCESS

Thesis: The United Nations is presently keeping the peace around the world.

1.   Middle East

Indar Rikye, "Peacekeeping and Peacemaking," *Peacekeeping,* ed. Henry Wiseman (New York: Pergamon Press, 1983), p. 9.

"Similarly, UNTSO continues to perform an important role in the Middle East. It keeps the Security Council informed of incidents and other developments that threaten peace."

2.   Pakistan

Selig Harrison, "A Break Through in Afghanistan," *Foreign Policy* (Summer, 1983), p. 4.

"Second, critical, interrelated issues remain to be settled, notably, the time for Soviet force withdrawals and for the phase-out of Pakistani aid to the resistance, as well as the precise orchestration of these two processes. Much to the surprise of the American officials, however, the UN effort is now moving tantalizingly close to a successful conclusion. Some of the more optimistic Pakistani and Soviet sources say that implementation of the agreements could conceivably begin in early 1984."

3. Golan Heights

Indar Rikye, "Peacekeeping and Peacemaking," *Peacekeeping*, ed. Henry Wiseman (New York: Pergamon Press, 1983) p. 9.

"The situation remains unchanged along the Golan Heights, where calm continues to prevail. Thus, UDOF continues to play a useful role between Israel and its remaining serious Arab antagonists."

4. Southern Lebanon

"UNIFIL Mandate Extended for Six Months," *UN Chronicle* (May, 1985), p. 7.

"In spite of the difficult conditions in Southern Lebanon, UNIFL's presence continued to be necessary and constituted an important factor of stability in an international commitment to upholding Lebanon's independence, sovereignty, and territorial integrity."

Section Two

Applying the Theory

5

Debate Dynamics

---------- **Chapter Objectives** ----------

- ☐ Understand the rhetorical tradition of debate and why a rhetorical perspective is appropriate for viewing debate.
- ☐ Be able to use principles of good style and delivery in debating.
- ☐ Identify the steps of four-step refutation.
- ☐ Be able to effectively cross-examine and answer questions.

This chapter marks the transition between discussing the primarily theoretical and the mainly practical debate dimensions. The preceding chapters have identified the various parts of arguments, values, and debates. You probably are ready and anxious to apply these ideas in actual debates. Application of these theoretical ideas is the focus of the remaining chapters. This chapter begins the application process by introducing the elements of the competitive debate process.

DEBATE AS A RHETORICAL ACTIVITY

In chapter 1 we alluded to the rhetorical tradition of debate. Many of the earliest references to "rhetoric" (the classical study of persuasion) discuss the creation of arguments or the process of arguing. Scholars consider Aristotle's classic work, *The Rhetoric*, as an important communication text. That book has significantly influenced the communication discipline and is especially important to the fields of persuasion theory and argumentation. Aristotle introduced and discussed fundamental arguing concepts including "proofs," "audiences," and "types of claims," and his views of argument and rhetoric still strongly influence our academic debate practices.

Debate is a well-known learning tool in Western civilization. Debating societies existed hundreds of years ago at British universities, reflecting the great importance that society placed on parliamentary debate and rational problem-solving. British immigrants formed colonial debating societies soon after coming to New England. Classroom debating, however, is a much more recent activity, dating back only about 100 years. Adam Sherman Hill's book, *Argumentation*, published in 1894, is generally considered the first formal debate textbook and accompanied the formation of high school and college debate leagues around 1900.[1]

Early debate programs existed either as extracurricular clubs or were associated with various academic disciplines such as speech, political science, philosophy, or English. Gradually, however, most debate programs came to be associated with university speech departments. In fact, there is a correlation between the growing interest in debate at the college level and the creation of speech departments at many universities in the early years of this century. By 1915 the academic discipline of speech formed a national professional organization (now known as the Speech Communication Association) and began publishing the *Quarterly Journal of Public Speaking* (now the *Quarterly Journal of Speech*), whose early tables of contents make reference to many articles about debate training.

Why is debate usually considered a part of the speech communication discipline? After all, political scientists concern themselves with public policy disputes, philosophers analyze arguments and claims, and teachers lacking formal speech communication backgrounds often direct high school debate programs. Although part of the answer is contained in the historical connection between debate and speech, the uniquely oral character of debate also explains why communication study includes debate.

The variable of oral presentation makes debate a special decision-making form. Oral argument, less common than written argument, is saved for "special" contexts, such as courtrooms, legislative assemblies, and even academic debate contests! Oral argument is unique for several reasons. There has to be an occasion (such as the debate round and tournament), rules (structural and situational), and an audience (such as a debate judge). These dimensions give oral debate an immediacy and liveliness not typically found in written argument. We instinctively know that oral presentation of arguments differs from written arguments. The basic differences lie in the spontaneity and unpredictability of the context, as well as the chance for refutation and rebuttal.

You probably join millions of Americans watching political debates. Perhaps you saw the 1988 presidential candidate debates and doubted that they were really spontaneous. Although that may be true, think about the advance preparation of the candidates, the negotiations about the format and questioners, and the intense media-inspired public anticipation of the debates. These debates had a high degree of unpredictability because the candidates could not completely anticipate the questions they would face.

Similarly, the potential for refutation makes oral debates special. Many of the dramatic and interesting turning points in political debates occur when candidates respond to or refute opposing claims. Richard Nixon's famous "kitchen debate" with Soviet Premier Nikita Khrushchev is one example of the significance of refutation in energizing an oral debate. Another example occurred during the vice-presidential debate in 1988, when Senator Lloyd Bentsen rebutted a claim by Senator Dan Quayle with the observation "You're no Jack Kennedy!" This carefully planned rejoinder placed Quayle on the defensive and tightened the presidential race. Although political campaign debates often exhibit far too little spontaneity and refutation, they have the potential for creating levels of interest and excitement in the political process that would not exist if the candidates were to simply exchange campaign platforms and position papers.

You probably sense the direction we are going with this discussion. We intend to make a case that your debate practice ought to strongly emphasize good oral communication skills. The rest of this chapter looks at four communication-related debate elements: delivery, style, refutation, and cross-examination.

DELIVERY

According to classical rhetorical thought, good delivery was essential to effective persuasion. After inventing the message by selecting appropriate subjects and forms of proof, arranging the message, and choosing an appropriate style, the speaker practiced a delivery style complementing the message. Communication theorists have always recognized that effective communication combines a carefully crafted message with a compelling presentation. Delivery influences a debate in several ways.

1. *Good delivery enhances speaker credibility.*

Aristotle was probably the earliest theorist to recognize that persuasive success is partially a product of the speaker's "ethos" or credibility. Also well known is that audiences use a speaker's delivery as one of the major considerations in deciding whether a speaker is credible.[2] You may recall our discussion of substantive and motivational proofs in chapter 3. Debaters must recognize that their persuasiveness is as much a function of their ability to motivate the listener as it is to present logical proofs. Your own communication experience no doubt confirms this idea. You know that it is more difficult to believe an uninteresting speaker even if you sense why you should pay attention to the message.

2. *Good delivery enhances message comprehension.*

Good delivery makes the message easier to understand. Debate is a unique form of public speaking in which speakers sometimes deliver their message at a rate of speed faster than normal conversation. Although sophisticated note-taking in the form of flowsheets have evolved to help the listener keep track of the statements and evidence introduced, listening to a debate requires well-developed listening skills.

An important ingredient of this listening is the speaker's ability to present the message as clearly as possible. Listeners have difficulty understanding and ultimately accepting incomprehensible messages. As a person speaks faster, he or she has a corresponding tendency to speak less plainly. When speaking more rapidly, speakers tend to articulate sounds less effectively. You probably have seen commercials featuring an actor talking very quickly and you understood everything the speaker was saying. This is because the actor emphasized his articulation so that the audience understood his words. A good debater follows this example.

3. *Good delivery enhances debate as an aesthetic experience.*
Good delivery helps make debates more pleasing to hear. Early academic debates happened in front of large audiences. Gradually, the tournament model of competition led to most debates happening in front of a single listener or a small group of listeners performing the role of judge. Even though few academic debates have a large audience, aesthetic elements of debate still must be considered. Debate ought to be training for other public speaking situations.

In every context outside of the academic debate, aesthetics are important. Speakers who ignore the aesthetic dimension in "real-world debates" will fail miserably. A speaker has the duty to be lively and interesting and to show evidence of caring for the audience. This caring takes the form of delivering the message in ways that will enhance the audience's ability to listen to and enjoy the information presented.

Good delivery is important for three reasons: It builds credibility for the speaker; it aids the audience in assimilating the information presented; and it makes the debate a more aesthetically pleasing experience. Unfortunately, the role of delivery in debate is a controversial subject, because of very different perceptions among scholars about the relative importance of delivery when compared to other situational components in the debate.

The Controversy about Delivery in Debate

When participating in a debate tournament, some debaters speak rapidly; and some judges prefer debates in which the speakers present a lot of statements and evidence at a rapid pace. Beyond doubt, the single most-criticized element of the debate situation is the rapid and often incomprehensible delivery used in many academic debate rounds.[3] Competitive debates have evolved toward much faster delivery since the 1950s. Although not all debaters speak quickly, even the delivery of inexperienced debaters can seem hard to follow to untrained listeners.

Some debate judges and theoreticians defend rapid delivery. Situational and structural variables explain the commonalty of rapid delivery. One structural model of debate views debate from an information-processing perspective. We often characterize our times as the "information age," in which information has replaced goods and services as the most important force shaping society. Proponents of this view assert that "information is power," and that good decision making depends on access to as much information as possible.

Using the information-processing model, debaters attempt to present many assertions and claims, giving the judge as much information as time permits, to help him or her in making the most rational decision. Because the debate time limits are for the most part unchanging, the only way for the debater to present more information is to speak more quickly, cramming as much information as possible into the limited speaking time. And because many judges are veteran debate judges, accustomed to rapid delivery and able to keep an accurate flowsheet of the debate, debaters are able to practice maximizing their presentation of large quantities of information without fear of penalty.

Rapid delivery is also explained partially by situational variables. We discuss the game-playing nature of debate at various points in this text when we analyze the situational elements of debate. Two common game-related elements are the equating of quantity with quality of issues and claims and the use of decision-making models that reward debaters for making unanswered statements. These two strategies lead to debaters' winning debate rounds by advancing more issues and claims than their opponents can successfully refute in the time allowed.

The concept of *clash* helps to explain why debaters sometimes win through the sheer quantity of issues and claims presented. Audiences expect arguers to clash or respond to opposing assertions and claims. Although clash may come about in many ways, clash depends on the goal of responding to each opposing statement. This creates the perception that failing to respond to multiple assertions and claims, regardless of their individual quality, is bad or unsuccessful debating.

The strategy of winning a debate by advancing more positions than can be refuted is called "spread debating." This approach, like an arms race, feeds upon itself. The Soviets and Americans (at least before glasnost and perestroika) see each other stockpiling more and more arms and think they can guarantee their security only by out-stockpiling their rival. In debate, teams discover that judges reward other debaters for having unanswered positions and, to be competitive, create their own arsenal of positions. You know, of course, how difficult arms control is for the superpowers. This attitude of mutual distrust sometimes pervades the academic debate context.

Proponents of the spread strategy sometimes justify this approach by contending that debate is an academic game most appropriately conducted in front of trained listeners who know the structural and the situational rules. Thus, tournaments do not regularly encourage using untrained (lay) judges to critique debate rounds. Students who want to be successful must adapt to their judges—who sometimes are less concerned with presentation than with content. Judges often reward debaters for deemphasizing good delivery skills in favor of presenting more assertions and claims.

The information-processing model of problem solving has encouraged debates in which the quantity of statements seems to be more important than the quality of arguments. This approach deemphasizes delivery in favor of presenting as much information as possible. The information-processing model has at least two fundamental weaknesses when used in debate:

1. *More information does not always result in better decisions.*

Scholars who have investigated information theory agree that more information does not always improve the final decision. Decision-makers must determine what information is important, and in doing so, they have their own biases, negating the supposed advantage of having more information. Or the decision-maker may delay making the decision in hopes of getting more and better information.

2. The spread strategy undermines the ethical and rational bases for the debate activity.

Deemphasizing delivery undermines the justification for learning debate skills. This approach assumes that good rhetorical skills can be compartmentalized—that a student can learn good analysis skills without having to learn good delivery skills. This contradicts the advice of rhetorical teachers from Aristotle to those of the present, who emphasize the interrelationship of the various parts of the speech act (speaker, message, audience). By comparison, it would be like learning baseball by working on hitting only, and ignoring fielding and base running. You might learn to be a great hitter but ultimately end up to be a lousy baseball player!

Communication is, fundamentally, interaction between people. Good communication necessitates an appreciation and empathy for other communicators in every context. Delivery is one of the important interfaces between the speaker and the audience, and poor delivery suggests that the speaker is not concerned about the audience, defeating any hope the speaker harbors of successfully persuading the audience.

Elements of Good Debate Delivery

Good delivery is based on sincerity and comfort. A good speaker articulately and passionately states a position while simultaneously showing concern for the listener. Good delivery can be learned. Some people are "natural" speakers, but any person can learn the techniques of good speaking. Probably the best way to improve speaking is to practice. Practice allows the speaker to overcome anxiety and anticipate potential problems before they occur. Your college probably has public speaking classes that could help you to be a better speaker. Good debate delivery emphasizes the dual needs of *clarity* and *persuasiveness*.

The audience must understand the speaker. The speaker must speak loudly and clearly enough for the audience to hear and understand him or her. The speaker also must use nonverbal elements of delivery to help persuade the listener. Some suggestions for debate delivery are:

1. Stand close enough to listeners (judges) to be understood but not so close that you intrude upon their space.

2. Speak in as natural a style as possible. Use gestures and body movements you are comfortable with.

3. Closely monitor the judge's nonverbal cues. This will give you feedback about the success of your attempts to persuade that person.

4. Be passionate about your position. Act enthusiastic and confident about your claims. Behave like you are having fun.

Good delivery also involves creating for the listener an image of yourself. You want the listener to perceive you as dynamic and passionate about the positions you are arguing. This makes you more interesting and persuasive.

In summary, then, delivery is one of the important characteristics of debate. Oral argument differs from written argument. The rhetorical tradition of communication strongly influences our conception of good delivery. Delivery is a controversial area of debate, as many debate teachers believe that delivery is less important than other debate elements. This perspective is based on an information-processing model of debate. Although it is popular, this model has several weaknesses. Finally, good delivery combines clarity and persuasiveness and is an important element in persuasion.

STYLE

Style, a second rhetorically grounded debate variable, is defined as *the speaker's language-related choices*. As communicators, we are always making stylistic choices. We use different language in front of our friends than we do in front of our grandparents. We use different language in our writing than we do in our speaking. Oral language, for example, tends to be briefer, less complex, and more descriptive.[4]

The importance of style to good debating should be somewhat apparent. Language has an almost infinite capacity to shape our perceptions of the world. Great speakers are often known by their ability to use language powerfully. Winston Churchill is a case in point. Churchill was a great orator but not an especially good speaker.

He succeeded through his legendary ability to use language powerfully. In probably his most famous address to Parliament, Churchill inspired his listeners:

> I would say to the House, as I have said to those who have joined this Government: "I have nothing to offer but blood, toil, tears, and sweat."

> You ask what is our policy? I will say: It is to wage war, by sea, land and air, with all our might and with all the strength God can give us. . . . That is our policy.[5]

Contrast this passage with an alternative style: "I will work hard. We will try to win the war any way we can." Both passages give the same message, but Churchill's style is much more interesting and compelling.

We can't all be Winston Churchill, but debaters, too, make stylistic choices in speaking, and these choices affect their success or failure. Some suggestions for good style in debate are:

1. *Be positive.*

A debater should constantly use language that frames his or her issues in the most positive light possible. Statements such as, "We have proven that . . ." or, "We are winning this issue . . ." are examples of a positive style. A debater must be somewhat like a sports announcer, always describing the action in the debate to the judge. Of course, debaters always have the responsibility to be ethical; they may not distort the debate simply in an effort to be positive about the issues. The sample debate has examples of being positive.

2. *Be economical.*

Another important stylistic goal for a speaker is to be as economical as possible in the number of words used. As few words as possible should be used to express the point. The rationale is simple: Speaking time is limited, and the speaker wants to present enough issues to help win the debate.

3. *Be humane.*

Being humane in using language simply means attacking the opposing claim rather than the opposing debater. Humane use of language never confuses an attack on an issue with an attack on a person. For example, a speaker might say, "The negative's third subpoint is wrong, based on a faulty study" rather than, "The negative is lying on the third subpoint by basing it on a faulty study"; or, "We are winning the third subpoint" rather than, "We are killing the negative on third subpoint."

This probably indicates the difference between debate and sports. Metaphors such as "killing," "beating," and "destroying" are often used in sports contexts. These are not appropriate words in debate contexts; debaters have to remind themselves that the game is only part of the debate process rather than the end. Our language choices symbolize our attitude about life, and we want to communicate to others our acceptance of their humanity and our unwillingness to treat them as objects rather than as people.[6]

4. *Signpost flagrantly.*

Signposting means telling the listener what assertion, claim, or issue you are discussing. "I am now on their B subpoint" and "I will have three responses to their third contention" are examples of signposting. The most important role of signposting is to help the judge "flow" the claims being made. If the judge does not understand what point you are responding to, you are unlikely to persuade that person.

REFUTATION

One of the most important goals of a debater is to overcome opposing attacks. We call this refutation. Refutation is defined here as *answering or overcoming opposing assertions, claims, and issues.* We all use refutation regularly in our interactions with others. An example is:

Dave: Devo is the hottest group of recent years. They're fun to listen to and easy to dance to.

Mike: How can you say that? U–2 sings much more socially relevant songs, and they're better musicians.

This imaginary example shows how refutation works in its simplest form—presenting a counter-claim or assertion. You might look ahead to chapters 6 and 7 to read about more complex ways in which debaters refute opposing claims. Any time debaters respond to a real or an anticipated opposing position, they engage in refutation.

Refutation is used in two ways. It describes a form or type of claim, as you will recall from chapter 2, and it also describes a process or form of communication. The latter sense of the term is discussed here. It helps to explain why we discuss refutation when outlining the debate process.

Good refutation is systematic; the debater uses the same general form each time he or she answers an assertion or claim and ensures that the speaker is doing the best possible job of overcoming opposing claims. The four steps to refutation are:

1. *Mention the assertion, claim, or issue you are refuting.*

This is simply to help the judge and opponents know what you are attacking. For example, "Go to their B subpoint, UN peacekeeping is effective." Claims and issues sometimes resemble other claims, which creates confusion if the speaker does not include this step. Here is an example from the sample debate:

> Contention number two. Tugwell evidence there in '84 says the safety valve theory has been turned on its head. She says Heritage Foundation.[7]

2. *State your counter-claim.*

Here you tell what your claim is. For example: "I will have several responses. First, peacekeeping efforts worsen conflict situations." Again, the purpose is to make it easy for the judge and the opponents to flow your attacks. It also provides a point of reference for knowing whether the claim and evidence directly clash with the opposing point. Again, an example from the debate:

> First argument is, who . . . is the *Atlantic Monthly*?[8]

3. *Present your evidence or reasons.*

This step of refutation entails presenting the evidence or reasons you are using to justify your refutation. In the sample debate, the second affirmative continued:

> How come that beats the Heritage Foundation? She doesn't even read a source.[9]

4. *Show the effect of the refutation on the debate.*

The final step is to show the judge why the refutation is important to deciding the issues in the debate. For example, "Since we have shown peacekeeping to be ineffective, the affirmative case lacks any real significance." The purpose of this step is to help the judge determine how to weigh the issue in the debate. The judge must compare both sides of the issue and may not follow the importance of the refutation presented.

In systematic refutation these four steps are followed every time you respond to a claim. Although cumbersome at first, with a little practice systematic refutation becomes almost second nature. Do you have to refute every opposing point introduced in the debate? You probably see the difficulty of trying for complete refutation of every opposing claim. Time constraints alone make it unlikely that you can give sufficient attention to every point. More significant, is that not every issue and claim is equally important. Debaters sometimes introduce issues simply to entice their opponents to use valuable time refuting the issue while ignoring more critical issues. This is similar to a strategy the Allies used during World War II. The Allies created a fictitious army under the command of General Patton. They dropped false hints to the Germans that this army would be the main force invading France, at Callais, some distance from Normandy. This strategy caused the German high command to keep several Panzer divisions waiting for the imagined invasion that might have turned the tide at the actual Normandy invasion.

You have to learn *what* to refute and *how* to refute. One valuable technique in this regard is to "group" assertions and claims and refute the group rather than each individual point. Grouping issues helps you to keep the focus on the issue as a whole rather than to get lost in trying to deal with the individual assertions and claims that make up the issue. The speakers in the sample debate used this technique in a number of instances. Although they did not group every issue, they did group issues they perceived to be less important to the outcome of the debate.

CROSS-EXAMINATION

Any television watcher already has an idea about the nature of cross-examination. The merciless defense attorney uses wily tricks to make the guilty party break down on the witness stand and confess. If only life imitated art! Even real-life attorneys recognize that cross-examination is rarely as clear-cut and dramatic as it is portrayed. Trying to compare debate cross-examination to television cross-examination is even more difficult. The main point the two have in common is the label—cross-examination. Beyond that, the dissimilarities become more important.

Definition and Purpose of Debate Cross-Examination

Debate cross-examination means *asking and answering questions to clarify, refute, and anticipate issues*. Debate cross-examination is different from legal cross-examination in at least three important ways:

1. In debate, all speakers ask and answer questions. In law, lawyers ask and witnesses respond.

2. In debate, no limits are placed on the kinds of questions that may be asked. In law, strict rules are applied in regard to leading questions, inadmissible questions, and so on.

3. In debate, strict time limits influence the number of questions and the ability to follow up questions. In law, time limits do not limit the questioner's ability to follow up questions.

Cross-examination serves several purposes in debate:

1. *To clarify assertions, claims, or issues that are ambiguous.*
The most obvious cross-examination purpose is clarification. You often have to ask and answer questions to help clarify ideas that were not clear from presentation in the speech. This is similar to asking questions of your professors in class. It can be more important in the debate context, in which speakers often speak quickly and present a lot of information. Your attention is divided between listening to the speaker and thinking about how you will respond. You may have to clarify opposing positions to know how best to answer them.

2. *To distinguish between your position and the opponents' position.*
You may cross-examine to help the judge identify the points of clash in the debate.

3. *To set up future positions.*

Debaters use cross-examination to elicit information they can use to set up the positions they will develop in later debate speeches.

Cross-Examination Tactics and Strategy

Although judges pay attention to cross-examination, they sometimes do not keep careful flowsheets of the information presented and may treat cross-examination different from other speeches in the debate. This implies that judges probably consider cross-examination as an opportunity to make inferences about the debaters' ethics and arguing skills rather than as a time for creating, extending, or refuting issues and claims. *Demeanor*, therefore, becomes more important than content in many cross-examination situations.

This is similar to courtroom cross-examinations, in which juries and judges use cross-examination, in part, to determine whether a witness is believable. A debater can use cross-examination to influence the judge's perception of him or her. This is done by combining *assertiveness* with *politeness*. In cross-examination the speaker must assertively request information and respond to opponents' questions while also appearing helpful and open, with nothing to hide. The problem, of course, is that cross-examination is confrontational—the only genuine opportunity speakers have to interact directly with each other during the debate. This creates the opportunity for lively discussion, and potentially for undesirable confrontation in the form of anger or evasion.

Strategies for the Questioner

The questioner should take the *offensive* during cross-examination by controlling the direction and tempo of the interaction. Good questioning is the product of preparation rather than luck. Good lawyers exhaustively prepare for cross-examination by trying to anticipate all the ramifications of the questions they ask. The worst outcome of cross-examination is being confronted with an unexpected answer that undermines the gains achieved by other questions. Some suggestions for the questioner are:

1. Ask questions in series, beginning by establishing common ground and moving gradually to questions that identify disagreements or uncertainties.

2. Maximize yes-no questions, and minimize open-ended questions.

3. Be assertive, polite, and confident.

Questioners should avoid asking questions randomly. Instead, they should identify several areas they want to ask about during cross-examination and ask questions in a serial fashion. A question series consists of questions that take between thirty seconds and one minute to develop. These series begin with questions establishing common ground ("Now your B subpoint says, UN peacekeeping efforts fail, doesn't it?") to help the respondent and the judge know what you want to talk about. The series then moves to increasingly pointed questions designed to elicit some final point or admission. Although not every series will lead to a damaging admission, the questioner can anticipate future positions by showing weakness or gaps in opposing positions.

Closed-ended (yes-no) questions are preferable to open-ended questions. The questioner wants to strictly control the information gained through the cross-examination. Asking open-ended questions gives the respondent an opportunity to expand upon or clarify information already in the debate that might be persuasive to the judge.

Finally, the questioner strives to be confident and polite even if confronted with a "reluctant witness." A reluctant witness tries to avoid answering questions by acting dumb or being confrontational. Sometimes respondents behave as if they do not understand the question, or they insist on explaining or arguing about the question. The appropriate strategy for dealing with the reluctant witness is: Ask the question; rephrase the question if it is not answered or if the respondent indicates that he or she does not understand it; and then repeat the question.

If after three tries you have not succeeded in getting an answer, go on to another question. You may also politely cut off the speaker if the person engages in a long-winded explanation of an answer. Although you must allow respondents to explain their answers, you are not required to give them unlimited time.

Strategies for the Respondent

The respondent is on the *defensive* during cross-examination. The respondent cannot completely anticipate the questions that might be asked and cannot know the ramifications of answers on opposing lines of attack. Thus, the major strategies of the respondent are to avoid volunteering information, to maintain a cool demeanor, and to use any opportunity to clarify or reiterate strong points that present themselves.

The respondent should clarify yes-no answers whenever appropriate. This is not an excuse for wasting time with unneeded explanations but, rather, is a chance to avoid admitting something that might support an opposing attack. In responding to a yes-no question that requires an explanation, the respondent might say, "Before answering yes or no, I would like to explain. . . ." The respondent's last strategy is to master the "poker face." Occasionally, skillful questioning will force a respondent to mistakenly make a damaging admission. The significance of a damaging admission may not be apparent to the opponent or the judge if the respondent manages to avoid verbal or nonverbal cues admitting error.

A written transcript is an imperfect way of illustrating some of the ideas regarding demeanor that we believe are important in effective cross-examination. The following excerpts from the sample debate, however, do exemplify some of the ideas introduced here. Consider cross-examination of the first affirmative by the second negative speaker:[10]

Benson: "The UN then consists only of the three major organs, correct?"

Crenshaw: "Yes."

Analysis: The question sets up common ground. It is designed to anticipate a future negative argument, by making the affirmative commit to a position, and it uses the yes-no format.

Benson: "OK, now, do the other areas of the UN contribute to the beneficiality of the UN?"

Creshaw: "Well, we're talking about membership in the United Nations according to the resolution. And

>membership in the United Nations only
>includes those three."

Analysis: The question fits with the previous question as part of a series, designed to acquire particular information. The answer is appropriate in using a qualification of an answer rather than giving a yes-no response without elaboration. The questioner is showing politeness by not cutting off the respondent before completing an answer.

Benson: "So only those three. But do the other
              organizations contribute to our beneficiality of
              being in that particular organization?"

Crenshaw: "I really don't know, and I would contend that
              is irrelevant, because it is not—"

Benson: "That is irrelevant?"

Crenshaw: "Yes, it does not fit under the topic in any way.
              It is not a resolutional discussion."

Analysis: The questioner tries to spring his trap by closing his line of questioning. The respondent attempts to avoid making a crucial admission. The questioner interrupts the respondent, which ought to be done only sparingly. The point of questions may not be completely apparent to the audience, which might undermine credibility of the questioner unless the first negative uses the answers.

Benson: "Now, the UN escalates these conflicts? Right?
              How many has it empirically escalated?"

Crenshaw: "I think there is one example of the Arab-Israeli."

Benson: "The Arab-Israeli dispute? Which one?" (laughter)

Crenshaw: "The conflict in that area."

Benson: "In that area. I mean there are all kinds of
              conflict. Are we talking, like—"

Crenshaw: "Israel and the PLO is what I believe Mr.
              Tugwell is—"

Analysis: This long exchange, later during the cross-examination period, shows the conflicting strategies of the questioner and the respondent. The questioner presses the respondent to be more specific about the examples and harm areas of the case. The questioner seeks to determine if the evidence in the case fits the analysis the affirmative advances. The respondent, on the other hand, attempts to avoid giving information that will help the negative, and tries to use the general, open-ended questions to extend the affirmative case. The questioner, realizing that strategy, interrupts regularly to keep the examination on track. The questioner also uses humor to show the generality of the respondent's answers. Humor can be an appropriate speaking tool.

SUMMARY

Delivery, style, refutation and cross-examination are techniques for applying communication variables to debate. Rather than being distinct from other communication constraints, debate is simply a communication context wherein principles of good communication can help the speaker to be a more successful debater.

Good communication depends on establishing a relationship between the speaker and the audience. Adapting to the listener, rather than expecting the listener to adapt to you is certainly one of the important keys to debate success.

ENDNOTES

1. Chapter 1 includes discussion of some of the history of academic debate. In addition, for information on the early history of debate, see E. R. Nichols' series of articles in the *Quarterly Journal of Speech*.
2. The relationship between delivery and source credibility is well known. Consult any textbook on persuasion or public speaking.
3. Herman Stelzner, "Tournament Debate: Emasculated Rhetoric," *Southern Speech Communication Journal* 27 (1961): 34–42.

4. Karlyn Kohrs Campbell, *The Rhetorical Act* (Belmont, CA: Wadsworth, 1982).

5. Winston Churchill, address to Parliament, May 13, 1940, in William Manchester, *The Last Lion* (Boston: Little, Brown and Co., 1988), p. 684.

6. Wayne Brockriede, "Arguers as Lovers," *Philosophy and Rhetoric* 5 (1972): 1–11.

7. Appendix A, Delao, p. 212.

8. Appendix A, Delao, p. 212.

9. Appendix A, Delao, p. 212.

10. Appendix A, Benson questioning Crenshaw, pp. 202-204.

6

Debating the Affirmative

──────────────── **Chapter Objectives** ────────────────

☐ Understand what goals the affirmative is trying to accomplish in its speeches.

☐ Know and be able to use proactive and reactive affirmative strategies.

☐ Understand the responsibilities expected of each affirmative speaker.

☐ Identify the types of affirmative statements and issues.

☐ Visualize strategies that the affirmative can use to
prepare to debate.

If you are new to debate or have limited experience, constructing an
affirmative case may be challenging. Successful experienced debate
teams often have more than one strong affirmative case. In this
chapter we offer some suggestions that may help in meeting the
challenges of affirmative case construction and rebuttal
presentations. We hope that you will come to see how the various
affirmative speeches are part of one coherent strategy.

OVERVIEW OF THE AFFIRMATIVE

The goal of the affirmative is to persuade the judge that the resolution should be adopted. At the end of the second affirmative rebuttal, the last speech of the debate, the affirmative will want to persuade the judge that the affirmative case and arguments were stronger than the corresponding negative ones.

The affirmative has several advantages at the outset. The affirmative begins the debate and has the last word. The affirmative has the right to define terms and present criteria for evaluation. The affirmative also has the right to identify the issues it hopes will be the focus of the debate. Although these advantages might seem overwhelming, they are balanced by the negative's ability to capture the debate by winning a particular issue, if it is important enough. The affirmative must win all the major arguments.

STRUCTURAL RESPONSIBILITIES OF THE AFFIRMATIVE

The following reveals the affirmative's structural, or constant, expectations; judges expect affirmatives, in most cases, to develop these lines of analysis:

1. To present and defend a topical case.

2. To present and defend definitions of resolution.

3. To present and defend contentions that justify the resolution.

4. To present a prima facie case.

5. To uphold the burden of proof.

The first structural responsibility of the affirmative is to introduce and define the resolution. The affirmative has the structural obligation to be reasonably *topical*. To be topical the affirmative will have to show that it has provided a reasonable interpretation of the resolution. Topicality is often a key issue in contemporary debate. In short, the affirmative must show the judge that its interpretation is reasonable and fair. At this point, you may wish to refer to chapter 3 to refresh your memory on topicality.

Judges usually expect the affirmative, in addition to presenting a topical case, to present *definition* and *criteria* claims. Affirmatives also are expected to present *contentions* in support of the resolution. These contentions should, in most cases, show that a significant problem exists that warrants attention and adoption of the resolution. These contentions analyze the stock issues that the affirmative must defend. You recall that the stock issues include the issues of definition, criteria, significance, and comparison. Affirmative contentions usually develop the latter two—significance and comparison. These contentions present the judge reasons why the affirmative's interpretations are strong and should be adopted.

At the end of the first affirmative speech, the judge must be convinced of a reason to debate. If, for example, the affirmative fails to present criteria to evaluate the competing claims, or the affirmative does not show a need to debate the resolution, the affirmative has failed to present a *prima facie* case. This Latin phrase means "at first glance." Negative debaters can argue that the affirmative has failed to present a case warranting debate. An analogy to the courtroom might help here. If a defendant is charged with murder and the prosecution is unable to produce a body or a motive for the murder, the judge might throw out the case for lack of evidence. In the same way, the negative might show that the affirmative has not upheld its structural obligations to show a need for the resolution.

Not only must the affirmative present a prima facie case, but it also must assume the *burden of proof*. Because most value resolutions challenge existing beliefs and values, the affirmative has a structural obligation to show sufficient reasons that will persuade the judge to consider altering existing beliefs and values.

Debate theory has borrowed heavily from the legal field. Existing values and beliefs, much like a defendant before a judge and jury, are often considered "innocent until proven guilty." The affirmative must provide proof justifying the changes proposed.

Although these structural expectations remain constant, every judge and negative team will respond to the affirmative in different ways. As a result, affirmative debaters will have to adjust to some of the situational constraints that might arise in a given debate round.

SITUATIONAL EXPECTATIONS OF THE AFFIRMATIVE

One goal of the affirmative is to present claims and issues for which the negative has not sufficiently prepared. During the course of the debate season, you might debate the same team two or three times. To keep a competitive edge, you will have to continually change and alter your case. The better affirmative teams seem to be one step ahead of the negative, even if they have debated the same team before.

Most important, the affirmative should remain responsive to all arguments the negative might choose to present. The affirmative will have to be ready for different kinds of arguments presented in a variety of ways. To remain in control of the debate round, the affirmative will have to anticipate arguments and refute arguments presented by the negative teams at a given tournament.

The affirmative also must adapt to the judge. Some judges enjoy a fast-paced speaking style and might be persuaded by innovative and unusual interpretations of the resolution. Other judges tend to be more traditional and will expect the affirmative speakers to present eloquent orations and arguments. Successful affirmative debaters are careful to adjust their case and their arguments to the specific judge.

AFFIRMATIVE SPEAKER DUTIES

Debaters have the responsibility to discuss particular claims and issues in a speech. Table 6.1 reviews the affirmative speaker duties introduced in chapter 2.

The duties of the first affirmative are relatively set: That speaker must present a prima facie case justifying the resolution. The second affirmative's duties, in many ways, depend on the nature of issues presented in the first affirmative and on the strategies of the first negative. In turn, the first affirmative rebuttal, one of the most difficult debate speeches, must answer all the major issues and claims of the second negative constructive, as well as the extensions of the first negative rebuttal. Finally, the second affirmative rebuttal has the duty to answer all remaining negative issues and summarize the reasons why the judge should vote for the affirmative.

Table 6.1   Affirmative Speeches and Duties

Type of Speech	Duties
First affirmative constructive	Primarily initiates issues, introducing them into the debate. Signifies those issues by anticipating possible negative attacks.
Second affirmative constructive	Primarily initiates, clarifies, refutes, and signifies. Occasionally questions and refocuses. Second affirmative is trying to rebuild affirmative case, after initial attacks of the first negative, and move the affirmative case forward (extending the case).
Affirmative rebuttals	Refutes, refocuses, signifies, clarifies, and questions. All rebuttals have the same basic purpose of refuting opposing claims, refocusing the debate on the issues signified most favorably to the arguer, and clarifying any issues that might be misunderstood.

To clarify the affirmative speaker's duties in value debate, Figure 6.1 outlines the flow of argument in the constructive speeches. It illustrates the flow of debate as it occurs in the constructive speeches. Note how the first affirmative initiates statements by defining the resolution (the first stock issue); presents criteria designed to measure the values (the second stock issue); presents contentions identifying the significance of the resolution (the third stock issue); and makes claims comparing the status quo and the affirmative's preferred value hierarchy (the fourth stock issue). The first negative follows with specific responses to issues presented by the first affirmative. The second affirmative responds to the issues and claims of the first negative and then attempts to extend the positions presented in the first affirmative.

Because debate rules and practice are in a state of constant change, the duties described here may be altered depending on the circumstance. We hesitate to present any rules of debate and are reluctant to tell debaters that they *should* do this or that. The following "rules" are provisional and are meant as suggestions rather than as immutable laws. But, we do believe that these principles can be useful guides.

Figure 6.1   Flowchart of Arguments in Constructive Speeches

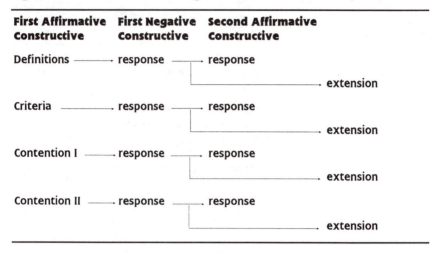

First Affirmative Constructive

We offer the following principles as a way of creating a coherent philosophy of the affirmative:

1. *The first affirmative should be constructed with the rest of the affirmative speeches in mind.*

The Florida State University first affirmative was well-constructed because it anticipated and refuted potential negative arguments. In reading the transcript of the debate, you get the sense that the two affirmative debaters had worked together in attempting to create a consistent, coherent affirmative strategy. The best affirmative teams seem to know what issues will be developed during the course of the debate; these teams anticipate and build their affirmative strategies around these issues. They seem to start with the last affirmative speech and work backward to the first affirmative. That is, the first affirmative speech is designed to initiate arguments that will be developed in later speeches.

2. *The first affirmative should be an eloquent oratory.*

Modern debaters tend not to spend much time practicing or working on the language used in the first affirmative. This tendency is unfortunate, for given the importance of initial impressions and of speaker points, the need to present an eloquent first affirmative seems obvious. Eloquence entails a careful delivery and an appropriate choice of words. The first affirmative should begin with a fitting introduction, seeking to get the judge's attention. A speech can be introduced effectively in many ways. Public speaking books have many good suggestions.[1]

Debaters should practice the first affirmative speech many times before presenting the speech in competition. They should refine, repair, and clarify the speech continuously. Most famous public speakers revise and rework their speeches meticulously. Successful debaters do likewise.

3. *The well-constructed first affirmative speech anticipates and inoculates against negative attacks.*

Various studies investigating persuasive strategies have revealed that the persuasive arguer should work to "inoculate" the audience against opposing arguments. Good affirmative speeches are written in anticipation of negative issues and strategies. Persuasion theorists note that if you forewarn your audience, you forearm your audience against negative attacks. The second contention in the Florida State first affirmative did, in a sense, anticipate and refute potential negative strategies. The negative debaters repeatedly argued that the United States effectively controlled international conflicts. The first affirmative forewarned her audience of that idea, illustrating the inoculation strategy.

> While it may seem obvious that conflict control is in everyone's interest, the UN only exacerbates conflict. Note contention two, the UN heightens conflict. The reason stems from how the UN functions.[2]

Here we see a concrete example of an advocate anticipating and refuting a possible negative response. We encourage you to make use of a similar approach when you construct your first affirmative.

At this point, you may want to reread the first affirmative presented by Florida State. As you can tell, this affirmative contained all the necessary components for a good affirmative case. Working with this example, let us consider, in some detail, the five components of an affirmative case, as presented in Table 6.2.

Introductions

In recent years, introductions have lost their importance in debate, so we hope you will consider the reasons why the introduction is an important part of a well-written first affirmative speech. The first affirmative should be an eloquent oratory in support of the resolution. The first affirmative should present compelling reasons why the judge should vote for the affirmative team. Based on evidence gathered by rhetoricians and social scientists, the introduction can be an important means of persuading an audience.[3]

The persuasive introduction is succinct and is a pleasure to hear. In our experience, we have seen first affirmatives present memorized introductions and others read a scripted introduction. Both styles can be satisfactory. Some first affirmative introductions are recitations of the resolution: "We stand resolved that . . ." Other introductions might display some humor. Witty introductions might revolve around a play on words, self-deprecating humor, or a joke. Other introductions might be constructed in the manner of the Florida State first affirmative.

An affirmative can use the introduction in many ways to advance its position. The affirmative should want the judge to understand the thesis of the affirmative case. Because many debates become muddled, the introduction is an ideal place to present a clear description of the affirmative's thesis. Judges often reward debaters who attempt to provide clarity in a debate. The introduction also should present the resolution to the judge. Ideally, the introduction should leave the audience predisposed in favor of the resolution. After

Table 6.2   Components of the First Affirmative Case

Component	Function
1. Introduction	Identifies case thesis and the debate resolution
2. Definitions	Provide the meaning(s) of key terms
3. Criteria	Establish the measures of the value terms
4. Contentions	Identify issues and claims justifying the resolution
5. Conclusion	Provides a synopsis of why the judge should adopt the resolution

presenting the introduction, key terms of the resolution may have to be defined.

Definitions

Chapter 3 introduced the stock issue of definitions. Because key value terms are often found in a debate resolution, a first affirmative may be wise to provide the judge and the opponents with the meanings of these terms. If the affirmative is advancing an unusual or a peculiar interpretation of the resolution, presentation of strong and persuasive definitions may be essential.

Definitions are open to argument. If the negative does not find the affirmative arguments to be reasonable or strong, the negative may attack those offered by the affirmative and may offer better definitions. A carefully and thoughtfully constructed set of definitions will greatly help the affirmative to win the argumentative ground.

Recall the debate over definitions in the sample debate. The first affirmative built a strong set of definitions by turning to authors and experts in the problem area. These authors and experts had considered, in a careful and scholarly manner, the meanings of key terms in dispute. Certainly the advocates could turn to a general dictionary for definitions, but (as discussed in chapter 3, on stock issues) strong definitions specify the definition's context and purpose in the debate case.

Good definitions provide careful distinctions between various meanings and for reasonable clarity. Good definitions allow the affirmative to distinguish itself from the negative. Judges expect the affirmative to give some argumentative ground to the negative. Thus, the affirmative will want to offer definitions that allow room for disagreement. Finally, the affirmative will want to avoid using idiosyncratic or profoundly unusual definitions. On occasion, an affirmative case may be based on an unorthodox interpretation of the resolution. Although innovative thinking should be encouraged in debate, some affirmative cases are designed to avoid discussion of the resolution. Such affirmatives often rely on definitions that may not be consistent with those offered by mainline authorities. Debaters sometimes base these affirmative cases upon the sixth or seventh dictionary definition of a term.

We encourage you to discover definitions used by experts in the field under discussion. We also encourage you to present definitions that provide clarity and precision. Reconsider the use of definitions in the sample debate. The affirmative had to define the meaning of the term "United Nations" and offered a definition in anticipation of a popular negative stance that the useful services provided by the United Nations were functions of agencies not "officially" part of the organization. Florida State wisely anticipated this negative stance by offering a contrary definition of the United Nations found in Thomas Franck's book. As noted previously, Franck is one of the best known experts on the United Nations topic.

If affirmative teams have to define key terms, they may be offered in the form of observations. These observations would organize the definitions for the judge and the opponents. An outline of a typical observation on definitions might be:

I. Definitions
   A. Word in resolution in need of definition
      Source of definition
      Definition
   B. Word in resolution in need of definition
      Source of definition
      Definition

After you have provided definitions of key terms of the resolution, you will need to construct criteria that will allow you to measure and to assess the desirability of competing values. To illustrate this model, consider the following example taken from the Florida State first affirmative:

> (A) subpoint, definitions. Initially, we'd like to note that the affirmative has the right to reasonably define terms because otherwise the negative could always define the affirmative as falling outside the scope of the resolution. The term United Nations implies only the General Assembly, the Security Council, and the Secretariat. Thomas Franck . . . explains what the UN is, in 1985.[4]

After presenting the definitions, the affirmative should provide a transition statement to the observation on criteria.

Criteria

Criteria consist of a series of standards for measurement. That is, if you are to measure the worth of an object, event, or activity, you will need a scale. This scale forms what debaters now call *decision criteria*. Note how the affirmative offers a decision criterion in the sample debate: "We support the contention that beneficiality should be evaluated according to the United States' national interests."[5]

Strong decision criteria are constructed the same way that decisions are constructed. Authors writing on topics related to the resolution often defend standards that are useful in measuring and assessing policies and values. In its case, the affirmative implicitly defended some specific standards, arguing that the UN does not achieve the desired conflict resolution goals. Decision rules should be designed to help advocates compare reasons. In this case, the affirmative presented an explicit decision rule asking the judges to determine if the UN serves the US national interests.

Several affirmative teams debating the UN resolution used criteria designed to persuade the judge and the opponents to ask if the UN had achieved its ends of helping to solve world problems. Such criteria might guide the rest of the debate. Good affirmatives are able to filter most of the arguments through their criteria. Well-constructed criteria help the judge compare the relative strengths of the affirmative and the negative positions. In addition, such criteria might help the first affirmative rebuttalist answer the arguments presented by the second negative constructive. For example, many affirmative teams were able to show that the useful UN functions could be fulfilled by other agencies and organizations.

To this point, we have discussed three of the essential components of the first affirmative: introduction, definitions, and criteria. All of the components should be part of an integrated set of claims and issues. The best first affirmatives carefully construct their speeches with well-designed transitions. Before discussing the fourth component, contentions—the heart of an affirmative—let us summarize what we have covered, with the following outline:

I. Introduction
   Statement of thesis
   Statement of resolution
   Transition to definitions

II. Definitions
    Presentation of definitions
    Citation of field sources
    Transition to criteria

III. Criteria
    Presentation of standards for assessing issues
    Citation of field sources
    Transition to contentions.

Contentions

The contentions present the concrete, documented reasons why the resolution, from the perspective of the affirmative, is true. The contentions develop analysis of the stock issues of significance and comparison. For example, membership in the United Nations may be unwarranted because the UN does not control conflict. Expert testimony that the UN is unable to control conflict substantiates the contention. Consider the following example, taken from the first affirmative speech:

> Note contention two, the UN heightens conflict. The reason stems from how the UN functions. Please note subpoint (A), the UN is used to blow off steam. The original purpose of the UN was to provide the countries of the world a place where they could vent their frustrations in the hope that the pressures which build up due to unsettled disputes would be relieved without the necessity of blood and agony. Mr. Tugwell, of the Center for Crisis Studies, establishes this in 1984.[6]

This example is a good vehicle for explaining how a contention should be constructed. First, note how the speaker titles the contention: "The UN heightens conflict." The entire label consists of four words. The judge can flow the contention with three symbols, "UN confl"—or with some other shorthand abbreviations. Chapter 9 presents techniques of flowsheets in greater detail.

The transition between the contention and the cited evidence leads the judge and the opponents to the supporting proof. Accordingly, the affirmative turns to an expert to support the contention that the UN had heightened conflict. The expert, Dr. Tugwell of the Center for Crisis Studies, seems to be well-qualified.

The affirmative does a nice job in providing these qualifications. In addition, the affirmative's citation is complete, as it provides the reasons behind Dr. Tugwell's conclusion.

The affirmative provides evidence to support the contention. Jeanne Kirkpatrick and Professors Yeselson and Gaglione echo the conclusions reached by Dr. Tugwell. This is an excellent example of how an advocate can strengthen a contention. Rather than relying on one source to support a key argument, the affirmative fortifies the argument with corroborating sources.

Contentions should be organized in such a way that they are mutually supportive. The contentions also should flow directly from the criteria and should allow the judge to conclude that the criteria are useful and helpful in assessing competing claims. If, for example, the affirmative had stated that utility should be a primary criterion of judgment, the first contention would have showed that US membership in the UN was not beneficial.

As we have mentioned, the contentions in a first affirmative speech should be designed to support the criteria and one another. Another example should help to illustrate how contentions might be constructed for mutual support:

> We note subpoint (D), the UN is used to mobilize for war. The UN may be intended to cool emotions, and plenty of lip service may be given by its supporters to that goal, but the actual participants of the UN use it for mobilizing war efforts. Professor Yeselson and Gaglione of Rutgers explain: "[The UN] is a weapon in international relations and should be recognized as such. As part of the armory of nations in conflict, the United Nations contributes about as much to peace as a battleship or an atomic bomb. Disputes are brought into the UN in order to weaken an opponent, strengthen one's own side, prepare for war, and support a war effort.[7]

Subpoint D of the second contention extends and supports the first contention. The second contention also anticipates the reactions of the negative team. During the course of the debate season on the UN topic, many teams argued that the UN defused conflicts. Here, the affirmative builds a strong contention anticipating this issue. Strong statements of transition and reasons are given for the conclusions reached. The affirmative contentions are supported and presented well. Another detailed outline will help illustrate why the contentions are useful models.[8]

Contention: The UN heightens conflict.

Theory: A brief, 4–6 word contention is easy to flow.

The reason why stems from how the UN functions.

Theory: The transition must be effective, particularly for an audience of debate judges, who tend to be experts in argumentation.

Subpoint (A), the UN is used to blow off steam.

Theory: The statement must be appropriate to the thesis of the contention.

Tugwell of the Center for Crisis Studies

Theory: The debaters provide the qualifications of the source. The judge can trust that the evidence comes from an authority.

Winston Churchill expressed it, "better jaw, jaw than war, war."

The UN is the one place in the world where representatives of nearly all countries—regardless of size, wealth, or power—are freely heard on the broad range of world issues. In this regard . . . the General Assembly is the principal forum for blowing off steam.

Theory: The evidence cited must be from a qualified authority. In addition, the evidence provides the reasons for the conclusions.

Conclusion

After presenting definitions, criteria, and contentions, the first affirmative speaker should summarize the thesis of the affirmative case. Clarity is critical to acceptance of the speech. Here, the affirmative might restate the thesis of the affirmative case and read evidence in support of this thesis. For example, the first affirmative concludes: "We now ask you to stand resolved that membership in the United Nations is no longer beneficial to the United States."[9]

Second Affirmative Constructive

The second affirmative constructive speech should be devoted to the reconstruction and extension of the first affirmative constructive positions. The second affirmative speaker has the duty to respond to the assertions, claims, and issues presented by the first negative. If the first negative elects to attack the first affirmative by making use of "straight refutation," the second affirmative will have to respond to that strategy. The second affirmative has to respond to all counter-claims, evidence presses, and any causal link attacks. In contemporary debate a popular strategy of the first negative is to present a "shell," or an undeveloped argument, which is "picked up" or developed by the second negative. The second affirmative will have to prepare for this strategy. The negative need win only one major issue to claim victory in the debate. Therefore, the second affirmative must prepare to deal with all claims and issues that the negative advances. Figure 6.2 illustrates the flow of statements up to and including the second affirmative.

As you can tell, the second affirmative must respond to the first negative's arguments. The second affirmative also has the responsibility to rebuild the case through extensions. The following argument was presented by the second affirmative in the sample case:

> Contention number two. Tugwell evidence there in '84 says the safety valve theory has been turned on its head. She says Heritage Foundation. First argument is, who . . . is the *Atlantic Monthly?* How come that beats the Heritage Foundation? She doesn't even read a source.
>
> Second argument is that evidence does not say they reach their opinions first. She merely asserts that. Third argument is she should just prove them wrong. If he is so incorrect, then just say why they are wrong. She says, number two, that they empirically prevented wars. Obviously not true. It is empirically false because we have wars all the time. And you have all this debate out there and they still go to war. Means at least

Figure 6.2 Flow of Analysis from First to Second Affirmative

first affirmative		**first negative**		**second affirmative**		
contention one	→	response	→	response		
				└	→	extension

venting does not lead to peace. Not that it necessarily leads to war, but it does not lead to peace.[10]

Notice how the speaker used four-step refutation and simultaneously extended the case and refuted the opposing positions. The speaker took this approach throughout the constructive. The constructive speeches primarily initiate, clarify, and refute issues, whereas the rebuttals compare and ultimately decide the final affirmative and negative positions.

Affirmative Rebuttals

Effective affirmative rebuttals retain command of the debate round. The negative has a 12-minute block of time between the second affirmative constructive and the first affirmative rebuttal. To counteract this negative advantage, the affirmative must enter the rebuttals with a strategy and some arguments to counter the negative block.

First Affirmative Rebuttal

The first affirmative rebuttal should attempt to answer all the issues presented by the second negative constructive and to respond to the major claims presented by the first negative rebuttal. This speech is difficult but challenging. Fortunately, some guidelines apply to this speech.

The first affirmative rebuttal must prioritize the issues in debate, giving special emphasis to issues that the affirmative has not addressed in the debate (usually presented by the second negative constructive) and issues that might lose the debate for the affirmative side. The first affirmative rebuttal usually adheres to the organization of the second negative constructive, while spending extra time on crucial issues. After answering second negative issues, the speaker spends whatever time remains on issues presented by the first negative rebuttal and the second affirmative constructive.

The first affirmative rebuttal should group the second negative arguments. The constructive speeches are allowed enough time for the advocates to provide detailed responses to particular arguments. In the 5-minute rebuttal speeches, advocates do not have time to offer the detailed analysis provided in the constructive speeches. The grouping strategy is designed to refute a series of arguments with a single, powerful response. Because the first affirmative rebuttalist has only 5 minutes to deal with both the value objections and the case side argumentation, the grouping strategy is often a necessity. Note how the first affirmative rebuttal in the sample debate responded to a value objection:

> Starting with the observations and going straight case. Observation number one. Please group her extensions. Subpoint one, membership in the UN is not membership in the agencies. Her definition by her author is the definition of the UN, it is not the definition of membership, and certainly that is the distinction in 2AC. Subpoint two, Franck extends that you could pull out and still belong to the agencies and that evidence is dropped.
>
> Subpoint three, her on-balance evidence is blurby and does not necessarily address the issues that the affirmative team does. And she grants the criteria of military security, so it is her burden to prove that evidence addresses that.[11]

These responses are not designed to deal with all the specific subpoints. Rather, they attempt to address most of the major issues embedded in the negative's value objections.

Another major goal of the first affirmative rebuttal is to respond to all major issues on the case side. Although the amount of time spent on case-side issues will vary from round to round, most effective first affirmative rebuttalists spend from 1 minute to 1 minute, 30 seconds on case-side issues. In the following excerpt, you can tell that the first affirmative rebuttalist is running out of time but still answers the negative's arguments and extends the arguments of the second affirmative constructive:

> Contention two, UN heightens conflict. (A) subpoint. The only thing he wants to extend is the Heritage Foundation indict. But I'd just like to point out . . . that we have other sources. Subpoint two, Tugwell is not Pines, you know. If you want to apply this indict, it has to be specific. Subpoint three, he drops Miguel's second answer that they assert it and his third answer is that you should just prove him wrong.[12]

The first affirmative has responded to the major claim presented in contention one in the first negative rebuttal. In addition, she extends the positions of the second affirmative that were not discussed by the first negative rebuttal. A good first affirmative rebuttal also should set up the second affirmative rebuttal for the final speech of the debate.

Second Affirmative Rebuttal

The second affirmative rebuttal is the last speech of the debate. Four constructive speeches, four cross-examination periods, and three rebuttal speeches precede this speech. As a result, the final speaker has much to draw upon. The goal of the second affirmative rebuttal is to refute all the major issues and claims the second negative rebuttal emphasizes and to explain why the affirmative has won the debate. The second affirmative has the last, and perhaps the best, opportunity to persuade the judge.

The general organizational pattern this speaker follows is to begin the speech by trying to defeat any outstanding negative issues that might cause the affirmative side to lose the debate and to end the speech by extending issues that are most favorable to the affirmative side. This strategy ends the debate by leaving the judge with the clearest, most recent memory of the important affirmative issues.

As with the first affirmative rebuttal, the second affirmative rebuttal addresses the value objections and then the case arguments. On occasion, the second affirmative might want to begin with a strong case argument that might refute a major value objection. Regardless, the second affirmative must address all the major arguments extended by the second negative. The last rebuttalist usually does not discuss arguments not extended by the second negative rebuttal.

In the sample debate, the second affirmative addresses the peacekeeping issue by arguing:

> But last thing Carrie says, you know, in 1AR was . . . you have to extend all the evidence I read in the 2AC on peacekeeping. And my evidence says, they don't want the United Nations, they won't go there, and it says because they're getting shot at; and that is why I think I made the distinction why the US is good; that evidence says that the Netherlands is sick and tired of getting their people killed. The US fights back. And the evidence I read there said that the UN would not have been any more successful at Lebanon and therefore should not be taken out. That evidence was granted. He had arguments there, but still granted what, everything the evidence indicated. I think that one card said they are getting shot at and therefore don't want to contribute soldiers, indicates why the US is better. What it comes down to is, you are not going to get

the US. The question is, is there a better solution? I mean in any sense is there a slightly more optimal solution? To the extent that we can defend ourselves, we at least guarantee that there is possibility for more peacekeeping. Because you're not going to get it from the UN. That Cuellar evidence is dropped. All he can win is that it used to be great, and you know, I have to agree with him on that.[13]

This excerpt illustrates the kinds of arguments presented in the second affirmative rebuttal. This speaker must address all the major claims and issues, and show why such statements do not warrant voting for the negative team.

PROACTIVE AND REACTIVE AFFIRMATIVE STRATEGIES AND TACTICS

The affirmative position should be carefully thought out and well-integrated. You and your partner will have to develop and to anticipate strong positions that you can defend and extend throughout the debate. For example, you might want to construct the first affirmative in such a way that the affirmative can anticipate and refute the negative's positions. You might want to present claims in the first affirmative that can be used to refute value objections. The second affirmative should remain flexible and ready to answer a variety of negative attacks.

The affirmative has the advantage of justifying the resolution with the first and last speeches and of defining the issues that might be argued in the debate. During the course of a debate season, affirmative debaters will want to anticipate, through proactive strategies, the positions that the negative might advance. In addition, the affirmative will want to remain flexible by calling on a variety of reactive strategies that can be used in response to a specific negative attack.

SUMMARY

The affirmative strategy should be responsive to the structural and the situational demands of the debate round. We hope that you now better understand how to debate the affirmative by responding to these demands. The affirmative case should be designed to uphold the resolution, and the affirmative strategy should lead a judge to vote for the affirmative.

ENDNOTES
---

1. Jo Sprague and Douglas Stuart, *The Speaker's Handbook, 2nd. ed.* (Chicago: Harcourt, Brace, Jovanovich, 1988).
2. Appendix A, Crenshaw, p. 200.
3. Mary John Smith, *Persuasion and Human Action: A Review and Critique of Social Influence Theories* (Belmont, CA: Wadsworth, 1982).
4. Appendix A, Crenshaw, p. 199.
5. Appendix A, Crenshaw, p. 200.
6. Appendix A, Crenshaw, p. 200.
7. Appendix A, Crenshaw, p. 201-202.
8. Words in italics are from p. 200, Appendix A.
9. Appendix A, p. 202.
10. Appendix A, Delao, pp. 212.
11. Appendix A, Crenshaw, p. 223-224.
12. Appendix A, Crenshaw, p. 225.
13. Appendix A, Delao, pp. 228.

7

The Negative Side

---
chapter Objectives

- ☐ Understand what goals the negative is trying to accomplish in its speeches.
- ☐ Know and be able to use proactive and reactive negative strategies.
- ☐ Understand the responsibilities expected of each negative speaker.
- ☐ Identify the types of negative statements and issues.
- ☐ Visualize strategies that the negative can use to prepare to debate.

Preparing to debate on the negative side is probably more difficult than preparing for the affirmative. After all, the affirmative can anticipate the direction of its case and prepare for how the issues will unfold. The negative, on the other hand, does not have access to the affirmative case beforehand. It must prepare for any number of different case areas that fit under the resolution. The negative must prepare to respond to an even larger number of assertions, claims, and issues that the affirmative might present in its chosen case.

This does not mean that the negative has a hopeless task. The negative can use some strategies to its own advantage, and they can present claims and issues that the affirmative may not anticipate and can prepare more completely on ones that the affirmative has anticipated.

OVERVIEW OF THE NEGATIVE

The goal of the negative is to persuade the judge that the negative side should win the debate. Although the various structural paradigms introduced in chapter 8 require the negative to win certain issues in order to win the debate, these share the common principle that the negative needs only to win *some* issues to succeed, whereas the affirmative must sustain the burden of proof by winning *all* the stock issues in the debate.

The reason for this apparent difference in what is required to win the debate is the fairness principle created to sustain debate as a game. Because the affirmative chooses the case and is given the opportunity to define the terms of the resolution, the negative is given an *artificially assigned presumption*. This is distinguished from the *contextual presumptions* that exist in any controversy and may be very different from controversy to controversy. For example, if we were to debate the proposition, "God is alive and active in our lives," the artificial presumption would be assigned to the negative, although most audiences probably would believe the contextual presumption exists for the affirmative.

You might review the discussion of presumption in chapter 2 to refresh your understanding of presumption. Artificial presumption does not usually come into play in a debate, because its function is simply to allocate the debaters' duties. Contextual presumptions, on the other hand, can readily influence how much proof is needed to convince a listener to accept an issue or idea.

Table 7.1 summarizes the duties and types of claims used by the negative speakers. The primary structural responsibility of the negative is to show flaws in the affirmative's reasoning and evidence. The negative tries to show why the affirmative has failed its burden of proof to provide a prima facie case in favor of the resolution. This is typically done in one of two ways. First, the negative creates *reasonable doubt* about the case. It creates reasonable doubt by showing many small flaws in the affirmative's analysis, suggesting to the judge that because the negative wins many claims and issues, even

Table 7.1   Negative Speeches and Duties

Type of Speech	Duties
First Negative Constructive	Has two primary functions: refuting and initiating. Begins the process of responding to and tearing down the affirmative issues. Refutes and initiates issues the negative will ultimately rely upon to win the debate. Also will question affirmative assertions and begin to signify why negative issues are more important than affirmative ones.
Second Negative Constructive	Initiates, refocuses, and signifies. Although the speaker may use the other strategies, this speech primarily attempts to initiate issues that will be more important than the affirmative case (compound issues) and refocus the debate on those issues and signify issues the negative will use to win the debate.
Rebuttals	Refutes, refocuses, signifies, clarifies, and questions. All rebuttals have the same basic purpose: to refute opposing claims, to refocus the debate on the issues signified most favorable to the arguer, and to clarify any issues that might be muddled or misunderstood.

if no single one of these issues is sufficient to defeat the case, enough doubt has been created about the sufficiency of the case to justify the judge voting against it. This would be like a technical knockout in boxing, in which the referee stops the match when a boxer is unable to continue defending himself.

The other negative method is to show a *fatal flaw* in the affirmative case. Here, the negative wins a single major issue that presumably is sufficient to defeat the affirmative case. This fatal flaw issue is often drawn from the debate stock issues. The negative chooses one issue—for example, topicality—and attempts to win the debate by pulling through that issue and arguing that the affirmative has not successfully presented its case because of this fatal flaw.

The negative also has some situational responsibilities. The main situational responsibilities are to adapt both to the affirmative strategy and to the judge's expectations. The negative cannot flawlessly anticipate the affirmative's strategies. One situational goal of the affirmative is to catch the negative unaware.

The debate situation, as noted in chapter 5, sometimes rewards the affirmative for presenting its case and its extensions in a way for which the negative is not completely prepared. Sometimes the affirmative uses trickery to accomplish this end. Other times the affirmative uses a case approach or case extensions that the negative has not anticipated. These difficulties compel the negative to prepare as many arguments as possible ahead of time. The negative must always prepare for the unknown. Although preparation cannot cover all possible circumstances that are encountered, it can at least cut down the number of unanticipated cases and issues.

The negative also must adapt to the judge. The judge, is, of course, the most important element in the debate context. Chapter 8 discusses paradigms and offers some suggestions about analyzing judges. Both the affirmative and the negative must carefully consider the peculiarities of the judge and how that judge is analyzing the debate situation and issues. Often the debaters' choices are a direct result of their attempt to adapt to their judge's preferences.

NEGATIVE SPEAKER DUTIES

Speaker duties refer to the debater's responsibility to present and defend particular issues in a debate speech. The division of responsibilities between the speakers represents the strategic choices the debaters make in attempting to win the debate. Successful debating requires a "division of labor" between the two negative speakers. Each negative speaker must be responsible primarily for initiating and extending issues presented in the debate. Although the other speaker may occasionally build upon those issues, the difference between the issues for which each speaker takes primary responsibility should be clear.

The reason for dividing labor is to make the best possible use of time in the debate. The negative must carefully plan its use of time because the negative does not know what the affirmative will argue or how it will extend the affirmative case. The negative must advance various positions to discover one or more that might successfully defeat the case.

Before outlining specific duties of each of the negative speakers the responsibilities expected of every speaker in the debate round are recounted:

1. *The responsibility to be clear.*

Every speaker should debate as plainly as possible. The judge and the opposing team should understand the speaker's delivery and follow the logic of his or her assertions and claims. The negative should avoid equivocation or intentionally misleading its opponents.

2. *The responsibility to be persuasive.*

Speakers should use every opportunity to persuade the judge to accept their positions. They do this through a persuasive delivery and by "weighing" issues. Debaters weigh an issue by showing its importance to the judge or by asserting that their position is superior to an opposing one. The first affirmative rebuttal in the sample debate gives an example of weighing:

> Extend Miguel's second answer from 2AC, peacekeeping worked in the past but has changed. Of course, that Tugwell evidence has been dropped by both negative speakers throughout this round. That means that you have no more peacekeeping after his examples that he provides. And that evidence is dropped.[1]

3. *The responsibility to be ethical.*

Every speaker, of course, ought to debate ethically. The principles of ethical debating are explained more explicitly in chapter 10. We simply remind you here that one of the most important debate concepts involves behaving fairly and ethically. This means that debaters should not intentionally misinterpret the positions of their opponents or mislead their opponents or the judge about the strength of their own positions.

Before describing the speaker duties of the negative speakers, we must caution you not to consider these duties "etched in stone." This description is only a guideline for the negative speeches. Speaker duty schemes are not debate "rules." Debaters are always free to use any strategy they desire. The advantage, however, of following commonly held expectations for the debate speeches is considerable. It allows the debate judge to concentrate on listening to the claims and issues rather than having to figure out the structure the negative is using. This probably makes the judge feel more comfortable about the negative positions and more likely to accept the issues and claims.

Figure 7.1 diagrams negative speaker duties.

First Negative Constructive

As the negative's first chance to present its position, this speech is important in shaping the judge's perception of the negative team. First impressions are, of course, important. Like a lawyer making an opening statement to the jury, the negative is trying to create a good impression and to undermine the impression that the affirmative has made. The first negative constructive can take two approaches.

The first approach is *straight refutation*. The first negative approaches the affirmative case in the order that it was presented and attempts to respond to all or most of the affirmative case, using one of the types of claims: counter-claim, evidence press, or causal link attack (presented later in this chapter). The first negative might present an issue that does not respond directly to a point made in the affirmative case (called an *overview* or *negative observation*), but this issue typically is not developed in much depth. This approach *reacts* to the affirmative case and gives virtually equal attention to all parts of the affirmative case.

Figure 7.1   First Negative Speaker Duties

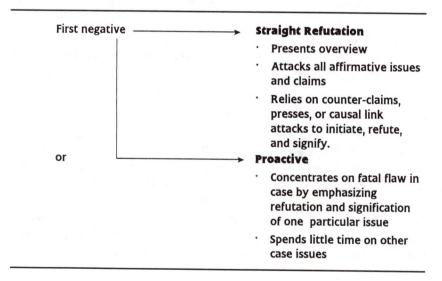

In the second approach, the first negative spends most of its time attacking one or more debate issue in depth while giving considerably less emphasis to other issues presented by the affirmative. The negative might choose one of the issues presented by the affirmative (such as one of its contentions) or an issue unique to the negative case (such as justification or topicality). The negative uses this approach when it sees a flaw in the affirmative case that it wants to develop in detail. Table 7.2 lists some common proactive negative issues that the first negative constructive might develop.

Second Negative Constructive

The second negative, in value debate, usually argues against the desirability of the affirmative's case. This speech often identifies the unfavorable implications of the affirmative's analysis of values. These implications include comparisons of the affirmative's value perspective with that of the negative.

The second negative constructive develops issues that are different from the issues the first negative introduces or issues that

Table 7.2   Common Negative Proactive Issues

Issue	Brief Description
Justification	Argues that the affirmative has not met the requirements of all terms of the resolution[2]
Topicality	Argues that the affirmative case should not be debated on this resolution[3]
Hasty Generalization	Argues that the affirmative case example is not typical and does not provide an appropriate example of all the case areas on the resolution[4]
Alternative Causality	Argues that the affirmative has identified the wrong cause for the problem discussed
Counter-Value	Argues that another value must be considered more important than the value(s) underlying the affirmative case

are picked up by the second negative and developed in much greater detail. The options of the second negative are listed in Figure 7.2.

The traditional second negative approach introduces *off-case* issues. These are called *counter-value* or *value objection* arguments. These arguments are discussed in the next section. Their purpose is to identify costs associated with accepting the values embodied in the affirmative case.

The second negative also might extend issues initiated by the first negative constructive. This strategy was introduced in the previous chapter—referred to as picking up an issue. When the second negative picks up an issue, the speaker takes responsibility for the issue and the first negative does not extend the issue in the first negative rebuttal.

First Negative Rebuttal

This speaker extends the issues introduced in first negative constructive and refuted by the second affirmative. This speaker

Figure 7.2   Second Negative Speaker Duties

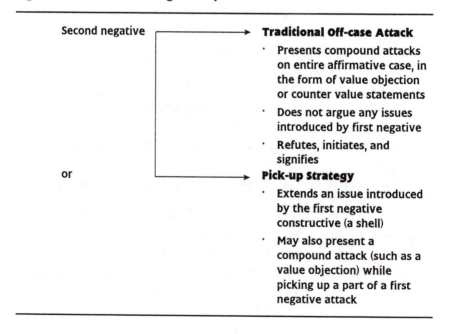

would not extend issues picked up by the second negative. The most important duty of the first negative rebuttal is to begin identifying the most important "voting issues" in the debate, or ones the negative believes the judge may use to justify voting for the negative.

Second Negative Rebuttal

This speaker—the last negative speaker in the debate—tries to extend and summarize all the issues in the debate from the negative's point of view. Because time is insufficient to adequately discuss every issue introduced, the speaker must emphasize the most important issues and claims. The speaker, in effect, "writes a ballot" for the judge, by identifying the reasons why the negative did the better job of debating.

TYPES OF NEGATIVE ISSUES
AND CLAIMS

Negative statements and issues are divided into two types: *elementary* and *compound*. Elementary attacks are assertions and claims that directly refute assertions, claims, and issues presented by the affirmative. They normally are simple in the sense that they do not have a complex substructure. Elementary attacks are the common form of *direct refutation* of the affirmative case. Compound attacks are assertions and claims that indirectly refute the affirmative case by creating a chain of reasons combining to refute a given issue in the

Table 7.3   Elementary and Compound Attacks

Elementary	Compound
Attacks on causal links	Counter-criteria
Counter-claims	Topicality claims
Presses	Observations
	Value objections

affirmative case. Table 7.3 lists the elementary and compound attacks the negative uses.

Elementary Attacks

The negative uses three elementary attacks: attacks on causal links, counter-claims, and presses. Elementary attacks include all six of the major and minor types of debate statements. An elementary attack is a singular statement that is not directly linked to other statements. The negative uses elementary attacks to directly refute affirmative claims. These attacks are usually simple in the sense that they do not have a complex chain of substructure or reasons.

Attacks on Causal Links

As we defined them in the previous chapter, causal links are the reasoning steps that connect evidence to a claim. Affirmative cases consist of complex chains of reasons leading to a conclusion. One important negative strategy is to "unlink" the affirmative case by refuting or undermining as many of the affirmative's causal links as possible. The negative attempts to point out flaws or deficiencies in the affirmative's causal reasoning. The first negative constructive in the sample debate gives an example. McGinnis is attacking the affirmative criteria documented by George Kennan:

> Second argument is why only this? Why are these the only three elements to talk about? Why can't we talk about health, welfare, and all that? Then they would argue that's within their third definition . . . which illustrates my point that they need sub-definitions before you can argue it.[5]

Counter-Claims

The counter-claim contradicts the affirmative claim by presenting counter-evidence or counter-reasoning. In the first negative, McGinnis made many counter-claims, one of which was a counter-claim to one of the claims of the substructure of the affirmative case:

> On the (B) point they state it equals the seeds for war. First argument is that they have a good track record. A. LeRoy Bennett, of the University of Delaware in 1984: "[T]he record of the UN in conflict resolution is

surprisingly encouraging. Of more than 150 disputes considered by the Council and the Assembly, not more than a dozen remain."[6]

Presses

A press is simply an assertion that challenges the affirmative to present more evidence or analysis. The purpose of presses is to get the affirmative to reveal more of its underlying evidence and reasons. When it does not have a causal link attack or counter-claim, the negative uses presses to respond to affirmative statements. The press gives the illusion that the negative is attacking the affirmative case—which is often a valuable situational strategy. An example of the press is again found in the first negative constructive of the sample debate:

> They argue from Franck in '85 that talks about political disputes. First argument is why is the affirmative definition distinct? Why is that the only definition? Why is the analysis I give above inappropriate?[7]

The negative combines all three of these elementary statements into the negative attack. This presents the affirmative with diversity in number and kind of attacks to be overcome in defending its case. Of course, as elementary attacks, unless there are too many for the affirmative to overcome or the affirmative makes errors in responding, transforming them into crucial issues, the negative will have to successfully initiate and defend its compound attacks to win the debate.

Elementary attacks can have any of the purposes of debate statements identified in chapter 2. They can initiate attacks, signify positions, refute opposing positions (probably the most common function), as well as question, clarify, or refocus issues.

Compound Attacks

Compound attacks are more complex negative claims that combine a series of assertions and claims into an issue that potentially can singlehandedly defeat the affirmative case. One tactical advantage of complex attacks is the negative's ability to initiate an issue of its choosing rather than having to react exclusively to issues presented by the affirmative.

Although every negative will use the elementary attacks introduced in the previous section, the choice of compound attacks depends upon the negative's choices of structural and situational paradigms. (Paradigms are discussed in chapter 8.) Some of the compound attacks fit well with the paradigms, and others do not fit well at all. Using compound attacks also depends on the affirmative case debated. Five compound attacks commonly used in value debates are discussed in the following pages.

Counter-Criteria Claims

The affirmative must present criteria to measure the values the resolution contains. As discussed in chapter 6, the affirmative can use a variety of criteria to analyze the resolution. The negative potentially can argue that the affirmative uses an inappropriate criterion to measure the effects of the resolution. The implication of the affirmative's using inappropriate criteria is that it will not be able to show the link between the value in the resolution and the significant harm shown by its case. The structure of a counter-criteria claim is:

1. Label of claim
2. Indictment of affirmative criteria
3. Presentation of counter-criteria
4. Justification of counter-criteria.

Topicality Claims

Topicality addresses the question of whether the affirmative case fits the resolution. An affirmative case must be topical to warrant consideration by the negative and the judge. Topicality is essentially an issue of fairness. If the affirmative case is not topical, the judge cannot reasonably expect the negative to effectively debate the case. The parts of a topicality claim are:

1. Standards for determining topicality
2. Affirmative violations of topicality standards
3. Presentation of alternative definitions
4. Effect of the claim on the debate.

A standard is used to measure whether a case is or is not topical. The two common topicality standards are *reasonability* and *best definition*.

The reasonability standard suggests that a case need only be "reasonably" topical. If there are definitions that an average person would accept, or ones that do not stretch the terms of the resolution to a large extent, the affirmative has reasonably defined the terms of the resolution. The best definition standard assumes that debaters should use the most appropriate possible definitions. This standard is based on the belief that in any given context certain definitions are the most acceptable for use. (The various methods of defining terms were discussed in the previous chapter.)

For the purposes of debating topicality, negative speakers rely primarily on the best definition standard, because the entire reason for arguing topicality is to show that the affirmative case does not properly fit under the resolution. The affirmative most likely would base a non-topical case on narrow or obscure definitions.

After presenting topicality standards, the negative identifies how the affirmative definitions do not meet those standards. The negative must show why the affirmative definitions are either "unreasonable" or are not the "best" definitions available. After making the indictment of affirmative definitions, the negative presents its own definitions and argues why the judge should consider the topicality issue.

Negative Observations

Negative observations are in-depth attacks on perceived weaknesses in the affirmative case that the negative wishes to emphasize. The negative emphasizes these attacks either by presenting them before directly refuting the points in the affirmative case or by spending time on the issue at the point the affirmative introduces it. The first negative constructive in the sample debate presented a negative observation at the beginning of her speech, defending the idea that membership in the United Nations is beneficial:

> Overview number one is that membership is inherently beneficial. (A) subpoint is that on balance, membership is beneficial and I'll cross-apply to their criteria on case side. Richard Gardner, Professor of Law at Columbia . . . [evidence] . . . (B) subpoint is that no U S means no U N . . . [evidence] . . . (C) subpoint is that specialized agencies go too . . . [evidence].[8]

The obvious purpose of this overview was to set up an issue that the negative intended to argue in depth. This is exactly what occurred in the debate.

Value Objections

Value objections are compound attacks comparing the benefits of accepting the affirmative's value to potential costs incurred. Cost-benefit analysis suggests that accepting any value as the basis for policy necessarily involves corresponding costs. A value objection attack argues that the costs outweigh the benefits that would be achieved. The parts of a value objection are:

1. Causal link to affirmative case

2. Harm or cost

3. Preemption of potential answers (optional).

The negative must identify what aspect of the affirmative value or case links to the problem or harm. The link should be as direct as possible. For example, a value objection on the United Nations topic might be: "Deemphasizing the UN undermines the value of peacekeeping." In the brief, the first subpoint of the case would link peacekeeping to the United Nations:

A. Peace is paramount.

    1. Peace is essential to national advancement.

Philip Aston, UN Division of Human Rights, *Bulletin of Peace Proposals*, 1980, p. 324.

"Every nation and every human being, regardless of race, conscience, language or sex, has the inherent right to life in peace. Respect for that right, as well as for other human rights, is in the common interest of all mankind and an indispensable condition of advancement of all nations, large and small, in all fields."

    2. The aim of the UN is peace.

Professors Goodrich, Hambro, and Simon, *The Charter of the United Nations*, 1969, p. 25.

"The order of listing, together with the content of subsequent Charter provisions, gives support to the view that the maintenance of peace and security is the primary purpose of the Organization and takes priority over other purposes."

   3.   Peacekeeping is the most important UN role.

Professor Debra Miller, Political Science, Columbia, *US, UN, and Management of Global Change*, 1983, p. 178.

"Perhaps the most important and effective role the UN performs in implementation is peacekeeping. Peacekeeping can be classified as an implementation function because it assists in keeping conflagrations from growing and in maintaining cease-fires with the aim of achieving a norm of the UN—the peaceful settlement of disputes."

The next part of the value objection isolates the harm or cost that results from accepting the affirmative value. This harm or cost can be measured quantitatively or qualitatively. A quantitative harm is one that can be measured in numbers. A qualitative harm is one that is intrinsically harmful regardless of the number of cases involved. Loss of freedom, for example, is a qualitative harm. The harm that is identified must be unique to the affirmative case. This means that the harm must occur only through accepting the affirmative's value. This is important because a valid comparison of alternatives can occur only when the alternatives are distinct. The harm and uniqueness are shown in the following example from the hypothetical value objection introduced earlier:

   B.   Support of peacekeeping forces is strong now.

   1.   Peacekeeping mandates have been extended.

UN Chronicle, February 1984, p. 94.

"During the year the Council renewed the mandates of the United Nations Interim Force in Lebanon . . . the UN Disengagement Observer Force . . . and the UN peacekeeping force in Cypress."

   2.   Both superpowers support peacekeeping forces.

Prof. Walter Jones (Political Science, Wayne State), *The Logic of International Relations*, 1985, p. 550.

"Even though the United States and the Soviet Union have grave disagreements over the uses and execution of peacekeeping operations, they have cooperated on all recent decisions regarding the Middle East and Cypress."

C. Peacekeeping facilitates deescalation of conflicts.

    1. Peacekeeping forces insulate the combatants.

David Wainhouse, of the Washington Center of Foreign Policy Research, *International Peacekeeping at the Crossroads*, 1978, p. 527.

"A most important aspect of peacekeeping is the insulation it provides where there is a real danger of superpower confrontation. Such an insulation is of paramount importance for US security."

    2. Peacekeeping forces provide diplomatic openings.

Indar Jit Rihkye, Director of UNITAR, *The Theory and Practice of Peacekeeping*, 1984, p. 245.

"It is generally accepted that peacekeeping is a diplomatic key opening the way to further negotiations for a peaceful resolution of conflicts."

    3. The alternative to peacekeeping is catastrophe.

Ramesh Thakur, Professor Political Science at the U. of Otaga, *The World Today*, March 1985, p. 101.

"Moreover they can help to contain sporadic incidents that are not meant to initiate a large-scale war. In other words, an important justification for peacekeeping is contemplating the alternatives, chaos or nuclear conflict."

    4. US abandonment of UN peacekeeping insures war.

Indar Jit Rihkye, Director of UNITAR, *The Theory and Practice of Peacekeeping*, 1984. p. 237.

"This campaign against UN peacekeeping seeks to damage the world organization's one really effective activity. The intention behind it is obvious: to persuade the United States to turn its back on UN peacekeeping, and rely on its own power. This suggestion is a sure formula for a global war."

Preemption of Affirmative Responses

The final element of a value objection is the preemption of affirmative responses. The negative must anticipate and attempt to answer potential affirmative responses to the value objection.

As was true of elementary attacks, compound attacks may also fulfill one of the six arguing purposes introduced in chapter 2. Compound attacks, however, are always major statements that either initiate, signify, and refute, or perform a combination of all three major strategies.

The negative uses elementary and compound attacks to attempt to defeat the affirmative case. Elementary attacks directly refute an assertion or claim. Compound attacks combine a number of assertions and claims into a more drawn-out attack on an affirmative issue.

NEGATIVE STRATEGIES

Two of the common strategies that the negative uses in preparing and executing its refutation of the affirmative case are negative briefs and picking up positions.

Negative Briefs

Debating successfully on the negative side requires anticipating the kinds of issues and claims the affirmative might present and then crafting a sound response. The negative must "brief out" their strategies. A brief is *a pre-planned group of assertions or claims that applies to an affirmative issue or claim.* Briefing out positions in advance of the debate gives the negative the luxury of being able to think about, research, and plan their lines of attack. During the debate round it is difficult to think of good attacks. Too much is going on to be able to plan for identifying the affirmative weaknesses.

By bringing as many briefs as possible to the debate tournament, the negative feels confident that they are ready for many of the recurring issues they will hear. That allows more time to cope with unanticipated issues.

Picking Up Positions

Sometimes the negative uses a strategy in which the second negative speaker extends an issue introduced by the first negative speaker. This is called picking up the issue. The purpose of this strategy is to give the negative an additional constructive speech to set up the issue in more detail and to expand the issue in later speeches. The negative uses this strategy when it believes it has an issue that takes considerable time to develop. The negative team in the sample debate used this strategy.

SUMMARY

The negative must find one or more issues to win in order to win the debate. This requires coping with both structural and situational responsibilities, planning carefully to use a variety of elementary and compound attacks, and preparing as many of the attacks as possible before going to the debate round. Choice of affirmative and negative strategies alike depends upon the preferences of the debate round judge.

ENDNOTES

1. Appendix A, Crenshaw, p. 224.
2. For further reading, see N. Adams and T. Wilkins, "The Role of Justification in Topic Analysis," *CEDA Yearbook* 8 (1987): 21–26; G. Turner, "Justification," *Debate Issues* (March, 1975).
3. For further reading, see David Thomas, "What Makes an Affirmative Case Topical?" in *Advanced Debate*, edited by David Thomas (Skokie, IL: National Textbook, 1979), pp. 72–74; Don Brownlee, "In Search of Topicality: Definitions and Contexts," in *Advanced Debate 3rd ed.*, pp. 443–448.
4. For further information, see David Berube, "Debating Hasty Generalization," in *Advanced Debate 3rd ed.*, pp. 483–489.
5. Appendix A, McGinnis, p. 206.
6. Appendix A, McGinnis, p. 207.

7. Appendix A, McGinnis, p. 206.
8. Appendix A, McGinnis, p. 204.

Section Three

Integrating Theory and Practice

8

Paradigms

─────────────── **Chapter Objectives** ───────────────

☐ Define paradigms and understand their use in a debate.
☐ Differentiate between structural and situational paradigms in value debate.
☐ Understand how to use and attack the paradigms debaters introduce in the debate round.

Before conducting an experiment, a scientist carefully maps out a systematic investigative plan, considering every possible contingency and variable that might affect the experiment. This systematic planning is called the *scientific method*. The scientific method is an example of a paradigm. Like a scientist, a debater must use paradigms in organizing, presenting, and refuting issues, assertions, and claims in the debate round. Paradigms guide the debater in presenting statements and guide the judge in interpreting and deciding the merits of those statements.

WHAT IS A PARADIGM?

A paradigm is a *prototype* or *model*. A paradigm provides an analogy for understanding one object or situation by comparing it to another.

Paradigms provide standards for thinking about and comparing issues, assertions, and claims in a debate. Judges use paradigms for judging the debate and determining which issues were most important and which team better analyzed those issues.

Paradigms can be found in every decision-making context. They help us to know how to act and make appropriate decisions in various situations. Scientists use the scientific method as their research paradigm. The scientific method helps the scientist to be logical and rational in investigating the unknown. The American legal system depends upon *common law* principles such as case law and legislative intent, which help litigants know how particular legal issues should be equitably resolved. The Ten Commandments are one of the bases of Christianity. These religious standards serve as a paradigm guiding personal behavior.

WHY DO WE USE PARADIGMS IN DEBATE?

Audience adaptation is fundamental to successful debating. Debaters have to predict how judges will respond to specific issues and debate strategies. Debate paradigms help debaters choose appropriate strategies for a wide variety of judges and ground debate in the real world by giving insight about various forms of decision-making.

Several structural and situational paradigms have emerged in academic debate.[1] Given the wide number of paradigm choices, debaters and judges must employ some rational criteria to guide their selection of paradigms. A useful paradigm ought to:

1. *Create good debating.*

A debate paradigm should produce debates that have good clash. A paradigm should not favor one side or the other.

2. *Produce clear and consistent debates.*

A paradigm ought to allow all the participants to know how issues will be evaluated and the debate decision made. The decision-making criteria should be consistent from debate to debate so that participants can learn how to make successful claims.

3. *Promote understanding of the underlying subject-matter issues in the debate.*

A paradigm ought to promote discussion of appropriate subject-matter ideas that help the participants better understand important policy and value issues.

4. *Create ethical and fair debates.*

A paradigm should be equally weighted for both the affirmative and negative and should maintain a sense of fair play for the participants so that the debate decision turns on evaluation of competing issues rather than on factors such as how quickly the debaters can talk.

PARADIGMS IN DEBATE

By now you are comfortable with the use of structural and situational elements of debate. Structural elements refer to aspects of debating that are for the most part predictable and unchanging. Situational elements are those unique to any given debate round. In earlier chapters we looked at the structural and situational components of arguing, use of evidence, and the debate process. There are also structural and situational paradigms. Structural paradigms are broad theoretical models used to structure the debate process by comparing debate to some other decision-making context. Situational paradigms describe strategic choices that debaters make by determining the specific debating preferences of debate judges.

Structural Paradigms

Structural paradigms are broad theoretical models that apply decision-making methods and standards from other arenas to debate rounds. Three structural paradigms are appropriate to use in value debates: the policymaking, the judicial, and the issues-agenda paradigms.

The Policymaking Paradigm

Policy debates often use the policymaking paradigm. Participants follow a legislative model and emulate legislators debating the merits of proposed pieces of legislation. The debate judge "votes on" whether to accept a "piece of legislation"—the affirmative case.

The Nature of Policymaking as a Paradigm

A policymaker compares the costs and benefits of the proposed policy to the status quo or to some other policy. The policymaker first determines whether a *significant* problem exists. The significance of the problem may be measured *quantitatively* (numerically significant) or *qualitatively* (aesthetically significant). The policymaker then considers whether the status quo has the means to remedy the problem without adopting a new mechanism. This is the issue of *inherency*. Presumably there is no reason to adopt a completely new mechanism when the current system has a way of dealing with the problem.

The policymaker then considers a potential solution in the form of a plan. Debaters compare the advantages of the plan to its potential disadvantages and consider whether the problem will likely be solved by following the plan. As noted earlier, this is the most common paradigm for policy debates. It also is often used in value debates.

Policymaking in Value Debate

How would a policy-oriented paradigm be used in a value debate? The answer lies in examining the close connection between value and policy disputes. Policy decisions are based on value judgments. For example, a decision to spend more money on national defense than on social programs would ultimately rest on accepting the value of defense as being more important than a competing social program. Policymakers, then, debate the underlying values before making a decision about adopting a particular policy.

Value disputes also have policy implications. These policy implications stem from the nature of debate resolutions, which are written in a unique way promoting discussion of the value implications of policies. Most *criteria* arguments used by both the affirmative and the negative suggest policy implications as the decision-making basis in the debate round. Negatives often present *value objection* statements that operate as disadvantage arguments used in policy debates. These value objections apply cost-benefit analysis to the affirmative case and argue that the benefits of accepting the affirmatives values are outweighed by the costs. This is the approach the negative took in the Macalester-Florida State debate used as the example in this book.

The decision-making criteria in a value debate using the policymaking model are:

1. What policy systems do the value statements in the resolution imply?

2. Are there policy-oriented decision-making factors that provide criteria for measuring the value statements in the resolution?

3. Applying these policy-oriented criteria, is there a problem that needs remedying?

4. Will the benefits of remedying this problem outweigh the potential disadvantages suggested by the value objections?

Merits of Using the Policymaking Paradigm

The policymaking paradigm has both advantages and disadvantages in value debates. The familiarity of this model to debaters and judges and the decision-making clarity it provides are the major advantages of the policymaking paradigm. Many debaters and an even larger number of debate judges are familiar with the policymaking model from their experiences as high school and college policy-debaters and judges. This is an advantage for debaters because judges have a well-developed understanding of what debaters have to argue to win a debate.

A second advantage of the policymaking paradigm is its decision-making clarity. Policymaking is based on cost-benefit analysis. In many debate contexts the potential costs and benefits of a policy are not difficult to compare. Assuming that the debaters identify the proper policy system value disputes, the judge may fairly evaluate the issues by considering the costs and benefits.

The policymaking paradigm does have some disadvantages. These include the blurring of policy and value controversies and the danger of misidentifying the relevant policy systems.

Use of the policymaking paradigm creates difficulty in visualizing the differences between policy and value debates. Considering public issues by taking into account only the policy-oriented factors involved in those issues ignores the many controversies that involve debate about important, if impractical, value-oriented issues. Further, using the policymaking paradigm may lock the debate into inappropriate reliance on cost-benefit analysis. The strengths and weakness of cost-benefit analysis were discussed earlier. The weakness of cost-benefit analysis as a decision-making criterion is that it is not always appropriate in evaluating value-laden questions.

The Judicial Paradigm

The judicial paradigm compares a debate to a courtroom proceeding, in which the judge determines whether the existing entity is innocent or guilty or uses legal decision-making principles to decide which of two competing positions to accept.

The Nature of the Judicial Paradigm

The judicial paradigm is probably the one first used in academic debates. So much of academic debate theory borrows from the legal system that the judicial paradigm has a natural logic or "fit." The judicial paradigm is based on analyzing debate stock issues. (You might want to go back and review the discussion of stock issues in chapter 2.) The affirmative must create a prima facie case by proving all the stock issues in the debate. The negative might win the debate by defeating any one of the stock issues.

The debate judge behaves as a neutral party, considering only the evidence and analysis the debaters introduce. The judge weighs the evidence the debaters present and decides which position has the greater probability of being true "beyond a reasonable doubt." This standard of proof makes debates evidence-oriented. Judges expect debaters to present proof for all assertions and issues advanced. This corresponds to the burden-of-proof requirement in courtrooms, where arguers are not normally permitted to advance assertions without proof.

The Judicial Paradigm in Value Debate

The judicial paradigm treats a value resolution as if it were a proposition of judgment. The judge determines not only the "facts of the matter" but also whether other factors should be considered in assessing a verdict. In a court of law, for example, a judge might have to decide whether a crime was committed and then consider whether other circumstances might justify the crime. This process has several steps:

1. Is there an *ill* that is significant enough to warrant consideration?
2. Can the *blame* for the ill be identified?
3. Does the ill have a *cure*?
4. Would the cure invoke *costs* that must be considered?

The first step is to determine whether a problem (ill) exists. The debaters identify the harm area that the resolution incorporates by *defining the terms* of the resolution, and then *establishing criteria* for determining if a problem exists. For example, in the resolution, "Resolved: that membership in the United Nations is no longer beneficial," to establish that a problem exists, debaters must define "beneficial" and then provide criteria for determining when membership is not beneficial.

The second step is to determine where the blame lies for the ill. If the debaters argue, for example, that US membership leads to a greater chance of nuclear war, they must prove that US membership is the primary reason for that increased chance of war. If the problem has other identifiable reasons, it can be inferred that the status quo is "not guilty."

The third analytical step is to identify a potential cure for the problem. This is a disputed area of value debate. One of the situational characteristics of value debate is a belief that presenting a plan is inappropriate. There is no strong theoretical reason why debaters cannot present plans, but it is customary in CEDA debate rounds not to do so. Even without presenting an actual plan of action for solving a problem, however, debaters often allude to the solution. For example, in the United Nations resolution, many affirmatives and negatives discussed US withdrawal from the UN as being either a good or a bad idea. Debaters have two ways to identify the cure for a problem, and thus assist decision making. Identifying the solution helps determine whether the correct blame for the problem is isolated and whether the implications of solving the problem outweigh the benefits.

The final issue is to analyze the cost of the solution. Solutions, or even allusions to solutions, involve costs. The costs might be economic, or they might be measured in other ways. For example, suspending constitutional search and seizure provisions might be a way of curbing drug use. We must compare this solution, however, to the cost that takes the form of losing an important freedom. The judge must weigh the costs versus the benefits of solving the problem.

Benefits of Using the Judicial Paradigm

The judicial paradigm uses familiar ideas and standards for discussing debate resolutions. Legal problem-solving methods are familiar to most people. They are employed even in non-courtroom situations. We know, for example, that a person is innocent until proven guilty. Using this paradigm makes it easy for debaters and judges to know what must be shown to prove or disprove a resolution.

The weakness of the judicial paradigm is that it emphasizes identifying a solution to a problem. As noted in the previous section, the CEDA debate context often discourages presentation of a plan. Further, not all value resolutions imply a plan. "Resolved: that *Gone With the Wind* is pure trash"—a resolution purportedly debated by Jimmy Carter during his school days—is an example of a value resolution without an apparent plan. Although most debate resolutions are linked to policy disputes, there is usually no problem in identifying the implied plan. But this does not mean that a different type of value resolution cannot be used in some situations.

The Issues-Agenda Paradigm

The issues-agenda paradigm is derived from the influence of the mass media on public decision making. The media, through coverage of issues, help to influence what decision makers see as the most critical issues needing solution. Using this paradigm, the debate judging behaves as an institutional or a societal decision maker whom the debaters attempt to convince that a particular issue or value should be accorded agenda status.

The Nature of the Issues-Agenda Paradigm

Decision makers cannot act upon every issue they confront. Time and money have limits, and any issue has its own advocates trying to convince decision makers that their issue requires greater time and attention. To achieve agenda status, an issue has to be perceived by institutional decision-makers or by the public as serious enough to warrant immediate attention.

The affirmative attempts to convince the judge that the resolution should be accorded agenda status, which ultimately implies that some societal or governmental action will be taken on the issue. The negative argues either that the value does not warrant agenda status or that giving the issue agenda status would needlessly harm the agenda position of some competing issue.

The issues-agenda paradigm is an audience-centered model of debate. The paradigm assumes that audiences use a wide variety of means of decision making and that the arguer has the responsibility to analyze the audience and make appropriate appeals to that audience. This process consists of four steps, or questions that the arguers analyze:

1. *How are the issues and values implied in the resolution defined?*

The way in which terms of a resolution are defined strongly influences how audiences perceive and ultimately accept or reject a value. You undoubtedly have observed this process at work in many contexts. Defining abortion either as "murder" or as a "woman's right" is an example. In many ways, the whole practice of public relations concerns defining events or issues. Recently the notion of "spin control" has been added to our political vernacular to describe how politicians define the significance of events.

2. *What assumptions can be made about the audience and its value system?*

The issues-agenda model is audience-centered. Various audiences have divergent value systems and decision-making criteria. Debaters must consider the value hierarchies of their audiences and the sources of information they hold as viable.

3. *Is this problem serious enough to affect this audience and its relevant value hierarchies?*

The significance of a problem is the most obvious measure decision makers use to determine if a problem requires action. Unless decision makers perceive the problem to be significant, either qualitatively or quantitatively, no action is likely to be taken. Furthermore, the problem must be contextually significant to the audience: it must affect the audience's relevant values. Hunger, for example, is a problem affecting millions throughout the world, but most Americans do not perceive hunger as significant enough to justify governmental action.

4. *Is this problem more worthy of audience attention than competing problems are?*

Problems do not exist in their own world. They must be compared to all other competing issues. This is not simply an economic decision but, rather, is one grounded in the amount of time and energy that audiences have to consider competing ideas. A newspaper has only so much space. Television has only so much news time to cover problems. Decision makers grant agenda status to only those problems they perceive as being significant, and the constantly shifting media focus from one problem to another suggests the difficulty some issues have in achieving agenda status as they are superseded by other, more "newsworthy" items.[2]

The issues-agenda approach gives the negative many options in attempting to defeat the affirmative case. The negative can dispute the decision-making criteria or the significance the affirmative attaches to the problem area, or it can present alternative values that may merit greater attention. This corresponds to the difficulty advocates have in actual decision-making situations in which they must overcome any number of barriers to convince relevant audiences to give their concerns agenda status.

Utility of the Issues-Agenda Paradigm in Value Debate

The primary advantage of the issues-agenda paradigm is its focus on the value-grounded implications of an issue rather than the policy implications. This paradigm assumes that a logical relationship exists between issues considered at the value and policy levels of decision-making. This relationship does not presume that there is a linear relationship between consideration of value and policy issues as the other paradigms do but, instead, conceives the value implications of policy issues as an intrinsic part of the decision-making process.

The major disadvantage of the issues-agenda paradigm is that judges do not have the same familiarity with, and understanding of, this paradigm as they do with the others developed so far. This makes debates a little less clear-cut, because the debaters and the judges continue to try to determine how to evaluate the issues presented in the debate round.

In summary, three major structural paradigms can be used in value debate rounds, all based on metaphors of how decision makers consider value claims. The policy-making paradigm is best-known; it bases debate on the decision-making process used by legislators. The judicial paradigm uses debate stock issues in a way analogous to courts of law. The issues-agenda paradigm compares debate to the process that the mass media use to bring issues to the forefront of consideration by institutional and structural decision makers.

SITUATIONAL PARADIGMS

The importance of the debate situation in dictating debaters' strategic and content choices cannot be overstated. Debaters must adapt to the situational constraints the debate format imposes and adapt to a judge who has particular preferences about debate strategies and content.

Situational paradigms evolved from debate practice, which has changed considerably over the years. Contemporary debates are more sophisticated in theory and content, place less emphasis on delivery, and often feature various game-playing elements. These situational paradigms are not as closely grounded to rational decision-making models as are structural paradigms. They are more pragmatic and flexible. Why, then, do we have to understand these "informal" paradigms?

Situational paradigms inquire into the complex ways that judges hear and evaluate debate rounds. In a perfect world, judges would consider only the assertions, issues, and claims presented in the debate. Those statements would be clear and precise enough for the judge to easily determine the winning side. Unfortunately, debates are not always clear. Structural paradigms do not explain the *communication environment* of debaters, in which illogical and extraneous variables can influence the outcome. Situational paradigms reflect debate strategies that are as important as content in determining success or failure in debates.

The Information-Processing Paradigm

Union Army General William Tecumseh Sherman acquired his Civil War reputation by his infamous "march through Georgia," in which he laid waste to everything the Confederate armies could use in maintaining their war effort. Similarly, using the information-processing situational paradigm, debaters attempt to defeat as many opposing arguments as possible. The quantity of assertions and claims in the debate round becomes the crucial measure of which team did the better job of debating, because, presumably, the presentation of more positions yields a greater likelihood of discovering better quality positions. This strategy is sometimes called the "spread" debate strategy.

Practice of the Information-Processing Paradigm

The debater's goal in using this paradigm is simple: to create and defend as many assertions, claims, and issues as possible while refuting as many of the opposing positions as possible. Debates are scored much like a checkers game, in which success is measured by capturing the most opposing pieces. In debate, the pieces take the form of opposing issues, claims, and assertions.

Following this strategy, attack and defense of *issues* are important in debates. Individual assertions and claims tend to be less significant because debaters probably cannot "cover" (answer) all the claims and assertions advanced in the debate. The judge in the debate will likely determine its outcome by comparing or weighing the importance of individual issues. The judge compares the significance of "dropped" (unanswered) issues by each team and formulates a rationalization for awarding the debate to one team or another.

This situational paradigm obviously favors the more experienced and the better prepared debate teams. To introduce or defend against many attacks without a lot of advance thinking about the ideas involved in the debate would be difficult. And mastering the skills of speaking quickly enough to use this strategy requires practice. Ethical questions involved with this approach are based on whether it is "fair" to base a debate decision on rapid speaking and quantity of assertions and claims rather than on the quality of arguments.

Debate critics often point to the rapid pace of debates as being unrealistic and uncommunicative.[3] This is an aesthetic problem and likely a valid criticism of debates conducted in front of lay audiences. But delivery speed does not in itself prevent audiences from understanding speeches. "Listening speed" and "speaking speed" have a significant difference that allows a listener to comprehend messages about four times as quickly as a speaker can present them.[4] Unfortunately, as speakers talk more quickly, they tend to speak less understandably. Considerable practice and some talent are required to overcome this comprehensibility problem.

Utility of the Information-Processing Paradigm

At first glance, this strategy seems almost antithetical to our justification for debate training. Debates that turn on delivery speed and the quantity of claims and assertions seem to reward strategy over substance. This is the position of many critics. Why does an apparently counter-intuitive strategy remain prominent?

The information-processing strategy is justified by a view of debate as being primarily a dispute over substance rather than consisting of presentational skills. Debates happen only after debaters go out and gather a lot of information and think about the implications of the assertions, claims, and issues they might present in the debate round. If one of the primary goals of debate is to encourage analytical and research skills, why shouldn't the judge reward the debaters' ability to present a significant number of well-reasoned assertions and claims?

Regardless of aesthetic and theoretical objections to the information-processing strategy, this paradigm is common in academic debate. It is the prevalent situational paradigm of the NDT (policy) style of debate and is typical in CEDA debate rounds. Regardless of speaking speed, debaters often speak more quickly than in normal conversation, and this difference can be highly significant. The reason for this gap between debate and average conversation is easy to identify: Debate judges are predominantly listeners who sometimes expect the presentation of many assertions and claims. The typical debate judge at a college (and often high school) debate tournament has considerable experience listening to debates. These people have developed listening abilities that allow them to understand and keep notes on information presented very rapidly.

Consider an analogy. Although you and I probably can engage in an entertaining basketball game, we would be lost and embarrassed if we were participating in a game against the running offense of the Los Angeles Lakers. The Lakers have honed their skills over many years according to a strategy that makes sense against the teams with which they compete. Any other strategy would disappoint their fans and probably lead to a losing record. The context, therefore, dictates their strategy. In some debate contexts, in which the debate judge expects a "fast debate" advancing many positions, a debater either must conform to the expectation or must prepare to lose.

The Game-Playing Paradigm

A second situational paradigm treats debate as an academic game wherein gamesmanship factors dictate how the debate happens. Games have formal and informal rules to guide the players, and success in the game depends on strategically using those rules. Debates using this paradigm emphasize strategizing in the form of using debate theory arguments and in-depth, technical assertions and claims about specific issues and the debate process in general.

Practice of the Game-Playing Paradigm

Whereas the information-processing paradigm emphasized the quantity of issues and claims, the game-playing paradigm emphasizes the strategic selection of issues, claims, and assertions introduced in the debate. Debaters must approach the debate as if they were playing any other game. They must probe the strengths and weaknesses of opposing debaters and attempt to determine if their opponents are vulnerable to particular issues or claims.

This approach emphasizes analysis of debate theory issues and claims. The game-playing model stresses the correspondence of debate theory issues with substantive debate issues when the judge determines which team should win the debate. The most important component of the debate activity becomes the determination of winners and losers. The debate topic is merely a subject area for discussion and is not necessarily the judges' focus or the debaters' interest. Topicality attacks, counter-warrants, "generic attacks," and other theoretical attacks typify debates that follow this paradigm.

The debate issue of topicality involves discussion of whether the affirmative case area properly fits within the debate resolution. Topicality has emerged in debate practice as a stock issue taking precedence over other substantive issues when determining whether the affirmative should win the debate. If an affirmative case is not topical, the negative is not expected to defeat it on other grounds.

Justification for the Game-Playing Paradigm

Game-playing is almost second nature to most people. We learn valuable social, intellectual, and physical skills by playing childhood games. Game-playing is an often-used educational and decision-making tool. So it should not be surprising that game-playing is the basis for a situational debate paradigm. To conceive of debate as a game does not take much stretch.

One important consideration of game-playing is the need for players to understand the rules of their game. Many games specify the rules in advance. Other games, such as debate, allow the participants wide latitude in negotiating the rules. Debaters often refer to "decision-rules," which are simply the guidelines they advocate for the judge to use in determining who should win the debate. Judges who use the game-playing paradigm allow the debaters to debate about the decision-rules for the debate round and do not consciously impose their standards on the debaters. Judges who take this approach may refer to themselves as "tabula rasa" or "blank-slate" judges who do not have any preconceptions about the debate round.

Whether it is appropriate for the judge to let the debaters determine the issues and decision-rules in the debate is the major criticism of this situational paradigm. Critics contend that this approach undermines the educational significance of debate by emphasizing competition and strategy at the expense of educational benefits.

The Speaking Skills Paradigm

The third situational paradigm emphasizes the persuasive elements of debate as a public-speaking activity. This is the most traditional situational paradigm for debate. Debate is an oral communication activity directed and judged to a large extent by teachers trained in the communication discipline. Many of these listeners critique debates from a communication perspective, which stresses the importance of oral presentation in the debate process.

Practice of the Skills Perspective in Value Debate

In taking this perspective, oral presentation is as important as content in debates. Debates are usually slower and are characterized by more persuasive language and efforts to involve the listener in the debate. Any substantive paradigm can be used to focus the debate, and the judge using this paradigm may also use another paradigm to think about the issues in the debate. The only difference is the emphasis on delivery skills.

Advantages of the Skills Paradigm

This paradigm is the most realistic substantive paradigm in the sense that it reinforces oral communication skills that a debater will employ in school or in a career. This paradigm fits with the popular conception of debate as a persuasive mechanism in the tradition of Abraham Lincoln and Stephen Douglas. A debater can use this situational paradigm in public debates or in academic debates in which a lay judge (a judge not trained in debate or a judge who has not listened to academic debates recently) is critiquing the debate.

The disadvantage of this approach is that less information can be presented in the debate. If the goal of debate is to exchange information about competing issues and claims, this paradigm probably does not accomplish that end as well as the other two situational paradigms. This might mean that debaters must pick out higher quality issues and claims to present, but there is no guarantee that they do so.

IDENTIFYING JUDGES' PREFERENCES

The debater cannot make broad generalizations about judges' situational paradigms. Determining a judge's preferences is often a case of trial and error and audience analysis. Although this lends some uncertainty to debate, it also helps to develop audience analysis skills—which is one of the goals of the debate process. There are ways of analyzing audiences before, during, and after the debate rounds:

1. *Ask the judges about their preferences.*

Many judges are willing to talk about their expectations. Judges are more comfortable in debate contexts in which they enjoy what they are hearing. They may see the advantage of disclosing their likes and dislikes.

2. *Observe judges' verbal and nonverbal behaviors.*

All people communicate a lot through their nonverbal behaviors. One of the most important skills debaters should develop is the ability to watch (in an unobtrusive and a nonthreatening way) what a judge does during the debate round. Judges give various nonverbal signals—nods, smiles, frowns, and the like—for what they prefer and do not prefer. Although analyzing nonverbal behavior is hardly a science, it provides a potential source of information about the listener.

3. *Use any known information about the judge.*

Well-prepared debaters ask other people what they know about judges' preferences. They consult ballots they or others received from a judge for indications of the judges' preferences. They might even ask students from the judge's school.

4. *Use common sense.*

Although analyzing the judge's preferences for issues and strategies is important, the debater also must use the structural and

Table 8.1 Summary of Situational Paradigms

Paradigm	Key Element	Judges' Role
Information-Processing	Data	To process data objectively, deciding debate on the basis of who presents the most data
Game-Playing	Strategies	To "referee" debate, deciding debate on whatever criteria debaters determine should be used
Speaking Skills	Persuasion	To decide debate on the basis of which team makes the most persuasive presentation of issues and claims

situational paradigms that fit the debaters' style and debating abilities. Trying to debate in a manner inconsistent with existing abilities is fruitless and unsuccessful.

Table 8.1 summarizes the elements of and judges' roles in each of the three situational paradigms.

SUMMARY

Paradigms are models that guide debaters and judges in determining appropriate ways for approaching the debate topic and debate situation. Paradigms give the debate judge a decision-making model. Structural paradigms are problem-solving models that provide analogies for the debate process. The policy-making model compares debate to legislative decision making. The judicial model uses legal principles. The issue-agenda model compares debate to the media process of making issues significant enough to warrant consideration by problem-solvers.

Situational paradigms explore the strategic choices debaters and judges make. The information-processing model views debate as a process of comparing quantities of information. The game-playing model views debate as a process of using debate strategies. The speaking skills model considers the persuasive and communicative elements of debate. Judges and debaters use both structural and situational paradigms, and part of the debater's responsibility is to use audience analysis techniques to understand how the listener is judging the debate round.

ENDNOTES

1. A good discussion of paradigms appears in David Thomas and Jack Hart, editors, *Advanced Debate, 3rd. ed.* (Lincolnwood, IL: National Textbook, 1987), pp. 165–241.

2. David Althiede and Robert Snow, *Media Logic* (Beverly Hills, CA: Sage, 1979).

3. Delivery speed is often criticized in debate. In addition to articles in academic journals, occasional mention of debate delivery is made in popular journals, such as a recent article about high school debate: M. McGough, "Pull it Across Your Flow," *New Republic* 199 (Oct. 10, 1988): 17–19.

4. Ralph Nichols, "Do We Know How to Listen? Practical Helps in a Modern Age," *Speech Teacher* 10 (1961): 118–124.

9

The College Debate Tournament

---------------------------------- **Chapter Objectives** ----------------------------------

☐ Know why the tournament format is an important part of debate training.

☐ Identify all the preparations you should make before going to the tournament.

☐ Understand the basic theory of the debate flowsheet.

☐ Have a basic understanding of how tournaments operate.

☐ Know how to use the feedback you get to become a better debater.

The debate tournament has a special culture. The basic concepts and theories we have developed to this point should help you in organizing your speeches. Now we consider how you might prepare before you leave for a tournament: what you will face when you arrive at the tournament, what you might do after you leave the tournament, and how tournament competition will help you improve your debating skills.

THE ROLE OF TOURNAMENTS IN
DEBATE TRAINING

The biggest change in debate training in this century was introduction of the tournament format. Before the 1920s, debaters primarily debated among themselves on campus or against another college on a one-to-one basis. Southwestern College hosted the first tournament in 1924. The idea behind a tournament is to give students the inducement, through receiving awards, to debate a number of rounds against a variety of opponents. The tournament format was immediately successful. Within a few years, tournaments almost completely replaced other forms of speech activities, and today more than 300 speech and debate tournaments are held in the United States.

Hosting a debate tournament entails several steps. Host schools arrange for contest rooms and judges. They secure awards, invite other colleges to attend, and schedule rounds in the events that the tournament offers. Judges, who are college professors or instructors, or community judges, listen to the debates and complete a written ballot giving their decision of who won the debate and the reasons why. A sample debate ballot is included at the end of this chapter.

Debate teams typically debate four, six, or eight rounds, with an equal number of debates on both sides of the resolution. At the conclusion of the preliminary rounds, the teams with the most wins participate in a single-elimination playoff to determine the tournament winner. Tournaments often group teams by their level of experience or class standing to maximize the opportunities of debating people of similar background and preparation to improve in debate.

PREPARATION FOR THE TOURNAMENT

Before participating in a tournament, you should conduct in-depth library research, take part in discussions about affirmative and negative strategies, write affirmative cases and briefs, construct negative positions and briefs, and engage in practice debate rounds. All these activities contribute to the likelihood of tournament success.

Your library research should be extensive and thorough. The best debaters are often the best researchers. To become a good researcher requires familiarity with the library and the various methods of collecting evidence. Chapter 4 offers some suggestions for debate-oriented library research. You will spend most of your preparation time preceding the tournament doing library research. You may find that the amount of evidence you collect far exceeds the amount you would normally gather when writing a research paper for class. Debaters typically collect several thousand pieces of evidence during the course of debating competitively for a semester or a year.

If you are a member of a program with several debaters, the program may wish to divide the labor; each debater may be assigned a particular issue to research. As a result, no one debater will be obligated to assume the full burden of research. Nevertheless, you are responsible for the accuracy of any piece of evidence you read in a debate round, regardless of whether you personally collected it.

Before you attend a debate tournament, you will need to talk with your partner, other teammates, and your coach at some length about the various issues. These discussions are invaluable, for they stimulate thought and allow you to test the ideas you have formed as a result of your library research. Discussions between you and your partner should take place as often as is possible and convenient. These discussions should lead the team to formulate strategies and tactics for both the negative and the affirmative.

The library research and the discussions with colleagues and coaches will lead you and your partner to create affirmative cases and negative positions. The first affirmative should be a finished product before you leave for the tournament. The first affirmative speaker should practice the speech many times before presenting it in competition. The affirmative briefs should be finished. Additionally, negative briefs and evidence should be organized and filed. Value objections should be practiced and timed.

There is a strong correlation between success at a debate tournament and the number and quality of practice debates a team has prior to the tournament. Practice rounds allow you and your partner to test your positions, delivery, and evidence before entering tournament competition. Practice rounds also enable you to help your teammates develop their positions. Your teacher and other debaters may pose as "typical judges" to help in the evaluation of cases and positions. Practice rounds should permit you to discover flaws in your reasoning or case before participating in the tournament.

Most college debaters are full-time students, enrolled in a variety of courses. Responsible college debaters let their teachers and professors know before they leave for tournaments that they will miss some classes. Often, the director of forensics will write a letter explaining that debate students will miss a designated number of classes. If tests or assignments are due on tournament days, debaters should ask the professor if these could be rescheduled for them or if they could turn in their assignments before leaving for the debate tournaments. The credibility of a college or university debate program is based in part on the debaters' academic success in the regular classroom.

The last area of preparation is to develop a note-taking system, allowing people to efficiently listen to a debate and accurately record the debate content. This technique called "flowsheeting," is discussed next.

FLOWSHEETS

One of the practical benefits derived from debate training is improved note-taking abilities. An essential ingredient of debate is listening. After all, you spend half the debate listening to the other team talk, and half of your own team's presentation listening to your partner talk. This corresponds to other communicative situations. As a general rule, we listen a lot more than we talk.

Good listening skills are an essential part of good communication. A debater who accurately understands and records opposing statements will inevitably respond better to them. In the debate context listening and note-taking are combined under the term *flowsheets*. A flowsheet is a debater's or a listener's systematically recorded notes of the statements presented in the debate.

Unlike a courtroom, where a court reporter keeps accurate notes by using a recording instrument and shorthand, debaters and judges keep their own records of the debate. A flowsheet ought to be *complete*, recording all statements and evidence presented by every speaker in the debate. It also should be *accurate*, recording that information objectively and completely so that the speaker's meaning is not distorted or misunderstood.

This is easier in theory than in practice. Debates occur in difficult listening environments. The physical set-up and acoustics can make hearing difficult. The pressure of trying to prepare a speech while also listening adds to the problem. Finally, because the debate participants are students learning how to debate, they do not always speak as clearly as we might wish, to help us record notes. Some suggestions for good flowsheets and listening in the debate are as follows:

1. *Minimize distractions.*

The most important aspect of good listening is *concentration*. It is very easy to be distracted. You can minimize distractions in the debate round in several practical ways. First, sit where you can hear your colleague and opponents. Although it is customary for debaters to sit at the front of the room (if the debate is held in a classroom), be sure to sit where you can see and hear your opponents when they talk. Second, prepare as much of your content as possible before the debate. The importance of making briefs was discussed in a previous chapter. A pragmatic benefit of having briefs prepared ahead of time is that it frees up time to listen. By listening, you can adapt your briefs to the specific issues and claims your opponents present.

2. *Have the right tools.*

At a minimum, you need paper and a pen. But it is not quite that simple. For most debates you will need a lot of paper and perhaps pens of two different colors, one color for your speeches and the other for your opponents' speeches. Debaters often use legal pads or larger art pads to flow the debate. Pads of this size allow debaters to write large enough and legibly enough to read their writing. You can imagine how embarrassing it is to stand up to speak and not be able to understand what you wrote down!

You also must have enough paper so you can follow an issue or assertion throughout the debate without having to write notes about that issue on different pages. Knowing that any statement the first affirmative introduces might be discussed throughout the debate, your flowsheet should allow you to see how that statement progresses. It follows this sequence:

1AC —→ 1NC —→ 2AC —→ 1NR —→ 1AR —→ 2NR —→ 2AR

Your flowsheet should have eight columns to provide room to flow what each of the eight speakers might say about that issue.

3. *Develop abbreviations.*

Debaters often adopt a shorthand or system of abbreviations. Abbreviations save time and energy. They allow you to write down the essence of the statement and give you enough time to think about how to respond. You should not try to abbreviate every statement, though. Instead, you should abbreviate commonly encountered terms or phrases. Some examples include:

CL, $\longrightarrow$,	Causal link or causes
Sig	Significance
T	Topicality
$\downarrow$	Decrease
$\uparrow$	Increase

Whatever abbreviations you come up with should be ones you and your partner understand and can use consistently and quickly in the debate.

4. *Flow the content.*

Flowing the content and labels means that you need to develop the ability to record evidence or reasons debaters use to justify their statements. You might flow, for example, Smith, 82, "UN stopped Arab-Israeli conflict"—which is not, of course, a complete precis of the evidence but should be enough to help you remember the claim. Sometimes the evidence or analysis will not fit the label the arguer uses, and the only way you can use that information is to flow it at the time it is presented.

Good flowsheeting takes practice and hard work. It is one of the more difficult technical skills to master. The key is to keep trying, never getting discouraged if you lose track once in a while in a debate. Over time your abilities will improve, and this skill will carry over to your note-taking in class. To summarize the key aspects of flowsheeting:

1. Use a lot of paper.

2. Write large enough and legibly enough to read.

3. Follow a given issue or claim from beginning to end on the flowsheet.

4. Flow content as well as labels.

5. Develop a workable abbreviation scheme.

6. Flow every speech.

TOURNAMENT BEHAVIOR AND THE TOURNAMENT CULTURE

A debate tournament is very different from a typical classroom learning environment. The competitive element of the tournament, in which people compete to win awards, interacts with the educational element of debate, in which people debate to learn skills. This creates an extremely stimulating environment. It is also an environment that introduces ethical concerns (the topic of chapter 10).

The Operation of Debate Tournaments

Every debate tournament is different. Unlike a basketball game or other competitive event, there is not a set method of running a tournament. But some aspects are common to most tournaments:

1. *Teams debate a number of rounds with an approximately equal number of rounds debating both sides of the resolution.*

The number of rounds in a tournament depends upon how long the tournament lasts and the number of teams participating in the tournament. A typical 2-day tournament, for example, could consist of six debate rounds. The usual format calls for a team debating on both sides of the resolution an equal number of times. The competitive reason for this is to ensure that the eventual winner of the tournament shows skill on both sides of the resolution.

2. *Debates are judged by listeners who render decisions about which team did the better job of debating.*

The competitive element of a debate is simply the process wherein the debate judge gives a win/loss decision after listening to the debate, and writes comments about the debate issues and the debaters' skills. The tournament manager records the wins and losses for each team, and this record helps to determine which team wins the tournament.

3. *Tournaments often group students according to the level of their skill or age.*

In many tournaments the competition is grouped into divisions, in which teams debate at a level suggested by their experience or their age. A tournament might have an "open" or "senior" division, available to experienced students or those wishing to participate at that level. A "junior" division might be designated for less experienced students or freshmen and sophomores. A "novice" division might be offered for students without prior experience. Those involved in tournaments often set their own rules for determining who should participate in each division. Dividing tournaments into divisions improves the debaters' educational experience by allowing them to match their skills with people at a similar level.

Competitive fairness suggests that inexperienced students should not always have to compete with experienced students. Some tournaments, however, do group all teams into a single division or combine divisions when the number of students in a division is not sufficient.

4. *Tournaments often use "power matching" to ensure a competitive balance.*

Power matching is a process—of which there are many different methods—for matching teams with similar records against each other. As the tournament progresses, power matching is often used to equalize competition. A team having a 3-0 record, for example, would be matched with another team having the same or a similar record. Power matching creates the best competition possible. It ensures that all teams have a chance to win the tournament by debating other teams with a similar chance. It means that no team loses simply by the "luck of the draw" or by manipulation.

In any competitive context, some teams will be better prepared and more competitive than others. Power matching can prevent a team from winning the tournament by debating only the teams that are less proficient—which could happen if the tournament were to match debates randomly.

5. *Tournaments often use elimination rounds to determine the ultimate winner.*

In an elimination round, the teams with the best records debate each other in a single-elimination debate, often with multiple judges. The team winning the debate advances to another debate and, ultimately, to a final round in which the winner is considered the tournament champion. The number of elimination rounds in a tournament depends upon the number of teams entered. A tournament might only have one elimination round, or it could have as many as six—as was the case in the tournament where the sample debate occurred.

The Culture of Debate Tournaments

Personal experience has no substitute in discussing the special culture of debate tournaments. And we reemphasize that debate tournaments are unique. But some cultural variables typify debate tournaments in general.

1. *Debaters dress appropriately, often more formally than when attending class.*

Competitors and judges often perceive tournaments as a special occasion, where people dress appropriately. Tournaments do not specify a dress code, but competitors often wear nicer clothing (e.g. suits and ties, dresses) than they wear to class, where more informal dress tends to be the norm. Clothing obviously plays a role in communication. Although clothing may not be a distinct form of persuasion, it probably contributes to establishing credibility as a speaker and to enhancing the tournament as a special occasion.

2. *Tournament results usually are kept confidential until the tournament concludes.*

The judge does not usually orally disclose to the competitors the decision in a debate round. The judge records the decision on written ballots, which the teams receive after the tournament. It is not unheard of for a judge to disclose his or her decision to a team, but tournaments often have rules discouraging that practice, and many judges follow that rule. This practice keeps the uncertainty and excitement high, as it is not known which teams are winning or which teams will advance to the elimination rounds.

3. *Tournaments can be intense, stressful environments.*

People vary in their reactions to competition. You probably know people who hate to lose or who become "Little League parents." Even an educational context such as a debate tournament is not immune to people who react to competition in less than desirable ways. Another source of stress comes from the very act of debating, wherein a person must stand up in front of strangers and speak. In the first chapter of this text we noted that debate can constitute an important method of building personal confidence.

4. *The debate situation is ambiguous.*

A debate round is unpredictable in the sense that each debate is a unique experience combining debaters, judges, and issues within a given physical and social context. Neither the debaters nor the judges can predict the progression of an issue completely. The interaction between debaters can influence the debate. The judge may use a whole range of obvious and subtle criteria in arriving at a decision.

Unpredictability characterizes almost every communication context. You meet a person for the first time and instinctively don't like him or her. You may not be able to put your finger on the reasons, but they are real just the same. Your reaction may be the result of interpreting some nonverbal cue, or some information you received about the person from a third party, or your own biases. This same process obviously is at work in a debate round. Although debate is based on the foundation of fairness, a debate judge cannot be expected to completely shut out the interpretive variables that continuously guide communication.

This implies that a debater should constantly monitor the communication environment of the debate to assess what is happening. A debater has to use all available skills to present a positive image. Honesty, openness, empathy, and good humor are some of the skills people use to influence others' perceptions. Communicators typically react unfavorably to people who do not show those traits.

Because debate is a social activity, you will have to be courteous to your opponents. Some debaters take attacks on and criticisms of their arguments personally and are unable to separate their arguments from their egos. The debate round is a laboratory for testing ideas. A judge might vote against you and your partner and still think both of you are good human beings. In the same light, your opponents are not angry with you as persons. They also are attempting to persuade the judge. You should treat your opponents with the same courtesy you would want from them. Debaters from different schools often become friends. They enjoy spending time with and debating against one another. We suggest that you attempt to make friends with your opponents.

The ambiguity of the debate also creates the need for adaptation. A debater has to prepare to change or adapt issues and claims when faced with a judge who does not accept them or when the debater finds that those strategies are not working effectively. A football player, for example, changes a play that ended in lost yardage. The same principle operates in debate.

A debater should be ready to alter strategies, briefs, affirmative cases, and negative positions. You want to be a moving target, because other teams will be attempting to prepare for your affirmative and negative positions.

5.   *The tournament experience combines success and failure.*

Competitive debate is similar to baseball. Even major leaguers make errors, strike out, and lose games. This is also true of debaters. Even the best preparation will not ensure that a person will do the best possible job of debating or prevent the person from debating someone else who has more skill. As with all communicative encounters, we experience varying degrees of success every time we debate or interact with others. Accepting the inevitability of only partial success is an important part of the debate culture. Because debates, unlike most sporting contests, depend on the subjective evaluation of a third party, a person inevitably will not be completely successful in arguing individual issues or in winning the debate contest.

ACCEPTING AND USING CRITICISM

An important element of the debate tournament culture is criticism. Judges write comments about the debates they hear, and they sometimes direct oral comments to the debaters. Criticism is the vehicle for self-improvement. After the tournament is over, debaters must carefully consider the criticism they receive and attempt to make necessary changes in their debate techniques.

The Debate Ballot

When the tournament is over, you will have an opportunity to read the ballots your judges have authored. These ballots are used to record the reasons the judge decided which team won, as well as comments directed to each speaker. Figure 9.1 gives a truncated example of a debate ballot.

No two debate ballots will have exactly the same content. Each debate judge uses a ballot to emphasize different ideas. You probably inferred this from the discussion of paradigms in chapter 8. But we can make several generalizations about ballots and their function in debate.

1. *Ballots are imprecise devices for communicating what took place in a debate*.

Although your paying attention to comments on debate ballots is important, so is your realizing that judges may not effectively communicate their perceptions of the debate. Judges operate under time constraints in deciding a debate and turning in a ballot; they usually are required to judge many rounds during a tournament; and they are subject to the same communication constraints as any other person.

Figure 9.1   An Example of a Debate Ballot

Debate Ballot

Round: __2__   Room: _Old Main_   Judge: _Rindo_____

Aff: _State Univ_____   Neg: _You and Your Partner_____

1st Aff: _John_   2nd Aff: _Susie_   1st Neg: _You___ 2nd Neg: _Your Partner_
_____26_____28_____27_____25____

The better debating was done by (Aff): _State U._____

Judge's signature: _G. Rindo_____ School: _____Alaska_____

This was a good debate. The negative did not extend arguments as well as they might have in the rebuttals. The topicality argument didn't seem strong to me. This affirmative seems reasonable and clearly in the middle of the road. I also thought the negative spoke too quickly. I haven't watched college debate for some time, and I wish the negative would have been more clear. Both teams have good potential. Good luck.

---

2. *Comments on ballots are often contradictory.*

Judges sometimes contradict each other in their comments about your performance. This does not imply that one judge is right and another is wrong. It simply points up the wide variety of perceptions about debate issues and skills.

One role of the debate teacher is to help students interpret comments they receive on their ballots. The teacher may look at many ballots written for a student, identifying various repeated comments. Consistently repeated comments probably reveal areas in need of improvement.

Reacting to Criticism

Accepting criticism is not easy. Debating requires a lot of time and preparation, which invests the debater with a large personal commitment to particular claims, issues, and strategies. Debaters may find it difficult to have a listener critique this effort and commitment. The debater must prepare for criticism by keeping in mind that criticism of a debate statement or strategy is not a personal judgment. Learning to gracefully accept criticism is an important life skill. Successful people adapt and learn from their mistakes.

After you have read the ballots and reflected on the debate tournament, you will want to create an agenda for the next tournament. No matter how well you did, or how poorly you did, you will need to make some improvements. As you did before the tournament, you will have to go to the library. You will have to talk with your teammates, your partner, and your teachers about strategies and tactics for the next tournament. You also will want to again have useful and productive practice rounds.

If you lost two of three affirmative rounds, you may need to consider some major revisions of your affirmative case. You may need a *new* affirmative case. If you lost two or more negative rounds, you will have to work on negative strategies and positions.

Even if you did well at the tournament, you should work to maintain your success. The teams you defeated will be thinking of you and what they will argue the next time they debate you. The teams that lost to your affirmative will discuss approaches they will use to defeat you the next time they debate you. Teams that lost to your negative position and strategy will also work to improve their affirmative cases and extensions. Characteristics exhibited by successful tournament debaters can be summarized as follows:

1. *Successful tournament debaters are well prepared.*

Successful debaters prepare their affirmative cases before they reach the tournament. They have exhaustively researched the negative and are able to present a variety of strategies and tactics, regardless of what they might confront.

2. *Successful tournament debaters are flexible and adaptive.*

On occasion, debaters must respond to unusual and innovative issues and claims. Successful debaters are able to adapt and retain control of the debate round even in the face of unexpected strategies. They identify ways of using their previously prepared evidence and briefs to respond to unexpected claims. They are able to dissect opposing positions and identify weaknesses in reasoning.

3. *Successful tournament debaters are aware of and responsive to their judges.*

Good debaters know they are debating to persuade the judge, not their opponents. Good debaters try to discover as much information as possible about the judge and make use of this information in their choice of strategies and tactics. Most important, successful tournament debaters read their ballots carefully and remember what their judges say—particularly if they have had the same judge at a previous tournament.

4. *Successful tournament debaters enjoy the social environment.*

Successful debaters talk with their opponents and treat them as human beings before, during, and after the debate round. Successful debaters talk and joke with their competitors. In addition, successful debaters enjoy working with their partners and their teammates.

5. *Successful tournament debaters are moving targets and learn from their mistakes.*

The best debaters we have known are not satisfied with victory or immobilized by defeat. These debaters continually revise their affirmative and negative strategies.

6. *Successful tournament debaters are open to constructive criticism.*

After a debate tournament is over, successful debaters carefully read the debate ballots. With the help of their teachers, successful debaters make use of the ballots and other information to improve their performances during the next debate tournament.

SUMMARY

The debate tournament culture produces some unusual but interesting demands on the college student. College students should carefully prepare for the tournament, be ready to make some changes while at the tournament, and spend time after the tournament reflecting upon their performance during the tournament.

Appendix to Chapter 9
Sample Debate Ballot

FORM A

CROSS EXAMINATION
DEBATE ASSOCIATION

DIVISION [   ] ROUND [   ] ROOM [   ] JUDGE [   ]

AFF. [   ] NEG. [   ]

INSTRUCTIONS: Fill out ALL shaded areas of the ballot (even if ballot label is attached). RATE all speakers on a scale from **30** (superior) to **1** (poor). RANK each speaker in order of excellence (1-4; ties are not permitted). If you are awarding the decision to the team with fewer speaker points, check the appropriate box. The boxes should be checked according to the following scale (the boxes do NOT have numerical significance):

P - poor/needs improvement   F - fair   A - average   E - excellent   S - superior

1st Affirmative	2nd Affirmative		1st Negative	2nd Negative
P F A E S	P F A E S	Analysis/Definition	P F A E S	P F A E S
		Evidence		
		Refutation/Rebuttal		
		Cross-Examination		
		Organization		
		Delivery		
		Language/Style		

NAMES

Pts. (30 max) [   ] Rank [   ]   Pts. (30 max) [   ] Rank [   ]   Pts. (30 max) [   ] Rank [   ]   Pts. (30 max) [   ] Rank [   ]

I am persuaded to vote for team [   ] (aff. or neg.)   REPRESENTING: [   ]   CODE: [   ]

Low point win? [   ]   [   ] JUDGES SIGNATURE   AFFILIATION [   ]

REASON FOR DECISION/COMMENTS:

_____
_____
_____
_____
_____
_____
_____

10

Ethics in Academic Debate

--------------------- Chapter Objectives ---------------------

☐ Understand the role of ethics in the context of the debate activity.

☐ Differentiate between aspirational and regulatory functions of ethical judgments.

☐ Understand the difficulty in applying ethical judgements to various case situations.

Ethical standards are crucial to the debate activity. Ethics help define the goals of the activity and identify the kinds of regulations necessary to ensure that competition will be fair.

There is considerable disagreement regarding what is and what is not ethical. Some of these disagreements are healthy, compelling forensic students and educators to consider the propriety of various practices. We highlight here an ethical posture we hope you will consider adopting as your own to guide you when making ethical decisions.

ETHICAL STANDARDS OF DEBATE

Debate ethics are not a new concern. Perhaps it was Socrates who initiated the philosophic concern with ethical choices in communication. Regardless of the birthplace, critics have always conducted vigorous discussions of ethical questions. We noted in chapter 1, for example, the concern over whether debating both sides of a resolution is ethical. Inevitably, as academic debate came to rely more on the competitive tournament model, ethical considerations of tournament-related practices became more timely.

The American Forensics Association is a professional organization of people interested in argumentation and debate. The association publishes an academic journal about argumentation and debate and sponsors national championship tournaments in policy debate and individual speaking events. This organization responded to the growing interest in identifying and codifying ethical standards by creating a document entitled "The Ethics of Forensics".[1] This document discusses ethical guidelines for teachers and participants, and the association has a code of ethics for participants as well.

"The Ethics of Forensics" approaches ethics from two perspectives: creating *aspirational goals* for competitors and identifying *regulatory standards* for competitive behaviors. These dual functions are the heart of ethical discussions. Ethics, or standards of right and wrong, function to help people know what they ought to aspire to become (e.g., "You should be a good person") and to know what specific behaviors are not acceptable (e.g., "Stealing is wrong.").

Aspirational Standards

Aspirational goals are sometimes easier to identify and agree upon than are regulatory standards. As an educational activity, debate shares the aspirations of all components of higher education. We sometimes group these aspirations under the heading of acquiring a liberal arts education. The document on ethics, for example, identifies the major goal of forensics as achieving an educational mission. Education, not competition, is the primary concern of academic debate.

A second goal of forensics is to promote effective communication practices. The document reads:

Students participating in forensics are obligated to adhere to high ethical standards. Here we are concerned with the ethical choices of students made for themselves. . . . An ethical commitment by students is essential because the value of forensics is directly dependent upon the integrity of those involved.[2]

As such, forensic educators and students should be expected to practice ethical communication behaviors. Students should not use their rhetorical abilities to knowingly argue what is not true. Ultimately, the goal of forensics is to teach students how to become competent and ethical rhetorical scholars.

Academic debate should do more than teach people how to do good research and to present this research persuasively. It should inspire students to present strong arguments in an ethical manner. *Ethical behavior and arguments are essential, for in a democracy, people make decisions based on the arguments they hear and the communication behavior they observe.*

Thus, the aspirational element of ethics suggests that students ought to behave in ways that help them become better scholars and communicators. Behaviors must be evaluated in that context. Aspirational goals are, of course, very broad.

Regulatory Standards

The purpose of regulatory standards is to identify those behaviors that are unethical. "The Ethics of Forensics" contains the following statement:

[I]t is the duty of each student to participate honestly, fairly, and in such a way as to avoid communication behaviors that are deceptive, misleading or dishonest. Students should strive to place forensic competition in a proper perspective when ethical decisions are pondered. The goal of winning must be evaluated within a framework of educational values. Forensic contests are not ends in themselves but means to an end.[3]

Students compete in forensics for a variety of reasons. Some enjoy the competition; others wish to conquer their opponents; still others wish to learn. When the desire to win overshadows all other goals, there is cause for concern. The desire to win might lead a student to give in to temptation. A student's overall academic performance may suffer because the student has devoted too much time to debate. A student might falsify some evidence to win a debate round. A student might alter the meaning of a piece of evidence by deleting a line or a key word. When the student gives in to such temptations, he or she diminishes the educational value of forensics. Surely debate students should strive for success—but not at the cost of the integrity of the activity.

The statement of ethics also calls for:

> . . . student participants [to] remember that forensics is an oral, interactive process. When ideas are expressed in an unintelligible manner, the forensic process is abused. The interactive dimension of forensics suggests that behaviors which belittle, degrade, demean, or otherwise dehumanize others are not in the best interest of forensics because they interfere with the goals of education and personal growth. The ethical forensic competitor recognizes the rights of others and communicates with respect for opponents, colleagues and critics.[4]

Some students are not as kind as they might be when responding to their opponent's arguments. Through their language and communication behavior, they may dehumanize their opponents, the judges and their partners. We should not tolerate personal attacks, racist/sexist remarks, and other comments designed to demean other human beings. This type of behavior is obviously unethical in any communication context. Academic debate should teach students how to deal with others in situations designed to stimulate and simulate conflict. The student has an obligation to treat the judge, the opponents, and the partner with the respect due any person.

In search of debate victories, unethical students resort to distorting the meanings of words and to specious reasoning. When students use distorted definitions and specious reasoning as purposeful strategies, they demean the integrity of the debate activity. If, for example, a negative side were to present an implausible value objection or if the affirmative case were to skew a definition, it would show a lack of respect for the importance of debate training as preparation for democratic decision-making. Thus, the statement of ethics suggests:

> Student advocates should compete with respect for the principles and objectives of reasoned discourse. Students who invent definitions involving unwarranted shifts in the meanings of words fail to maintain respect for the integrity of language. Students who deliberately employ specious reasoning as a strategy fail to maintain a respect for the integrity of the forensic decision-making process.[5]

We agree with this statement. We hope that you do as well, and that you see the reasons for adopting an ethically grounded view of forensics.

To summarize, debate ethics have two aspects: (1) aspirational standards, or ethical goals sought for participants; and (2) regulatory standards, which attempt to identify specific types of behaviors that are unethical. The ethical goal of debate is to create good scholars and communicators who are committed to fairness and humanity toward others.

CASE STUDIES IN DEBATE ETHICS

Codes of ethics or any perspectives on morality have little meaning until they are tested in actual situations. We are relatively conservative when it comes to matters of ethics. When you read the following case studies, you may have different reactions than ours. We realize that honorable and ethical people can react in different ways to problems of ethics. In light of the previous discussion, we invite you to consider how you would respond in the following situations. We begin by considering some rather obvious cases of unethical behavior and then move to some cases that are much more problematic and difficult.

Case Study One: Use of Ethical Evidence

> A student is doing debate research on the topic of abortion. The article she is reading attempts to summarize the impact abortion has on women. She is considering using the following evidence:
>
> "Several studies have suggested that women who have abortions often suffer deep post-abortion depressions. However, recent studies demonstrated that these particular studies were flawed. In fact, the vast majority of studies suggest that most women who have abortions do not suffer from post-abortion depression."
>
> The student uses the first sentence as evidence in support of a claim that abortions harm women.

Is this is an ethical use of evidence? Most forensic educators would agree that this is an unethical use of evidence. The student might claim that the evidence was properly used because she has not altered the wording. But she has altered the author's intended meaning. Consider the following guideline established in the statement of ethics:

> In determining whether evidence has been distorted, the advocate should ask if the evidence deviates from the quality, quantity, probability, or degree of force of the author's position on the point in question. Any such deviation should be avoided, because such alteration can give undue rhetorical force to an advocate's argument.[6]

The debater's use of the evidence obviously is not consistent with the author's position on abortion. As a result, the student would have committed an unethical act. Although this example is obvious, use of evidence often falls into a "gray area," where ethical dimensions are harder to evaluate.

Problems with evidence are usually divided into the categories of "falsification" and "distortion of meaning." Many times the distortion of meaning may be a result of genuine misunderstanding rather than bad intent. The judge may have to determine whether the distortion is intentional.

You also will need to think seriously about how you will react to and present ethical challenges concerning evidence. Your program might have some guidelines dealing with such issues, or you may debate in a region that abides by a code of ethics. You and your coach should discuss how you plan to deal with and react to evidence challenges.

Case Study Two: Using Evidence Researched By Others

> The debater who cut the evidence in question contributes the evidence to a team evidence pool. One of her team members uses the evidence at the next tournament. Who is responsible if this team member reads this evidence in a debate round and a student from another program points out that the evidence is out of context?

The statement of ethics takes a position on this issue:

Advocates are responsible for the integrity of all the evidence they utilize, even when the evidence is not researched by the individual advocate.[7]

Again, most forensic educators agree with this standard. The student reading the evidence in the round is personally responsible for the veracity of the evidence. The response, "I didn't research the evidence," does not relieve the debater of the responsibility for its integrity.

A debater using evidence researched by others ought to make the effort to ensure that other researchers understand their responsibility for accurate scholarship. Another implication of both this and the prior case study concerns the appropriateness of making evidence challenges in the debate round.

A debater certainly has the right, and possibly the duty, of pointing out the misuse of evidence in a debate. Should the debater always do so? We believe that caution should be exercised in making evidence challenges in a debate. This caution takes several forms. First, a debater should make the challenge only when he or she has proof, in the form of a copy of the original source of the evidence. Second, the challenge should be made only after consulting your debate teacher to make sure that the challenge would be appropriate. Third, the challenge should be offered in a neutral fashion, in which the challenger does not make judgments about the person reading the evidence but simply indicates to the judge the problem with the evidence.

Case Study Three: Ethical Attitudes Toward Others

> You hear a student leaving a round saying: "Boy, we sure killed them. We demolished their arguments; they were pathetic. Too bad the judge was a plant species." Is this ethical communication behavior?

The communication behavior this student exhibited is less than ideal and is probably unethical. The statement of ethics views dehumanizing communication behavior as unethical. In this case, the student has dehumanized the judge and used unfortunate language in characterizing the opponents.

Is language use that important? After all, examples of dehumanizing language are often found in sports and other competitions. We think that language use is an important ethical aspiration in the debate activity. Our language choices reflect on our underlying values—a point made articulately by Wayne Brockriede, in a discussion we began in chapter 5. Brockriede used the sexual metaphor to describe arguing stances or attitudes. Arguers, in Brockriede's view, could be considered "rapists" or "seducers" or "lovers." An aspect of being a "lover" is accepting the humanity of others and making a commitment to behave in ways confirming that humanity.[8] Ethical language choices are one element of this process.

Case Study Four: The Ethics of Fast Delivery

> You are participating in a debate in which your opponents speak very quickly. You can't keep up, and you are unable to flow the arguments. Is your opponent's speaking style unethical?

Rapid speaking is probably not unethical. This case study involves a matter of style, not ethics. If the judge can flow and is willing to hear a fast-paced speech, the debaters will have to adjust. Debaters may prefer a slower-paced delivery, but an opponent probably has not committed an unethical act by speaking quickly.

We hasten to add, however, that rapid delivery may be ethically questionable in some instances. Sometimes debaters use rapid delivery simply to overwhelm the opposing team—which could be construed as an instance in which the debater has not met the aspiration of debate as a communicative activity.

Bad taste is not unethical. Participants ought to conduct debates using an appropriate, reasonable delivery rate. Rapid-fire delivery violates aesthetic communicative norms and subordinates form to content in debate, undermining the activity's social and educational value. But even the most rapid delivery is usually not considered an ethical issue.

Case Study Five: The Ethics of "Squirrel Cases"

> You are on the negative. The affirmative has presented a case that you have not considered, and you do not have evidence on the case. The case does deal with a minor part of the resolution. Has the affirmative committed an unethical act?

The choice of an affirmative case that deals with a minor part of the resolution is more a strategic choice than an ethical problem. If the affirmative has used sound definitions and has presented properly interpreted evidence, the strategy might work.

An unexpected or unusual case area presentation is sometimes labeled a "squirrel case." Should we penalize debaters for presenting the unusual or the unexpected? The motive for negatively labeling this strategy probably comes from the belief that debate is best when there is clear clash between well-prepared teams. Although this is undoubtedly true, there is no reason to believe that simply lacking evidence on a case dooms a negative to inevitable defeat. The negative might succeed by relying on logic and on analytic abilities.

American society emphasizes strongly the values of free speech. Debaters are free to present any statements and evidence they wish, subject to close scrutiny by their opponents. Unusual or unexpected cases may show either original or insightful understanding of the resolution or may even show up the negative's failure to adequately prepare. Cases must be judged on their soundness, not on whether the listeners could reasonably expect to predict the case ahead of time.

Case Study Six: Audiences in Debate Rounds

> You and your partner notice that a student from another school is in the back of the room flowing your affirmative case. You know that the student will share the flow of your case with his team. As a result, the debaters from his team will be prepared for your case. Is it unethical for this student to flow your case and then to share it with other debaters?

The student has not committed an unethical act. Debate tournaments are open to the public, and the First Amendment to the Constitution guarantees the right to create and to hear arguments. The student has a perfect right to record and to share your ideas.

Although it may be aggravating to know that others will learn about your affirmative case strategy, or negative positions, scouting you and other teams is not unethical.

As we have mentioned, you should be ready to alter your strategy as the tournament proceeds. This is true particularly if other teams know about one of your affirmative cases.

Case Study Seven: Research by Coaches

> You are a member of a large program. One of the graduate assistants does original research for the team. He cuts evidence; he writes briefs; and he often writes affirmative cases. Is the behavior of this graduate assistant ethical?

This is a difficult question. The statement of ethics notes that "coaching efforts should supplement, not substitute for, student efforts."[9] The graduate student is serving as an educator in his role as graduate student. When he does the original research and writes affirmative cases for debaters, he is "substituting for student efforts."

When, however, a coach is attempting to teach novice debaters how to construct a brief or an affirmative case, it may be more appropriate for a coach to write a brief to illustrate the principles of brief construction. Because forensic education is a difficult profession, forensic educators should be given broad leeway in the teaching techniques they use. Some would argue that the graduate student's behavior is appropriate, for it is almost impossible in modern academic debate to prepare without assistance for all the affirmative case possibilities. This argument has some strength. Yet, debate students should create arguments and find the research. Learning the process of argument invention and discovery of proof are major reasons that students should debate. When a coach or a graduate student performs these functions, the student cannot learn.

SUMMARY

This chapter has identified the major principles of ethical intercollegiate debate. We believe that the statement of ethics produced by the American Forensic Association is a useful guideline for forensic students and encourage you to read this document and discuss it with other students. You will be faced with ethical dilemmas. There is no one right response to ethical problems.

We hope that you will aspire to achieve higher ethical standards. Such aspirations are particularly timely in light of the unethical behaviors exhibited by some public officials, athletes, and business people. The forensic activity exists, in part, to foster the best and most ethical rhetorical behavior. We hope you will do your best to enhance the integrity of the forensic activity by actively promoting and exhibiting ethical debate practices.

ENDNOTES

1. "The Ethics of Forensics," in *American Forensics in Perspective*, edited by Donn W. Parson (Annandale, VA: Speech Communication Association, 1984).
2. "The Ethics of Forensics," p. 17.
3. "The Ethics of Forensics," pp. 17–18.
4. "The Ethics of Forensics," p. 18.
5. "The Ethics of Forensics," p. 18.
6. "The Ethics of Forensics," p. 18.
7. "The Ethics of Forensics," p. 18.
8. Wayne Brockriede, "Arguers as Lovers," *Philosophy and Rhetoric* 5 (1972), pp. 1–11.
9. "The Ethics of Forensics," p. 16.

Appendix A
Sample Debate

First Affirmative Constructive:

Carrie Crenshaw, Florida State University

Miguel and I stand resolved: That membership in the United Nations is no longer beneficial to the United States.

In beginning our affirmation of the resolution, we wish first to note one observation. Observation number one. Criteria for evaluation of the resolution. (A) subpoint, definitions. Initially, we'd like to note that the affirmative has the right to reasonably define terms because otherwise the negative could always define the affirmative as falling outside the scope of the resolution.

The term United Nations implies only the General Assembly, the Security Council, and the Secretariat. Thomas Franck, Director of Research for UNITAR, the UN's think tank, explains what the UN is, in 1985:

> This impression [of disillusionment and disappointment with the UN] cannot be rebutted by reference to public opinion polls demonstrating continued support for selected UN activities such as help to developing countries, the eradication of malaria, or the useful activities of the World Bank and the International Postal Union. The American public is sophisticated enough to know that these praiseworthy activities are carried out by agencies that are largely independent of the principal institutions of the UN. When the laity think of the United Nations, they have in mind the organs which deal with highly visible political disputes: the Security Council, the Secretariat, and especially the General Assembly. [These three organs] which deal with the big political disputes . . . are essential core of the system. (6–7)

In fact, Mr. Franck argues that membership to the UN is only really confined to those three areas when he writes:

> Between World Wars I and II the United States belonged to some specialized agencies, such as the International Labor Organization, even while refusing to join the League of Nations. Even now, we could continue to belong to the best of the functional bodies such as the World Health Organization and the World Food Programme, even if we decided to withdraw from the UN itself because of the initiatives of the core political organs no longer coincided with the US national interests. (7)

The final term needing definition, of course, is beneficial. According to *Webster's New World Dictionary* in 1979, beneficial means: For one's own interest.[1] Thus, we support the contention that beneficiality should be evaluated according to the United States' national interests.

Additionally we'd like to note subpoint (B). The US national interest defined. George Keenan, noted International Relations expert and Professor at Princeton, quoted in the December 16th, 1985, issue of *Newsweek*, gives guidelines by which to determine the US national interest: "[T]he United States should be guided by three basic concerns—military security, the integrity of its political life, and the well being of the American people" (47).

Thus if we succeed in proving that the UN no longer acts to serve the interests set forth by Professor Keenan, the resolution can be affirmed.

The grounds for our claim are offered in contention one. United States military security is endangered by conflict. Subpoint (A) conflict control ensures military security. If we wish military security then we must limit conflict. Michael Klare, analyst at the Institute for Policy Studies, notes in 1984: "Looking at the world as it is, and wishing to avert a global catastrophe, our goal must be more expedient: the deterrence, containment, and control of military conflict" (247).

Subpoint (B) small conflicts pose the greatest threat of global disaster. Former President Nixon points out this first in his 1984 book *Real Peace:* "The greatest threat to peace comes not from the possibility of a direct conflict between the United States and the Soviet Union, but from the chance that a small war in the Third World will drag in the two super powers and escalate into a world war" (73).

While it may seem obvious that conflict control is in everyone's interest, the UN only exacerbates conflict. Note contention two, the UN heightens conflict. The reason stems from how the UN functions. Please note subpoint (A), the UN is used to blow off steam. The original purpose of the UN was to provide the countries of the world a place where they could vent their frustrations in the hope that the pressures which build up due to unsettled disputes would be relieved without the necessity of blood and agony. Mr Tugwell, of the Center for Crisis Studies, establishes this in 1984: "[A]s Winston Churchill expressed it, 'better jaw, jaw than war, war'. . . .The UN is the one place in the world where representatives of nearly all countries—regardless of size, wealth or power—are freely heard on a broad range of world issues. In this regard . . . the General Assembly is the principal forum for blowing off steam" (158).

However, things haven't turned out quite as Mr. Churchill expected. Subpoint (B), venting sows the seeds for war. The General Assembly is used to mobilize emotions, which cause conflicts. Mr. Tugwell continues in 1984:

> It cannot be said that this beneficial outcome has never occurred. It must also be said that in today's General Assembly, such occurrences are very rare. All evidence points to the safety valve theory being turned on its head. The venting of steam is for the most part hypocritical,

---

[1] Source indicated.

stage-managed and conflict-oriented. Far from cooling passions, the techniques of name-calling and lying are intended to mobilize the Assembly on the side of the speaker, to discredit and isolate adversaries, and to cultivate climates of opinion inhospitable to national argument. (163)

UN involvement in every problem only causes conflict to become extended. Jeanne Kirkpatrick, former US ambassador to the UN, examines this reality in 1983:

In the process of being transformed from actual problems outside the United Nations to United Nations issues, the number of parties to a conflict is dramatically extended. A great many countries who would never be involved at all in the issue of the Golan Heights, for example, become involved in that issue as the conflict is extended inside the United Nations to become a matter of concern to all the world. The United Nations is an arena in which many countries are brought into conflicts they might not otherwise become involved in. (96–7)

As the conflict becomes extended, everyone must choose sides in the issue, and this causes more conflict. Professors Yeselson and Gaglione of Rutgers University explain in 1974:

If a particular black African state wishes to maintain a neutral and helpful position vis-a-vis the Arab-Israeli dispute, it must consider the risk of alienating other Afro-Asian states in respect to issues on which it seeks their support. Politics at the UN, by constantly forcing states to choose up sides, progressively destroys neutral havens, which may mean the difference between war and peace. (175)

This conflict extension precludes the UN from peaceful settlement of conflict. Subpoint (C), venting precludes peacemaking. Mr. Tugwell continues in 1984:

Nor is the UN's record in controlling regional conflict very impressive. In the Middle East, for example, fluttering blue and white UN flags and contingents of UN observers or peacekeepers never once prevented an Arab military or terrorist attack on Israel. . . .In recent years, undisguised UN hostility toward Israel has effectively disqualified that organization from its supposed pacific role in the Middle East. Significantly, the latest peacekeeping force in the region was sponsored outside the UN. (160)

We note subpoint (D), the UN is used to mobilize for war. The UN may be intended to cool emotions, and plenty of lip service may be given by its supporters to that goal, but the actual participants of the UN use it for mobilizing war efforts. Professors Yeselson and Gaglione of Rutgers explain:

[The UN] is such a weapon in international relations and should be recognized as such. As part of the armory of nations in conflict, the United Nations contributes about as much to peace as a battleship or an atomic bomb. Disputes are brought into the UN in order to weaken an opponent, strengthen one's own side, prepare for war, and support a war effort. (x)

While the UN would be a good forum for discussing the solution to real problems, it is instead exploited for the mobilization of war efforts. Mr. Tugwell agrees, "The plight of Palestine Arabs is real the UN ought to be a good forum for reconciliation, compromise and settlement. However, instead of venting steam one day and returning the next to contribute to rational debate, the supposedly injured parties in these disputes vent steam to mobilize for war" (165).

While the past has been more successful than portrayed here, that is only the past. Please note finally subpoint (E), the UN has had successes but is now an enemy of peace. Kurt Waldheim notes in 1984: "The system on paper is impressive. It has frequently helped to avoid or contain international violence. Yet in recent years it has seemed to cope less and less effectively with international conflicts of various kinds, and its capabilities in other areas of international cooperation have also seemed to dwindle." (93).

In addition, any past success cannot be taken as indicating of any future trend. Mr. Tugwell explains:

> The UN has enjoyed some success in peace-maintenance, particularly in the prevention of escalation and in helping parties in a dispute to disengage. Although nuclear war has been avoided, this is more to NATO's deterrence policy than efforts in the UN. Moreover, a reluctance on the UN's part to recognize or address the reality of Soviet expansionist policy, coupled with disarmament proposals that may undermine deterrence, could diminish rather than strengthen the preservation of peace in the future.(157)

The only conclusion Miguel and I can reach is that peace can be better assured by not employing the UN in conflicts. Yeselson and Gaglione note: The overwhelming majority of quarrels among allies are settled secretly or bilaterally. Even states basically at odds with each other forego the UN when they are unwilling to exacerbate tensions (165).[2]

We now ask you to stand resolved that membership in the United Nations is no longer beneficial to the United States.

Cross-Examination:

Paul Benson questioning Crenshaw.

Benson: The UN then consists only of the three major organs, correct? Crenshaw: Yes. Benson: OK, now, do the other areas of the UN contribute to the beneficiality

---

[2] "The overwhelming majority of quarrels among allies are settled secretly and bilaterally or within the confines of an alliance setting. Even states basically at odds with each other forego opportunities to utilize the UN when they are unwilling to exacerbate tensions."

of the UN? Crenshaw: Well, we're talking about membership in the United Nations according to the resolution. And membership in the United Nations only includes those three. Benson: So only those three. But do the other organizations contribute to our beneficiality of being in that particular organization? Crenshaw: I really don't know, and I would contend that is irrelevant, because it is not— Benson: That is irrelevant? Crenshaw: Yes, it does not fit under the topic in any way. It is not a resolutional discussion.

Benson: OK. Now the CIA was established by Congress, correct? Crenshaw: That's correct. Benson: OK, and when we discuss the beneficiality of Congress, would we not look at the actions of the CIA as part of that? Crenshaw: No, you wouldn't. In fact that's the analogy that Miguel uses most of the time. He says— Benson: Yeah, I know. Crenshaw: Oh, good. Benson: Miguel is a nice guy. Crenshaw: If you're a member of the CIA, that does not mean you are a representative or a senator. Benson: That's irrelevant. I mean, doesn't, when you're evaluating beneficiality of Congress, would you not consider then— Crenshaw: But, see you— Benson: The actions of the CIA in that, you know, on balance calculus? Crenshaw: No, you must take the resolution as a whole. Benson: Resolution as a whole? Wouldn't we be taking the resolution as a whole if we did this? Crenshaw: No, you wouldn't because you have to deal only with membership in the United Nations. That is the only way you determine the benefits. That is the only thing that you are determining the beneficiality of.

Benson: OK. I need the national interest (A) subpoint. And all of contention one.

Benson: Now, the UN escalates these conflicts? Right? How many has it empirically escalated? Crenshaw: I think there is one example of the Arab-Israeli. Benson: The Arab-Israeli dispute? Which one? (laughter) Crenshaw: The conflict in that area. Benson: In that area. I mean there are all kinds of conflict. Are we talking, like — Crenshaw: Israel and the PLO is what I believe Mr. Tugwell is— Benson: Israel and the PLO? Is that like UNIFIL? Is that what you're going to defend? Crenshaw: That was a peacekeeping operation. We're talking about venting. The blowing off of steam in the general assembly debate. Benson: OK. So blowing off steam is the impact then? Crenshaw: That is the link. Benson: That is the link to the impact. And the impact is what? Crenshaw: The fact that the UN exacerbates conflict and it contributes to— Benson: Well, what's the impact of exacerbating the conflicts? Are we talking war here or what? Crenshaw: The nations use the UN to mobilize their war efforts. In fact Professors Yeselson and Gaglione say that— Benson: Yeselson and Gaglione in '74, right? That's '74 evidence, correct? Crenshaw: Yes it is. Benson: Now you argue that, you know, we have to talk about current examples. OK. Now if that's true, how does this Yeselson and Gaglione even matter? It's twelve years old. Crenshaw: Well, you know, if you want to press the evidence. Benson: Why, I am. Will you answer my question please? Crenshaw: Well, it is 1974. Yes, it is.

Benson: OK, the Tugwell evidence. Tugwell's Heritage Foundation, correct? Crenshaw: No, he is not. He's from the Center for Crisis Studies. Benson: Isn't he published in *The World Without a UN*? Crenshaw: Yes, he is, but that does not— Benson: And isn't that where you got the cite? Crenshaw: Yes, but that does not mean that is where he is from.

First Negative Constructive:

Molly McGinnis, Macalester College

We were told we would get time for thank you's, so I'd like to do that first. Macalester College is very proud to be in the first final round of the National CEDA Debate Tournament. We would like to thank the members of the team that are here with us: Grant, Barb, Peter, Brenda, Steve, and Chris,[3] and our coaches Dick Lesicko, Tim Baker, John Jackson, and Dr. Scott Nobles.

Overview number one is that membership is inherently beneficial. (A) subpoint is that on balance, membership is beneficial and I'll cross-apply to their criteria on case side. Richard Gardner, Professor of Law at Columbia, 1982. "[W]hen we look at the activities of the United Nations *as a whole*, the evidence leads us to the unavoidable conclusion that the advantages of the UN to our national interest outweigh the disadvantages" (50-1).

(B) subpoint is that no US means no UN. *Harpers* in January of '84 cites an anonymous high official of the administration who says, "With us out, our Western allies would soon follow . . . along with many pro-Western countries in the Third World . . . and the UN would soon collapse" (29).

(C) subpoint is that specialized agencies go, too. Thomas Franck, who they cite, says in '85: "As for wider withdrawal from the entire UN, the State Department has pointed out that financial loss would constrain UN organization drastically and force them to cut back programs, including many regarded as especially important; refugee, health, and technical programs, for example" (264-5).[4]

Overview number two is that they suffer from lofty expectations. And lofty expectations says that they expect too much out of the peacekeeping forces, and it's not surprising that they conclude that they fail. (A) subpoint is the purpose of peacekeeping mission. Donald J. Puchala, professor of government, University of South Carolina, in 1983: "The primary purpose of these UN missions has been to deter the renewed fighting, to gain time for diplomacy, and to discourage external and especially superpower intervention that could lead to . . . escalate to larger wars (578).[5]

(B) subpoint is that they are not supposed to shift parties. Alan James, Professor of International Relations in '83: "But if the parties refuse to move, it is not the peacekeepers' job to shift them" (633).

---

[3] Grant Killoran, Barb Birr, Peter Richardson, Brenda Smith, Steve Appelget, and Chris Cloutier.

[4] "As for wider US withdrawal from the entire UN system, the State Department has pointed out that the financial loss would constrain UN organizations drastically to cut back programs, including many regarded as especially important; refugee, health, and technical programs, for example."

[5] The primary purposes of these UN missions have been to deter renewed fighting, to gain time for diplomacy, and to discourage external, and especially superpower, intervention that could escalate into larger wars."

(C) subpoint is failure is the fault of outside diplomacy. Indar Rikhye, professor of political science at Yale in '84: (Which takes out their final argument on Yeselson and Gaglione, which indicates they are becoming other than the UN): "The lack of peaceful resolution of conflict has more often been due to the failure of diplomacy outside" (224).

OK, overview number two or overview number three, excuse me, is that the UN slows proliferation of nuclear weapons. (A) subpoint is that US is key to the IAEA [International Atomic Energy Agency]. Dr. Scheinman announced in '85 that to insure an effective agency, a leadership role by the United States is needed (67).[6]

(B) IAEA benefits the US. Robert Keohane, government professor at Harvard in Fall of '85: "[A]n international regime discouraging proliferation has greatly aided American policy . . ." (152).

(C) subpoint, key to the regime. Joseph Nye, professor of government at Harvard in Summer of '85: "The main norms and practices of this antiproliferation regime are found in the NPT, the nuclear nonproliferation treaty, and the IAEA."[7]

Debra Miller, a political science professor at Columbia, says in 1983 that the UN itself has also contributed to the articulation of norms against the use of nuclear weapons. The reluctance of weaker states to use nuclear weapons in local disputes may derive in part from the UN's norm against such an action from the perception that sanctions would be employed (136).[8]

(D) subpoint is that the regime is effective. Leonard Spector from Carnegie Endowment for Peace in 1985: "Safeguards probably detect most illegal uses of these plants and therefore pose a significant deterrent to proliferation" (55).[9]

(E) subpoint. It slows the prolif rate. Lewis Dunn is from the ACDA in October of '84: "Without the NPT, political constraint to the bomb's spread would be undermined . . ." (15).

---

[6] "One of the most important measures to assure an effective and credible agency enjoying the broad-based confidence so necessary to its effectiveness is a strong and continuing leadership role by the United States both within the agency and among its principal members."

[7] "The main norms and practices of this regime are found in the NPT and in regional counterparts such as the Treaty of Tlatelolco, which aims to keep Latin America non-nuclear; in the safeguards, rules, and procedures of the International Atomic Energy Agency (IAEA); and in various UN resolutions."

[8] "The UN has also contributed to the articulation of norms against the use of nuclear weapons. While the restraint of the superpowers in this area is due more to their perception of self-interest than to UN norms, the reluctance of weaker states to use nuclear weapons in local disputes may derive in part from the UN's norm against such an action and from the perception that sanctions (e.g., the cutting off of military assistance by one's allies) will be applied within the UN context against countries that violate the norm."

[9] "Despite certain shortcomings, these safeguards can probably detect most illegal uses of these plants and therefore pose a significant deterrent to proliferation."

Finally, subpoint (F), and it says that proliferation is disastrous. Scheinman says in '85: "The proliferation of nuclear weapons to more countries would increase prospects for their use, risk involving the super powers, and raise the possibility of cataclysmic nuclear war" (1).

I'm on their observation number one now. (A) subpoint says definitions, that they have the right to be reasonable. First argument here is we will argue that they need to realistically define. And when the overview argues, you know, that there is a link between the United Nations and the specialized agencies in terms of funding, that is realistic.

They argue only General Assembly. First argument is parallel to Congress. Now when Congress debates and decides that something needs to be done, they delegate that to an agency which they set up, or a commission which they set up, and that's a delegation of responsibility. And we argue that there's the same delegation within the United Nations.

They argue from Franck in '85 that talks about political disputes. First argument is why is the affirmative definition distinct? Why is that the only definition? Why is the analysis I give above inappropriate?

They argue that between World War I and World War II we still belonged to these things. First argument is that a poor analogy between the League of Nations and the United Nations, because we argue now that the funding of both is inextricably tied.

They argue that beneficial means to be in one's own interest. And that's on observation two, the (A) point, where they talk about the definition of benefit. First argument is who is "one's own interest?" I mean is that your interest, or my interest, and how do you weigh those things? Second argument is we will maintain on balance. That you divvy up the costs and benefits of the United States membership in the United Nations and we will conclude that we win. Third argument is how do you weigh? If they prove a benefit and we prove a cost, or vice versa, I guess would be the case, you know, how would we decide who wins? Who is the individual cited in their definition?

The (B) subpoint is from Mr. Kennan in 1985. He says that we should be guided by military security, the integrity of political life, and the well being of American people. First argument is what are sub-definitions? That is, what is the integrity of the American people? What is military security? And those things are not defined, and if you're not certain whether or not the UN hurts those or helps those, then there can be no assertation of whether or not the UN is beneficial or not.

Second argument is why only this? Why are these the only three elements to talk about? Why can't we talk about health, welfare, and all that? Then they would argue that's within their third definition, which only, which illustrates my point that they need sub-definitions before you can argue it. Third argument is how do you weigh? And that goes back to the on-balance criterion above.

I am on contention number one, (A) point. They talk about how conflict control; the need for conflict control. First argument is they do not identify Third World conflict. Second argument is they do not identify UN-fostered conflict, in fact, there is no mention of the UN at all in the card. Which would indicate that

Klare is not really concerned about the UN conflict in particular, but, just about conflict.

Fourth argument is not only peacekeeping. Which would indicate that we will argue that peacekeeping is not the only [unintelligible] to peace, nor should peace be the only thing that is discussed because that's not what Kennan discusses only.

On the (B) point they talk about how small conflicts are the greatest risk. First argument is what are the scenarios? I mean, what does this author assume about what would be the greatest risk? Second argument is how large of a conflict is needed before this harm arose? And third, is this fostered by the UN? Does this piece of evidence indicate that such things are fostered by the United Nations?

Their contention number two. (A) subpoint says that the UN is used to blow off steam. Tugwell in '84. First argument is he's from the Heritage Foundation, and we would indict him in particular. *Atlantic Monthly* says in January of '86: "We're not here to be some kind of Ph.D. committee giving equal time, says Berton Pines, a vice president of the Heritage [Foundation]. Our role is to provide conservative public-policy-makers with arguments to bolster our side" (Easterbrook, 72). They reach their conclusion first.

Second argument is that debate is a substitute for war. Elliot Richardson is the Representative to the Law of the Sea in 1985. "[T]he long-winded debates are often surrogate for war . . ." (Fasulo, vi). Third argument is the war is over arms. C. Maxwell Stanley, from the Stanley Foundation in '82: "In the area of peace and security, the General Assembly provides a neutral forum where parties to a dispute can fight with words rather than weapons" (105). Third argument, excuse me, fourth argument is that third world gets to vent their aggressions. Seymour Finger says in '85 that "Sometimes, too, fiery statements at the UN by Third World countries are a substitute for redeeming their pride by going to war when they know going to war would be disastrous" (Fasulo 65). OK?

Final argument is that there are no empirical examples. No indication of where the UN has fostered this sort of thing.

On the (B) point, they state it equals the seeds for war. First argument is that they have a good track record. A. LeRoy Bennett, of the University of Delaware in 1984: "[T]he record of the UN in conflict resolution is surprisingly encouraging. Of more than 150 disputes considered by the Council and the Assembly, not more than a dozen remain"(130).

Second argument, nope that's enough there.

On the next argument from Kirkpatrick, they talk about how (unintelligible) is extended. First argument is, even if it is prolonged it's better than no peacekeeping. K. Venkata Raman, professor of law at Queens, in 1983 says that "It is true that in some situations . . . indefinitely extended peacekeeping operations have not served to produce a settlement. But the absence of peacekeeping would have aggravated the situation much further" (376).

Next card is from Yeselson and Gaglione. They argue that they choose sides. First argument is 1974 evidence, and they better show some empiricals since then in the twelve intervening years. Second argument is that the empirical needs to be the standard. We argue that the empirically peacekeeping is good. Third argument is that does not talk about the superpowers, which means they don't win the Nixon argument above. Fourth argument is that they do not show a snowball. That is, Yeselson and Gaglione do not say that these conflicts escalate into the types of things the impacts come off.

(C) subpoint they talk about how peacekeeping does not prevent. First argument is this is only talking about Israel. OK? And that's the Tugwell evidence again, the indicts cross-apply here.

They argue that outside the United Nations work. First argument is the MNF was not peacekeeping, it was war. Indar Rikhye, in '84: "The President thus categorically stated that MNF was helping to train and organize the Lebanese army and was needed to back it in maintaining order because Lebanon lacked the forces to do so" (235). Meaning we had to put a peacekeeping troop back in order to get these things to work.

Second argument is failure justifies UN. Dr. Cannon, from the Board of Governors of the UN, in 1984: "In the fall of 1982 the US organized . . . a MNF, outside of the UN, for Lebanon. It failed . . . The US should have learned that the UN peacekeeping forces are truly international and relatively impartial—a major advantage in seeking to resolve peacefully" (30).

On the lip service argument next from Yeselson and Gaglione. Again 1974, and they need to indicate that the present would be truly the same. Raimo Vayrynen, professor of political science, from the University of Helsinki, in 1985: "Peacekeeping forces are advocated both within and outside the UN. Peacekeeping will in the next decade and likely beyond be applied more frequently and with greater variety and complexity" (193).[10]

On the (E) subpoint they talk about how there have been success, but it's not enough. J.G. Ruggie, he's a professor of political science at Columbia 1985: "On the whole, peacekeeping has been a success story for the United Nations as even some of the fiercest critics of the organization are obliged to concede" (347).

Cross-Examination:

Carrie Crenshaw questioning McGinnis

Crenshaw: You argue that the UN causes a proliferation of nuclear weapons, is that correct? McGinnis: No. We argue that the United Nations' norms and the United Nations' agencies help to slow the rate of proliferation of nuclear weapons in the world. Crenshaw: So that's (D) subpoint that says it slows the proliferation rate? McGinnis: Right.

---

[10] "It is a sign of the times that peacekeeping forces are advocated both within and outside the UN framework. For instance, ASEAN has called for peacekeeping forces for Kampuchea, OAU even sent such forces to Chad—although they later had to be withdrawn—and the Carter Administration proposed the establishment of a UN peacekeeping force to pacify the border areas of Iran and Iraq. Obviously, Wiseman is right in observing that peacekeeping will in the next decade, and likely beyond, be applied more frequently and with greater variety and complexity than heretofore."

Crenshaw: Does the impact evidence deal with the rate of proliferation or does it deal with just whether or not proliferation is bad? McGinnis: It talks about whether or not proliferation is bad. Though we would indicate from the (E) point that, the (E) point is also impact, which says that a fast rate of proliferation is not appropriate for a safe world. Crenshaw: Can I see that piece of evidence? McGinnis: Well, I just gave it all back. Hang on a second. Crenshaw: Because I believe on your next subpoint the only piece of evidence that you read was that proliferation in general is bad. McGinnis: Right. That's the (F) subpoint from Schienman. Right.

Crenshaw: Could I see the (E) subpoint? McGinnis: Yeah, (E) subpoint is right here.

Crenshaw: Why is it that a rate of fast proliferation is worse than a rate of slow proliferation? McGinnis: It is the making of the INC argument about prolif that more nuclear weapons are not a good thing. And that the move toward that has been halted or slowed by the UN.

Crenshaw: Could you read this piece of evidence for me again please? McGinnis: Any one in particular? Oh, the (E) subpoint. Lewis Dunn in '84 says that without the NPT, political constraint to the bomb's spread would be undermined. That's all the card says. Crenshaw: What does that say about the rate of the spread? McGinnis: We argue that were it not for this organization, more people would have the bomb. That's all we argue. Crenshaw: But you just argued that the rate of proliferation has something to do with this argument. McGinnis: Maybe the words I used were inappropriate then. All I'm saying on this subpoint is that were it not for the UN, more people would have the bomb then do now. That's all I'm claiming. Crenshaw: OK. So the rate or the– McGinnis: No,– Crenshaw: The rate of the– McGinnis: All I need,– All I need by, not that it's irrelevant, all I'm arguing on this subpoint is that fewer people have the bomb. That's all I'm arguing.

Crenshaw: OK. Why is it that the United Nations spreads nuclear weapons? McGinnis: Why is it that they spread nuclear weapons? Crenshaw: 'Cause your link said that– McGinnis: I don't argue that they do spread nuclear weapons. Crenshaw: Wait now. OK. Correct me if I'm wrong, but didn't you just say that if it were not for the United Nations, then less people would have the bomb? McGinnis: No. Were it not for the United Nations, more people would have the bomb than do now. I argue that– Crenshaw: OK, I'm sorry. Correct. OK.

Crenshaw: So the United Nations promotes the spread of nuclear weapons? McGinnis: No. Crenshaw: It decreases the spread of nuclear weapons? McGinnis: Yes. Crenshaw: OK. I'm getting sleepy, obviously. Why is that? Through which agency? The International Atomic Energy Agency? McGinnis: Two ways. First is the United Nations itself sets the norms against such use. Crenshaw: What, the General Assembly? McGinnis: Right. The norms generated in the UN. And then I also argued that they delegate their responsibilities to enforce that sort of pledge, that norm, to the IAEA and through the UN treaty– Crenshaw: So, the norms evidence talks about the limited use of the nuclear weapons, does it not? McGinnis: It argues—stops the move toward that– Crenshaw: It's not obtaining the technology; it's talking about the use of.

Second Affirmative Constructive:

Miguel Delao, Florida State University

Their first overview is on empiricals. (A) subpoint is on balance. I would first argue that this is agencies. The evidence says when you look at the UN as a whole, as they argued in cross-examination, it should be wholistic. Second argument is vague word. It is not something you can vote for, it does not say exactly what is beneficial and certainly you cannot weigh exactly what they are talking about. You do not even know what was considered. They consider our arguments.

She says (B) subpoint, no US equals no UN. She is correct.

(C) subpoint says agencies would go. That is not true. That evidence only indicates that we actually left the agencies also. We could still fund the agencies by still being in them. We do not necessarily have to cut off funding to the agencies, and I think the Franck evidence at the top of the case indicates that.

Overview two, lofty expectations. First argument is, I don't think it's very unreasonable to expect the United Nations to not cause conflict. Certainly we can't expect them to stop every conflict, but you don't want them to create any of them. Second argument is that peacekeeping has worked in the past, but we are claiming that it has changed because of venting, as I will argue on case specifically.

Third argument is that we are not dealing with failure. We're not saying that they fail at all peace efforts, but that fact that they create conflicts means we do not need the United Nations because we will argue that it is not unique to the United Nations.

Prolif. First argument is that the IAEA is an agency. Evidence is from Ameri in '82: "Although not a specialized agency, the International Atomic Energy Agency (IAEA) is an autonomous intergovernmental agency under the aegis of the United Nations" (26). Second argument is that we must obviously have the bomb out there because the evidence that they read that says that the UN has these norms to stop the use—you only stop the use of nukes after someone has nukes. Which indicates that the UN has not stopped proliferation. Otherwise, the norms would not matter.

Third argument is that the debates actually lead to prolif. Becker writes in 1985: "Nuclear proliferation is not tackled as a security issue but rather as another source of 'discrimination' between 'haves' and 'have nots'. . . . The net result is that the United Nations debates undermine the status of the NPT and become instrumental in legitimizing nuclear weapons proliferation" (175).

Fourth argument is that the NPT spreads nuclear weapons capabilities. Becker in '85: "The NPT will in effect become a treaty for the peaceful uses of nuclear energy, and as such may be instrumental in promoting the very spread of nuclear weapon capability that it was intended to inhibit" (134).

Fifth answer is that the IAEA promotes nuclear proliferation. Becker in '85:

These deficiencies are particularly alarming because of the 'abrogation risk' inherent in the NPT system. . . . In other words, the IAEA system, and particularly its promotional role, allows a state to proceed under the guise of the NPT as far as possible with all its plans for making nuclear weapons and, when ready, merely notify the IAEA and the United Nation Security Council that it is withdrawing from the treaty. (126)

Sixth argument is that the experts agree that the IAEA cannot stop prolif. Becker in '85, quoting Epstine: "Experts agree, and the IAEA itself admits, that there are limits to the extent to which the agency is able to detect diversions and to guarantee an effective international response to a non-proliferation violation, even when it is detected" (126).

Criteria of our case. She says you need a realistic standard, and they have a funding link, but she never indicates that funding would actually be stopped, i.e. this is the same argument she makes as her overview.

She says number two, Congress equals delegates, and it is the same in the UN. But, if I'm a member of the CIA, I am not a member of Congress. And therefore, the US could still belong to the IAEA, still stop proliferation, and not have to be in the United Nations and stop this venting.

She then extends that, I can't read my own handwriting. Oh, I'm sorry, she says why is Franck correct? And I would argue that this. You can belong in these agencies and this is empirically true. You can belong in these agencies and this is empirically true. Bennett in '84: "Membership in the specialized agencies have a membership larger than that of the UN" (75). Switzerland belongs to a lot of these specialized agencies and they are not members of the United Nations.

She extends that the League is a poor example because there was no funding link. But she never indicates that there was no funding link between the League of Nations and these agencies. She merely asserts it. And Mr. Franck indicates that even if we leave the UN, you can still belong to these agencies. And that part of the evidence is granted.

Beneficial. She says, for whose benefit? Should balance. Of course, I would agree. She says, number three, how do you weigh? I would say you give articulate, eloquent reasons why your argument outweighs.

(B) subpoint, US national interests. Kennan in '85. She says what are the subdefinitions? I think we provide the subdefinitions on contention one, when we indicate that military security is in our benefit. Number two, I would argue, is that it outweighs everything else, because if we are not militarily secure and our country's involved in a war, or should have a nuclear catastrophe, then surely we cannot have political integrity or well-being.

She says number two, why not the others? As I argued above, this outweighs. She says number three how do you weigh? Not to be cynical or anything, but you use scales and when you weigh me, I'm a bit heavy. (Laughter) Pudgy.

Contention one. (A) subpoint, you need conflict control. She says this does not say UN fosters. Of course not. But it is true that if the UN leads to conflict, this evidence indicates you don't want that, because that would lead to catastrophe.

She says number two, peacekeeping is not the only thing. Fine.

She says (B) sub. On our (B) subpoint we argue small wars are the greatest threat. She says what are the scenarios? I think Mr. Nixon gives you excellent scenarios. He says we'll get sucked in; we'll get dragged in. She says number two, how large do they have to be? Clearly, the evidence indicates when you have these small wars, you have this political for escalation and we would ask you to vote for that, at least the evidence at top says you don't want all this conflict out there. That is the Klare evidence.

She says number three, does not say UN. You know, so what? We are arguing by links here. And this contention is merely establishing the criteria by which you weigh contention number two. And that is where the links are.

Contention number two. Tugwell evidence there in '84 says the safety valve theory has been turned on its head. She says Heritage Foundation. First argument is, who the hell, who the heck, is the *Atlantic Monthly?* How come that beats the Heritage Foundation? She doesn't even read a source.

Second argument is that evidence does not say they reach their opinions first. She merely asserts that. Third argument is she should just prove them wrong. If he is so incorrect, then just say why they are wrong. She says, number two, that they empirically prevented wars. Obviously not true. It is empirically false because we have wars all the time. And you have all this debate out there and they still go to war. Means at least venting does not lead to peace. Not that it necessarily leads to war, but it does not lead to peace.

She says that they get to vent. But, I want to extend the evidence there in the case that the safety valve has been turned on its head. So that venting is actually bad. Her last argument is no empirics. But the evidence down there that we read later on in the case, that the Arab-Israeli conflict is fueled by the United Nations.

(B) subpoint, venting—sow the seeds of war. She says that they have conflict resolution, but I would argue that they still cause conflicts, and that is not what you want. Kirkpatrick. She says it is better than nothing. But the UN is not going to get peacekeeping, as I will argue below. '74: She says show empirical example. I would argue that the problem is still around. *World Press Review* in December of '85: "Never before has the UN been so divorced from its functions of preserving peace, settling international disputes, protecting human rights, and creating an atmosphere of dialogue instead of vituperation" (Sethi 39).

Second argument, she says you need empirical standard. I got that above. She says three, no superpowers, do not show snowball. And this is the Nixon evidence that indicates when you have these conflicts, you have this potential for getting sucked in.

(C) subpoint, venting precludes. She says that it is only Israel, and that it is Tugwell. No, the evidence indicates in the whole Middle East, not just Israel. She says MNF equals war and this is all her peacekeeping stuff. Please group. First argument is the UN would not have done better. Nelson in '85: "To assert that the MNF role had been transformed from peacekeeping to enforcement is not to say that it failed per se, not emphatically, that a UN force would have been more successful in the same circumstance . . . " (82).

Number two, they don't want the UN there. Cuellar in '84: "But the difficulty is that some of those concerned don't want to have the United Nations involved in the Middle East problem. They object to the United Nations' presence" (Gauhar 18).

Number three, they will not go to the Middle East. That is the evidence from Tugwell there, indicating only the US can do it.

Number four is that there will be no more peacekeeping in the future because we've had the non-UN peacekeeping. Cuellar in '84: "On two occasions multinational forces were set up by the US, which is really tantamount to telling the UN that we don't trust you to handle difficult matters. With that background, it seems that the major powers might be unwilling to support UN peacekeeping operations" (Gauhar 17).

Number five—thank you—soldiers are dying and, therefore, no one will contribute soldiers to it. Cuellar in '84: "The growing reluctance of member countries to provide troops unless they have some guarantee that the troops will be protected. It is not developing countries who ask for such guarantees, it is the developed countries who insist on it. For instance, the Netherlands and Norway are hesitant to continue providing troops to the United Nation's UNIFL. The Netherlands have told me very frankly that they are prepared to extend their presence in Lebanon for three more months but not beyond" (Gauhar 16). You need the U. S. in there because, heck, we're really, you know, ready to shoot at them.

(E) subpoint is granted, which means you have no reason to. This peacekeeping stuff will come down to uniqueness. If the US can go in there, and at least shoot back and guarantee that people want them to be soldiers, and you can get all this conflict resolution outside the United Nations, that Yeselson card in '74 is granted, that says you go bilateral because you don't want to increase tensions, then the UN is not unique to get the peace.

Cross-Examination:

Molly McGinnis questioning Delao

McGinnis: Are there any peacekeeping forces in operation right now? Delao: Yes, there are. McGinnis: Yes, there are. How many? Delao: Two. McGinnis: Two? Delao: That's a guess. McGinnis: No, I'm asking you a question. Delao: Well, you seem to know the answer. McGinnis: Oh. Actually, not, that's Paul. Delao: Well, we'll take two. McGinnis: Any idea where these unnumbered peacekeeping missions might be? Delao: UNIFL is one of them. McGinnis: UNIFL is one of them. OK. And it's not working? Is conflict there? Delao: I don't remember making that argument. McGinnis: Now wait a minute. Delao: I'd love to make that argument. I probably will. McGinnis: You argue they extend the conflict, they institutionalize the conflict, they still cause the conflict, all that. Delao: Now that's the venting in the General Assembly.

McGinnis: Now wait a minute, the Kirkpatrick evidence says that UN involvement equals extension of the conflict. Delao: In the General Assembly. McGinnis: In the General Assembly only, right? So, there's no extension of the conflict on the battlefield? Delao: Not at. Right, not in that evidence. McGinnis: Not in that evidence. Anywhere in 2AC? Delao: Nope. McGinnis: Nowhere in 2AC? Delao: We're not saying peacekeeping is bad, we're just going to, we are going to argue we're going to get it more effectively. McGinnis: Oh. OK, sounds good.

McGinnis: Is there conflict right now? Delao: That's a vague question. McGinnis: OK, in terms of the definition of conflict used in 1AC, is there conflict now? Delao: In the world, yes, there is. McGinnis: OK. So, why haven't the super powers been sucked into the horrors of Richard Nixon's scenarios? Delao: Luckily, we don't all get sucked into every single conflict. McGinnis: Oh, so only a few conflicts do they get sucked into? Any possibility of where that might be? Delao: That just shows that it is not in our interest. And it doesn't have to happen every time, but since there is a potential, certainly it is not in our interest. And it doesn't have to happen every time, but since there is a potential, certainly it is not in our interest to want to risk that. McGinnis: OK. If it is in our interest to have MNF, or non-US peacekeeping forces, why haven't we sent them everywhere in the world where there is conflict? Delao: The last few times peacekeeping forces were used were outside the UN. The last time they were—

McGinnis: OK. In areas where there are no UN peacekeeping forces or no non-UN peacekeeping forces, why hasn't the US, like, gotten up and done something about it? Delao: Peacekeeping forces are not used all of the time. The only time that they have generally been used is when you had a more serious conflict. Its not like everyone uses them— McGinnis: A more serious conflict? Delao: Not using them is not necessarily a failure. It only means that—

McGinnis: Excuse me. What's the difference between a more serious conflict where there would be peacekeeping forces and a small conflict which is the greatest risk that Nixon talks about? Delao: Oh, OK. The one Nixon is talking about is when you have allies, like superpowers, and therefore you have to get involved. I mean when Israel fights somebody, like in the '73 war— McGinnis: OK, so now Israel is something that Nixon would talk about, right? Delao: That is certainly something.

McGinnis: Are there peacekeeping forces from the UN now in the area of Israel? Delao: Not in Israel. McGinnis: In the area of Israel? Delao: There is UNIFL. McGinnis: There is UNIFL? Would Mr. Nixon say that that peacekeeping, or that conflict, that area of conflict, would be enough to worry about sucking us in? Delao: Yup. McGinnis: Why haven't we been sucked in? Delao: Because there is a peacekeeping force there.

McGinnis: That works? Delao: Well when you make that argument, I assure you we will have lots of responses. McGinnis: Now wait a minute, your criterion is that we shouldn't get sucked in, and you just said that peacekeeping forces— Delao: I didn't say it works, I said there is one there. McGinnis: But, they aren't sucking us in, right? Delao: Not the peacekeeping forces, peacekeeping forces— McGinnis: Has the area sucked us in superpower? Delao: Obviously not. McGinnis: OK.

Second Negative Constructive:

Paul Benson, Macalester College

Lofty expectations, it gets big, contention two. Lofty expectations is overview number two. The criteria set up by the 2AC is if you can do it outside the UN better, then you vote affirmative. And what we will argue is, he will have to prove i.e., solvency for this, indicating that outside the UN is better. We will contend that UN is the best thing that you've got and it's the only empirical examples of solving for peace.

Please go to his first argument on lofty expectations. He says it's not unreasonable to say that they don't, you know, for them not to cause it. Of course, number one, I will argue they do not cause the wars. I mean the wars happen with or without the United Nations. And nowhere does he indicate that a war would happen because the UN existed.

Second argument is it prevents wars. This is from the *World Press Review* in '85: It would be unjust to consider only the organization's failures. How can we count the number of wars that, thanks to the UN, did not break out because of the Security Council (Balk, 4).[11]

Next argument is that they decrease tension. Ronald Falkner, who's a professor of political science at Tennessee Tech, in '83: "Its record in view of the tremendous tension reductions in the world has been a good one. The United Nations has served with remarkable effectiveness as a mechanism for reducing friction arising out of the process of change" (490).[12]

Next argument is it controls violence. Indar Rikhye, professor of political science at Yale, in '74: No one who has carefully studied the performance of these peacekeeping forces in a role closely dictated and controlled by the General Assembly and Security Council lightly dismisses that any of them has made a contribution to the overall control of violence.[13]

I will indicate that these peacekeeping forces are good.

---

[11] "Indeed, the prestigious *Le Monde* of Paris, ruminating on the UN four decades after the signing of its charter, observes [June 26], 'It would be unjust to consider only the organization's failures . . . How can we count the wars that, thanks to the UN, did not break out? Security Council meetings, however virulent, have the effect of a safety valve.'"

[12] "Its record, in view of the tremendous tensions in the world, has been a good one . . . . In 1981, [Secretary General Kurt Waldheim] observed that the United Nations had served with remarkable effectiveness as a mechanism for reducing friction arising out of the process of change."

[13] "No one who has carefully studied the performance of these international peacekeeping forces in a role closely dictated and controlled by the mandate that they have been given by the Security Council or General Assembly can lightly dismiss the contribution that any of them has made to the control of violence."

His second argument is that, you know, it has worked, but it has changed now. And I'll indicate below that, you know, even today it's doing some neat stuff.

His third argument is it does not deal with failure. Of course, number one, on balance we would indicate that they are beneficial. And you will answer yes to the resolution. And what we are arguing here is, and the evidence above talks about from the *World Press Review*, is that, you know you can't even count the number of wars that have been prevented because of the UN.

Second argument is he drops that the failures are the fault of outside forces. Indicating that the failures are not the fault of the UN, it's because of outside areas.

I want to extend here on lofty expectation. Argument number one is you should not blame them for no conflict resolution. Raman, who was previously qualified, in '83: "There is, consequently, little justification in blaming peacekeeping for a failure to reach a solution in a conflict" (376). It was never their responsibility.

Next argument is if they want to fight, they will. This is from Connor O'Brian, who is a UN secretary, in 1985: "In cases where both parties are prepared to go to the bitter end—as, for example, in the Falklands—there is no real role for the UN"(19). Indicating, you know, if Iran and Iraq hate each other that much, nobody is going to stop them from shooting each other.

Next argument is if the UN wants, you know if they want peace, the UN provides it, indicating beneficiality. Abba Eban, the Foreign Minister from Israel, in '85: "When the belligerents desire to formalize a measure of stability and mutual restraint, the availability of UN symbols and myth helps them to create periods and areas of restraint and then stop the conflict" (45).[14]

Final argument here is you cannot expect them to solve all conflicts. Edward Luck, in '85: "The United Nations obviously cannot manage all conflicts and resolve all disputes successfully" (149). Impact of this argument indicates, you know, that you can't expect them to do everything great, but, man, in the stuff they do, it's fantastic.

I want examples here, and I'm going to give you a ton of them. (A) subpoint are past examples. And he's going to say, well, these are in the past and they don't apply. But I will give you examples where the superpowers have been prevented from getting involved in conflict. And I'll contend that if these things hadn't happened, you may not even have a today.

First example is the Congo. And this is from Indar Rikhye, professor of political science, in '84. He argues international peacekeeping not only survived the challenge but established beyond any doubt that, without its involvement,

---

[14] "But it remains true when the belligerents desired to formalize a measure of stability and mutual restraint, the availability of suitable UN symbols and myths helps them to create periods and areas of restraints in what would otherwise have been an uncontrolled conflict."

the Congo would have ceased to survive as a unified nation and could easily have become a battle-ground of superpower warfare (89).[15]

Next argument is it justifies overall peacekeeping. Rikhye again, this time in '74: The part of the UN in the Congo played deserves its rightful recognition and can clearly be defined as justification for the UN's overall conflict resolution policy (91).[16]

Indicates justification on a big basis.

Next argument is it prevented superpower confrontation, and I mean that's the evidence that's above.

I'll give you the next empirical example of the Cuban missile crisis. Connor O'Brian continues. The Cuban missile crisis suggests that the world might have been more unsafe if it weren't for the UN's repertoire of tricks (18).[17]

Next argument is essential role by the UN. Brian Urquhart, Social and Political Affairs, in '81: The UN played an essential role in the Cuban missile crisis in '62, not only providing a forum where both sides could expound their positions publicly, but also in suggesting steps could be taken to deescalate the crisis (9).[18]

Final argument is Yom Kippur War. Sir Anthony Parson, in '83. He's a UK Ambassador. "At the end of the Yom Kippur War of October 1973, there was a situation of the most appalling danger to global peace. . . . The world came close to a naked confrontation between the superpowers on a battlefield. Neither side could find a way to climb down. At the last moment, they used the Security Council of the United Nations as a ladder from which to dismount their high horses" (106–7). I'm telling you, in the Yom Kippur war, we might not even have today if it were not for the UN.

Please go now on to the (B) subpoint, which will indicate, you know, current examples. Cyprus is the first one. *UN Chronicle* in '85: "The Secretary General said the continued presence of UNFICYP remained indispensable in helping to maintain the calm on the island . . . " (33).

---

15 "International peacekeeping not only survived the challenge but established beyond any doubt that, without its involvement, the Congo would have ceased to survive as a unified nation and could easily have become a battleground of economic and ideological warfare."

16 "The part that ONCU (United Nations' Congo Operation) played in this deserves its rightful recognition—and can clearly be regarded as a justification for the United Nations' overall conflict control policy of combining military operations with political and conciliatory efforts."

17 "More than any other episode in the UN's history, the Cuban missile crisis suggests that the world might have been more unsafe if it weren't for the UN's unimpressive repertoire of tricks."

18 "The United Nations played an essential role in the Cuban Missile Crisis in 62, not only providing a forum where both sides could expound their positions publicly, but also in suggesting, through letters from Secretary-General U Thant to Chairman Khrushchev and President Kennedy, steps that might be taken simultaneously by both sides to deescalate the crisis."

Next argument is in terms of the Middle East, UNTSO. This is from Indar Rikhye, professor of political science, previously qualified. "Similarly, UNTSO continues to perform an important role in the Middle East. It keeps the Security Council informed of incidents and other developments that threaten peace" (1983,9).

Next argument is Pakistan. It keeps the peace today. Rikhye again. Uhm, this is, oh excuse me. Selig Harris, [Harrison], Carnegie Endowment in '83: The UN effort in Pakistan has come close to successful conclusion, and has been successful in regard to the Soviet withdrawal from Pakistan (4).[19]

Next argument is UNDOF, that's the Golan Heights Force. And this is from Rikhye again. The situation remained unchanged in the Golan Heights, where calm continues to prevail. Thus UNDOF continues to play a useful role between Israel and its remaining, you know, Arab problem (62).[20]

Next argument is UNIFL. *UN Chronicle* in '85: In spite of the difficult conditions in southern Lebanon, UNIFL's presence continues to be necessary and constitutes an important factor in the stability in the international commitment to upholding Lebanon's independence, sovereignty, and territorial integrity (7).[21] I think I take all of that out. Man, the empiricals are with the negative.

Please go to contention two. He argues who's the *Atlantic Monthly*? Well, I'll argue the *Atlantic Monthly* is not an unbiased source that reaches its conclusions beforehand. And I mean if you want to call for the evidence at the end of the round, that is what the evidence does indicate. They reach their conclusions, then go off and research it.

I'll argue next argument is that, you know, the Heritage Foundation is basically a mindless organization. William Charles Maynes, Editor of *Foreign Policy*, in '85: "[T]he Heritage Foundation . . . has devoted so much of its budget to what seems to outsiders as a mindless assault on the United Nations" (237).

Next argument is, remember these guys? These are the guys who said fluoridation of water was a Communist plot. (laughter) I mean empirically, give me a break here.

---

[19] "Second, critical, interrelated issues remain to be settled, notably, the time frame for Soviet force withdrawals and for the phase out of Pakistani aid to the resistance, as well as, the precise orchestration of these two processes. Much to the surprise of the American officials, however, the UN effort is now moving tantalizingly close to a successful conclusion. Some of the more optimistic Pakistani and Soviet sources say that implementation of the agreement could conceivably begin in early 1984."

[20] "The situation remains unchanged along the Golan Heights, where calm continues to prevail. Thus UNDOF continues to play a useful role between Israel and its remaining serious Arab antagonists."

[21] "In spite of the difficult conditions in southern Lebanon, UNIFL's presence continued to be necessary and constituted an important factor of stability in an international commitment to upholding Lebanon's independence, sovereignty, and territorial integrity."

His second argument is, you know, empirically takes out debate, substitutes for war. Where are the empiricals? He doesn't indicate them. And he drops the Richman evi– I think it's Richman evidence, that indicates, you know, debates do substitute.

The third argument he says safety is turned, but all he does is say, you know, extend. I mean our arguments from the Stanley Foundation in '85 beat this.

His next argument, you know, he drops the fourth subpoint that says the Third World gets to vent their aggression, that's the Finger evidence and he grants it. He says, you know, we say no empiricals, he says it fuels conflict. No. I mean we argue here that the empiricals rest with the negative. And I think that our evidence pulls through. He does no extension here. All he does is repeat.

Please go now on to where he argues causes conflict. I will argue, no it stops. And I give empiricals. He says they do not keep the peace. That is wrong. He drops the Raman evidence that indicates even if its prolonged, it's better that you have the peacekeeping forces there.

Now on Yeselson and Gaglione. It's '74, the above evidence takes out anyway.

On empirical standards, he says above. I'll say above. He says Nixon takes out superpowers and no snowball. But he drops the answers.

Only Israel is the next argument Molly makes, and he says it's on the whole in the Middle East. Baloney: It's only Middle East, and I give other examples.

He then argues that there are these better ways to do it. Of course number one, only Middle East. Number two, drops Vayrynen evidence says we will use it in the future. Number three, drops the MNF evidence that says it wasn't even a peacekeeping force, it was a war.

Next argument is that bypassing the UN is bad. Houghton and Trinka, Center for the Study of Foreign Affairs, in '84: The UN has acquired a great deal of expertise in the field. To create a non-UN organization for the same purpose derogates the prestige of the UN and thus weakens the overall peacekeeping process of the world (79).[22]

Next argument is it prevents superpower confrontation. Houghton and Trinka again. "[T]he establishment of non-UN peacekeeping force, with US participation . . . is unacceptable to the Soviet Union, even if it is done under the banner of a peacekeeping force. A response by the USSR can be expected, thus creating the risk of a new direct confrontation" (95).

You know, those non-UN forces are nasty stuff.

Cross-Examination:

Miguel Delao questioning Benson

Delao: Can I have the last two cards? Benson: Sure. Delao: That's a really interesting last card. Paul, I get crucified in cross-ex because I say, you know,

---

[22] "The UN has acquired a great deal of expertise in the field. To create a non-UN organization for the same purpose derogates from the prestige of the UN and thus weakens an institution which the world looks upon as a major instrument for maintaining peace."

when you have conflict and it will escalate and everybody will die. That last card says that when you go outside the UN, the Soviets will nuke us or something to that extent, and we've had two outside the UN, when did they nuke us? Benson: Well, no, no, no, see like the MNF and MFO, I mean, we're not saying it definitely is going to happen— Delao: Well, what's the potential for it? (laughter) Benson: Well, I mean you argue. If you're going to contend potential, I will contend that there is a greater possibility of this happening here. Delao: Why? Benson: Because UN forces do not include the superpowers or any members of the Security Council. Non-UN forces— Delao: They never do? Benson: Huh? Delao: They never do? Benson: Not currently. I mean, if you want to bring that up, I've got the charter.

Delao: I thought the Cyprus forces had US people there. Benson: They did in the past, but they were withdrawn. Delao: They don't now? Benson: No. Delao: Can you prove it? Benson: Well, I mean the US is continuing to support it via funds, political stuff, and that, but our troops aren't over there. And I mean we commit our troops to these non-UN peacekeeping forces. We have to, that's the only way they can function.

Delao: Can you name me the wars we stopped? Benson: The wars we stopped? Yom— Delao: You want me to show you the wars we caused. Benson: Huh? Delao: You want me to show the wars we caused. Benson: Well, I'd say this is a little late— Delao: I'm referring to the *World Press Review* card that just says don't just consider the failures— Benson: OK. OK. Yom Kippur prevents superpower conflict. Delao: So you're going to refer to all the empirics then in 2NC, right? Benson: Oh no, I'll contend that all the empiricals that are going on now which I will claim as independent benefits to UN peacekeeping.

Delao: I think you have a really good argument here that— Benson: Well, thank you. Delao: Well, let me tell you which one— Benson: I think it's a good argument. Delao: You may be wrong. Well, I think they are all good.

Delao: You say it's reasonable that you should not have lofty expectations. Now all the evidence you read says that you should not expect them to stop every war, right? Benson: I agree with you. Delao: That's an unreasonable expectation. But is it unreasonable for the affirmative to say that the UN should not contribute? Is that unreasonable? Benson: Should not contribute to conflicts? Delao: Exactly. Benson: Well, I mean that depends like, what your, you know, what empiricals you bring up and whether or not I can turn them. (laughter) Delao: Whether we win them or not, is that an unreasonable standard? Benson: Well, I mean I don't think, you know, I'm not going to grant you that premise at all because I would contend that the wars would with or without the UN and for you to hypothesize that somehow the UN caused this to incrementally increase this much, I think that's baloney. Delao: That's if you win your argument. If the UN contributes— Benson: Even if I don't, I think it makes sense. Delao: If the UN contributes to it, why is it unreasonable to expect them to not contribute? Benson: You just lost me. Why is it unreasonable to expect them not to contribute? They don't— Delao: See, you're assuming you win your argument. I am saying— Benson: I don't plan on losing it. (laughter) Delao: I want to know if, I don't care who wins it, why is it unreasonable to not want them to contribute to it? This is your fourth chance to answer this. Benson: Oh, so you mean that the UN would actually like, cause more people to get involved. Is that what you're asking? Delao: Why is that unreasonable? Benson: You can bring up stuff that says like, it brings in like eight other countries getting involved, well then, yeah, I would say that the UN isn't beneficial in that instance. Delao: OK.

First Negative Rebuttal

Molly McGinnis, Macalester

His first answer on the overview says that my evidence talks about the UN as a whole, therefore it's obviously not talking about what the affirmative is asking about. First argument, they contradicted this definition. Now that means his definition is different from mine, but I'm arguing that that highlights that there is not definite definition of what is and what is not the UN. Why is my author inappropriate when he says the words UN in his piece of evidence and concludes that on balance, it's beneficial to the United States? And he needs to show that the assumptions my author, why those are different than his. And he has to highlight those distinctions before there can be any concrete definitions of UN.

Second argument is that the money is inextricably tied. And this cross-app's back to the (C) point. Nicholas Platt, from the Bureau of International Affairs, DOS, 1982: "The subsidiary UN bodies and the specialized agencies are another component of the UN, and their activities in fact consume the major portion of UN moneys and personnel" (13). UNA Publication, *Financing the UN*, says in March of '84: "Also included in the regular budget of the UN are the expenditures of the specialized agencies" (Formuth 2). We get to talk about all of them. OK.

Third subpoint is that, on balance the UN is good for us. Frank Church, who was a former congressional delegate to the UN in 1985: "[I]n our world and in these times, such an organization needs to function, and one would hope that it might grow more effective over the course of time. On balance, the UN is far more of a plus for the world than a minus" (Fasulo 114). OK. Which would indicate that no matter what else happens in the round, this author says, you know, vote negative. And there is no same, on-balance evidence by the affirmative.

I'm on observation number one on case now. He argues right to define. He argues there is no evidence that money can be cut. I talk about that on the overview. He argues that a member of the CIA is not a member of Congress. First argument is that it does not indicate that we should not add those folks into our calculus. You know, and that's the same money argument I made on the overview side.

He argues that we belong to the agencies without. First argument is that is arbitrary. And that's a cross-application of the definitional muddle that we talk about on the top of overview number one.

On between World War I and World War II, the League of Nations. He says I provide no evidence. You know he needs to indicate there is a distinction, because I argue now funding is inextricably linked.

He argues that beneficial is in one's own interest. This is observation number two. I argue, you know, he agrees that we need to argue on balance, which means

I win the Church evidence I just read. And I don't know how you weigh those sorts of things. He says eloquence. You know.

On observation number two, (B) point, he says national interest. OK, he says it outweighs anything, and this is only military security. OK, and so he indicates that it's our military security, which we will win on case. But, he does not indicate that the other things are not as important. And certainly Kennan does not make those distinctions as well, and he's arbitrarily inserted those distinctions.

Underview on this contention. First argument is that we should not contribute to conflict. That is 2AC's question to Paul in cross-ex. Second argument is that there is no affirmative contention that peacekeeping is bad, merely that it doesn't work. And remember we talk about that after 2AC cross-ex. He says that we will not contend that peacekeeping exacerbates the conflict. OK, only that the General Assembly exacerbates conflict. Third argument is only if GA debate spurred conflicts are uncontrolled is there a problem. And there is no indication that any of these are uncontrolled.

Contention number one, please group. First argument is that there are no empiricals, no indication why we need to fear this at all. Second argument is there is no reason for an increase in fear, especially when we win that we use peacekeeping. Final argument is that Nixon has no scenario. I mean we talked about this in cross-ex and he can't indicate when Nixon would indeed be true.

I am on prolif. First argument on Atomic Agency. I win the funding link below. Second argument is equal to UN because I argue the UN deserves the credit for what they sponsored via the IAEA and NPT.

His second argument talks about the norms. Now he does not address the Miller evidence that I read that says that the norms themselves mean we don't have proliferation of nuclear weapons. That's independent of the specialized agencies, and that's the UN in and of itself. Second argument is that there is no harm given to a mere holding of the weapons. OK. They are not used.

Third argument is that norms against harm are increased by the United Nations. This comes from Daniel Poneman from the Center for Science in Harvard, 1983: "As more and more countries become technologically able to produce nuclear weapons, that norm will become the main obstacle to nuclear weapons proliferation" (31).

He argues that Becker, and debate equals prolif. First argument is who is Mr. Becker? All his evidence comes from this man, and we argue from authorities, that I give the qualifications for, that conclude you should vote negative. Second argument is that you can't have a treaty without this discrimination. Joseph Goldblatt from *SIPRI* says in 1985 that "A non-proliferation treaty not containing a distinction between nuclear haves and have-nots would have had either to make allowances for a nuclear buildup in non-nuclear weapons states [which he says would contradict the very idea of arms control], or to provide for the elimination of all existing nuclear weapons, [which he says would be infeasible]" (21). This is the best thing we've got.

Third argument is that there are not more nuclear powers. Jozef Goldblat continues in January of '86: There appears to be no imminent danger of an open expansion of the nuclear club. The incentives to acquire nuclear weapons are still considerably weaker than the disincentives, which means that the status quo will be maintained for some time (30).[23]

So when he argues that debate legitimize, that's not enough to outweigh the disincentives. OK.

He argues next that it equals the spread of energy. First argument is that there is no evidence that energy equal the tech for prolif. He argues next that the IAEA is a guide. First argument is that there is no evidence here. Second argument, no empiricals, and I cross-app from above that there are no more proliferation nations. Third argument is that safeguards prevent, and that's evidence from 1NC. He says [unintelligible] are limited. First argument is limits, but not inability, and all my evidence says we have an effective nonproliferation regime right now. OK. Scheinman says in '85 that: "The IAEA has helped to avoid the further spread of nuclear weapons and deter the misuse of facilities and materials intended for civil nuclear purposes" (1).[24] And I think that's all we need here because we win that there is not enough, and let there be no new responses on this argument in rebuttals.

First Affirmative Rebuttal:

Carrie Crenshaw, Florida State

Starting with the observations and going straight case. Observation number one. Please group her extensions. Subpoint one, membership in the UN is not membership in the agencies. Her definition by her author is the definition of UN, it is not the definition of membership, and certainly that is the distinction in 2AC. Subpoint two, Franck extends that you could pull out and still belong to the agencies and that evidence is dropped.

Subpoint three, her on-balance evidence is blurby and does not necessarily address the issues that the affirmative team does. And she grants the criteria of military security, so it is her burden to prove that that evidence addresses that.

Observation number two on lofty. Please extend Miguel's first answer not unreasonable, UN causes conflict. Please group his four answers. Subpoint one, they should not contribute to war or exacerbate conflict and certainly that means that we should indict them for that. Subpoint two, [unintelligible] drops the case side evidence that indicates that these countries use the UN for mobilization for war. Three subpoint we are on the verge of new international anarchy now. Mr. Ruggie in '85: "With regard to peace and security, the UN Secretary General

---

[23] "There appears to be no imminent danger of an open expansion of the nuclear club. The balance of nuclear disincentives and incentives is not tipping in the direction of the latter, and the status quo will be maintained for some time."

[24] "For more than a quarter-century, an international organization—The International Atomic Energy Agency (IAEA)—has played a leading role in national and international efforts to avoid the further spread, or proliferation, of nuclear weapons and to deter the misuse of facilities and materials intended for civil nuclear purposes."

himself has remarked that the organization's machinery functions so poorly that the international community finds itself perilously near to a new international anarchy" (343).

Subpoint four, of course, all their extension evidence is in the past. Extend Miguel's second answer from 2AC, peacekeeping worked in the past but has changed. Of course, that Tugwell evidence has been dropped by both negative speakers throughout this round. That means that you have no more peacekeeping after his examples that he provides. And that evidence is dropped.

Extend Miguel's third answer that it creates conflict and please group his extensions with that. I would argue first of all, venting is not the same thing as peacekeeping. So if we win that they contribute to the conflict off of venting, that means that we still win, even if he wins his peacekeeping stuff. Subpoint two, UN should not contribute to the conflict, and therefore should be indicted. Subpoint three, peacekeeping fails, and I will extend those issues on case. Subpoint four, it is not unique benefit to the UN. It is only peacekeeping, and both countries agree. In other words, his Cyprus evidence admits that it could be NATO that could do it. And it's only when these countries agree that the UN is allowed to insert those forces. So certainly it is not a unique benefit.

Prolif. Please extend Miguel's first answer, the IAEA is an agency. The only thing that she has is all these links above. But first of all, she drops Miguel's specific evidence that says that the IAEA is affirmative. And that evidence is cold. Subpoint two, she loses safeguards if she loses agency topicality. And I will,– The others take out the NPT below. And those are the only two links.

Extend Miguel's second answer that they have bomb and the norms do not stop use. Please group her extensions. Subpoint one, they do have the bomb. Her evidence admits that, and her impact evidence assumes an accident scenario. So certainly you could still have the problems from proliferation.

Subpoint two, the norms are undermined and the NPT is undermined by the debate. The debates say that you actually legitimized proliferation by undermining the NPT. Extend the third answer, debates undermine proliferation by undermining the NPT. All the– The only answer– The first answer she has here is who is Becker? But she doesn't read all of the qualifications of her sources. Subpoint two, Becker is the former Israeli delegate to the UN, and he was one of the drafters of the NPT.

Extend her second and third extensions—those pieces of evidence. Subpoint one, that third card is not linked to the UN. Subpoint two, if you actually legitimized prolif by undermining the NPT, then that second answer becomes irrelevant. Extend Miguel's fourth answer, NPT spreads weapons capability. The only thing she says is there is no evidence and it says energy—energy is not technology. But if you read that evidence, or call for the evidence after the round, you will find that it says that it spreads the capability for nuclear weapons. And that evidence is dropped. She just misreads it. Now I think that's an independent turn.

As far as all the rest of it goes, the only link she has is the NPT, because agencies, the IAEA is out of there, and I would ask you to extend the fact that the NPT is undermined by debate.

Observation on criteria, case. The only thing she wants to extend is that, is dollars in terms of what membership is, whether or not it's agencies. Please group her extensions. Subpoint one, she drops the evidence on the IAEA is autonomous of dollars. Subpoint two, she also drops the Bennett card that's talking membership and not a definition of the UN. Please extend the definition of beneficial, and that should certainly address military security on balance.

Extend the (B) subpoint, national interest. Certainly that should address military security.

On her overview on case, please group. Subpoint one, venting prevents peacekeeping and that Tugwell evidence has been dropped throughout case. Subpoint two, I'll extend venting on case because she did cursory coverage there.

Contention one. The only thing she has here is that there are no empirics and that Nixon gives no scenarios. But I'll ask you to extend the Nixon evidence and indicate that her partner faces the same problem. And certainly you should grant us the risk evidence there because her partner faces the same problem.

Contention two, UN heightens conflict, (A) subpoint. The only thing he wants to extend is the Heritage Foundation indict. But I'd just like to point out, ladies and gentlemen, that we have other sources. Subpoint two, Tugwell is not Pines, you know. If you want to apply this indict, it has to be specific. Subpoint three, he drops Miguel's second answer that they assert it and his third answer is that you should just prove him wrong.

Please extend also specifically on the (A) subpoint the Arab-Israeli conflict is an empirical example. Two subpoint, the on-balance evidence that says this is true. Three subpoint, I'd like to point out that venting is different from peacekeeping. And four subpoint, I would extend the evidence that says, it takes out her evidence on case, that says, it indicates the fact that, it indicates the fact that venting would stop peacekeeping. OK? And it also says that venting no longer occurs regardless of what evidence she read.

I would just like to get down to the peacekeeping issues and extend Miguel's 2AC answers which I don't think, you know, have been addressed really by the 2NC or 1NR.

Second Negative Rebuttal:

Paul Benson, Macalester

Far too much is dropped in 1AR. She again indicates membership, not equal organizations. Of course drops all of Molly's funding evidence that indicates that funding is tied. Now her second argument is Franck indicates you could pull out. But, you know, we would argue the real world Congressional analogy, that, you know, if you were talking about in the real world, whether Congress was beneficial, you would talk about the actions the CIA takes because Congress established the CIA. Indicating, you know, that in the real world we are perfectly reasonable.

Third argument here is she says on balance, card is a blurb. No. She drops out Gardner evidence and also drops the Church evidence which is extended that indicates, on balance is beneficial. And when I talk about Heritage Foundation indicts, the scholars conclude negative.

Please go now on to lofty expectations. She drops off all kinds of things. She says, you know, extend number one. But drops my evidence that indicates it prevents wars, it decreases tensions, and it controls violence. All that is dropped, and I do not want 2AR giving new answers. She says should not contribute to war. I argue that they do not, and she doesn't give any empiricals.

Her second argument is, you know, case evi takes all this out. Of course I argue case, I spend lots of time on case. Third argument here she says we're on the verge of anarchy. Of course, number one, he's not talking about peacekeeping. Number two, you know, it does not indicate what the impact of all of this would be. Why this would necessarily be that bad. Third argument is does not indicate that, you know, the entire UN system will fall apart, you know. Fourthly, that this is brand new. I mean this thing should have been cut in. And I will argue the 2AC, because this is an entire position shift. If they're going to argue the UN is going to fall apart, by God they should have that in constructives.

She then argues extend the second answer that he gives. Of course, drops all my answers that indicates, you know, the failures are outside faults, and on balance. She says, you know, venting does not equal peacekeeping. Of course, it stops wars, and I indicate that that is good in and of itself. And if, you know, their national security criterion is number one, then that would, you know, make it relevant to the round.

She says they should not contribute. I argue that they don't. She argues peacekeeping forces fail. I say no, pull all the empiricals which she punts off. Fourthly, she says not unique to the UN. That would mean that she would have to indicate solvency for non-UN organizations. And she drops all my evidence that I read in the 2NC that indicates you can't do it outside the UN. And I'll talk about that when I get there.

Please go to prolif. On overview number one, she says money is linked directly to the UN. No. Number one, UN deserves credit for the safeguards. Second argument is safeguards take out impact on 2AC UN harm. She says, you know, countries have the bomb. Of course, number one, Goldblat evidence January '86 says no new members. She drops it. Second argument, no evidence about accidents which is what our evidence talks about. Third argument is 1NR Poneman evidence says you won't develop any/or use, and that's dropped.

On norms. Number one, must have discriminatory treaty. I mean that's dropped as well. Second argument that means the norms are upheld. And third argument is Goldblat says disincentives outweigh legitimization. She says energy equals development. Of course, no evidence here. My second argument is norms say does not develop. I mean she cannot get that off of this. No prolif equals big time benefit. And I mean that is UN-specific.

Please go to overview on criteria. Of course she says only numbers, IAEA autonomous, and Bennett is dropped. Of course she drops why wouldn't we add this to the calculus, and I talk about this above. She says definition of beneficial. Of course, Molly argues it's arbitrary, and where's the distinction, and she grants that. She just says extend (B) point. Drops on balance criteria should be applied here and that our scholars conclude with us.

She argues on the underview venting does not equal peacekeeping. Of course, she applies the Tugwell evidence again, which is Heritage Foundation, and even if you don't buy the indict, I beat it. She says case takes out, well let's go to case.

On contention one, she says extend Nixon. Drops Molly's third argument that says Nixon gives no scenarios, indicating the Nixon evidence is awful. Drops her first response that says no empiricals are given, which beats it at that level.

On contention two. She says we have other sources and Tugwell is not that bad. Of course drops basically our indict which indicates, you know, the Heritage Foundation, you know, reaches conclusions then does the study. I mean if we did that kind of stuff, we'd probably be shot by our coach. (laughter)

You know, she says we dropped two and three. No. I grouped that together. And I argue that it beats it on that level and, you know, this is brand new. I don't understand how it takes anything out any way.

She says extend Arab-Israeli. I beat that out with my empiricals. She then says extend another, you know, conflict. I think I beat that as well on balance.

She says on balance beats. Wrong. I read evidence that indicates on balance it works well, and I have all the empiricals in the round. I mean if you're going to decide peacekeeping, look at the empirical examples. And she drops when I talk about Yom Kippur, and all that type of stuff. We probably wouldn't even have a today if those conflicts had occurred.

She says venting does not equal peacekeeping. So what. It stops wars, which they indicate is the number one priority. And if that is true, you know, that it's irrelevant because it's not peacekeeping, then go down to the very bottom where she argues, you know, those outside the UN peacekeeping forces. They ain't peacekeeping forces. And so if my evidence gets kicked out, her evidence gets kicked out, and where's the only place you have peacekeeping? That is in the UN. OK. And I mean she drops the evidence that I read that indicates it prevents superpower conflict. I mean that evidence is cold.

All I want here is that the peacekeeping forces don't include the superpowers. This is from F. T. Lui, Assistant Secretary General of Political Affairs, in '84: Peacekeeping forces' presence in areas do not include the superpowers (25).[25]

I guess I'm supposed to say something nice at the end of this. And all I'd like to say is I've been involved with this activity for about seven years now and I've heard things about the fact that it's starting to die out in certain areas of the country. I don't think that should ever happen, and I think that we as members of this type of a community should do our best to keep CEDA, NDT, and other forms of debate alive. Thank you very much. (Applause)

---

[25] "Secondly, despite their weaknesses, UN peacekeeping forces have one important advantage. Their presence in an area of conflict serves to preclude direct intervention by third-party governments, including superpowers in that area and thus to insulate the conflict from a potential East-West confrontation."

Second Affirmative Rebuttal:

Miguel Delao, Florida State

I said exactly what I was going to do in 2AC, and I said what I was going to do in 2AR. I said we're going to go for uniqueness. All right, and that is what I'm going to try to win, because even though he can take out Tugwell, Cuellar evidence indicates that because we went outside the UN, there will be no more peacekeeping in the UN. He can win all his past evidence. The UN was wonderful at it, they will not do it anymore. Of course he raises a good issue, well now we have to show solvency. But last thing Carrie says, you know, in 1AR, was [unintelligible] you have to extend all the evidence I read in the 2AC on peacekeeping. And my evidence says, they don't want the United Nations, they won't go there, and it says because they're getting shot at; and that is why I think I made the distinction why the US is good; that evidence says that the Netherlands is sick and tired of getting their people killed. The US fights back. And the evidence I read there said that the UN would not have been any more successful at Lebanon and therefore should not be taken out. That evidence was granted. He had arguments there, but still granted what, everything the evidence indicated. I think that one card said they are getting shot at and therefore don't want to contribute soldiers, indicates why the US is better. What it comes down to is, you are not going to get the US. The question is, is there a better solution? I mean in any sense is there a slightly more optimal solution? To the extent that we can defend ourselves, we at least guarantee that there is possibility for more peacekeeping. Because you're not going to get it from the UN. That Cuellar evidence is dropped. All he can win is that it used to be great, and you know, I have to agree with him on that.

Prolif. I'm not going to go for this agency on IAEA, because what I want is the legitimization. Right. He extends that there are no new members. That is true, but the evidence; my second; my third answer in the 2AC—debate would undermine the NPT. That is granted. That is the only evidence that Carrie really goes for in the 1AR. She indicates that this takes out their links, because now the one thing that is bringing about these norms, the one thing that is deterring these people is NPT and it is being undermined.

He said they will not develop or use. But the evidence that was read there says they were legitimizing proliferation. Right. That is granted. He says norms are upheld. But they're undermining the NPT, that one card I think is what takes out all these links. Because it indicates that even though this may have been true, what is going on now in these debates is hurting their links.

He says norms mean they will not develop. I simply refer you to the phenomenal evidence that was read in the 2AC. That evidence says that the NPT is instrumental in promoting proliferation. It says the IAEA is also in the same vein. They do the same thing, they lead to proliferation. All he has here, he says, is that the norms mean they won't develop. I want you to weigh that, these norms they won't do it, versus evidence that indicates that it is instrumental. When he runs that, you know; we've always granted, of course, prolif isn't bad; I think that gives us all the military security we need. Because they argue it leads to cataclysmic nuclear war. And if we win that evidence that indicates that it's being legitimized; which now means that people will prolif; and that it is undermining the NPT, which undermines their norms, then I think we certainly outweigh all this peacekeeping stuff which was all in the past. At a minimum, I put a doubt in your mind. At the most, I think I win the turn on peacekeeping because you will not have any in the future. And that was because of the venting.

I'll go to the first observation. Now I granted agencies, so that will not matter. But the third answer, this is 1N overview. All they have is this on-balance stuff. You now, I think it's the same argument, 2AC's the same argument as 1AR. This is really blurby stuff. Does not say why it is good and you have to weigh this specifically against proliferation. And I think that is a perfect illustration why. Because these authors may be assuming, well, you know, the UN stops prolif. They did not necessarily take into account Mr. Becker's argument that it indeed leads to prolif.

We are giving you specific examples versus, you know, evidence that just says, well you know, the negative would always win every round.

Lofty expectations. He starts off again by saying it prevents war. That is only when you get the peacekeeping and you will not have peacekeeping in the future. That means UN will not, no longer will stop war. The only thing you have to look at is, is there a chance outside the UN, and I think we give you that because of the fact that we can shoot back.

My evidence on the verge of peace; of anarchy. He says that it is not peacekeeping. That may be true, but it indicates that in general there is going to be war. He says number two, why is that bad? Certainly, I mean it has to be bad, there is no conflict control. We're going to have anarchy, and Klare says you want to have conflict control. He says number three, does not mean UN falls apart. That is certainly not the argument we are trying to make. And he says it is new, and the reason he says it is new is because he thinks I'm arguing the UN will fall apart. But he read a lot of evidence in the 2NC indicating that right now the UN is good. I don't see why it is illegitimate for Carrie to stand up and read evidence saying no that is not true, right now the UN is bad. That is not new. He thinks we made a different argument about the UN falling apart, which is not what we are claiming.

I think that's all I really want. But I will go to case and take a glance. US national interest. All they extend, on B subpoint of their first observation, must be on balance. I agree, I think the cataclysmic nuclear war on prolif wins it for us, and the fact that only we can get peacekeeping in the future.

Contention one. He says scenarios. Certainly we get a scenario off prolif and we get an empirical scenario off peacekeeping. That's the Cuellar evidence I read in 2AC, and it's empirical. It says because we went outside the UN, you will not get peacekeeping in the future. And the evidence says empirically the last two were outside the UN.

I want to thank several people, and I'd like to start off with Curtis Austin, our coach. At the beginning of this year, I was not going to debate. And it is because of the fine human being that he is, that I decided to stay, and I'm really glad that I did. I'd like to thank Carrie. Before this tournament she said the one thing she wanted was for us to get here to the final round. And she was going to work her butt off to see that I got here, and she did it for me, and I can't thank her enough. And Carolyne, who makes my every day. I enjoyed it fully. Thank you. (Applause)

WORKS CITED

Ameri, Houshang. *Politics and Process in the Specialized Agencies of the United Nations*. Aldershot Haunts: Gower Publishing Company Limited, 1982.

Balk, Alfred. "The Editor's Corner." *World Press Review* (August 1985).

Becker, Avi. *Disarmament Without Order*. Westport, Conn.: Greenwood Press, 1985.

Bennett, A. LeRoy. *On International Organizations: Principles and Issues*. Englewood Cliffs, New Jersey: Prentice Hall, 1983.

Cannon, Carroll. *Shaping Our Future Together*. San Diego, California: United Nations Association, 1984.

Dunn, Lewis. "Controlling Nuclear Arms Includes Curbing Their Spread." *Christian Science Monitor* 11 October 1984.

Easterbrook, Greg. "Ideas Move Nations." *The Atlantic Monthly* (January 1986).

Eban, Abba. "Multilateral Diplomacy in the Arab-Israeli Conflict." *Multilateral Negotiations and Mediation*. Ed. Arthur Lull. New York: Pergamon Press, 1985.

Falkner, Ronnie. "Taking John C. Calhoun to the United Nations." *Polity* (Summer 1983).

Fasulo, Linda. *Representing America: Experiences of US Diplomats at the UN* New York: Praeger Special Studies, 1984.

Formouth, Peter. *Financing the United Nations*. New York: United Nations Association, 1984.

Franck, Thomas. *Nation Against Nation*. New York: Oxford UP, 1985.

Gardner, Richard. House. Committee on Foreign Affairs. *US Participation in the United Nations* 97th Congress, 2nd sess. Washington, D.C.: GPO, 1982.

Gauhar, Altaf. "North-South Dialogue: An Interview with Perez de Cuellar." *Third World Quarterly* (1984).

Goldblat, Jozef. *Nuclear Proliferation*. London: Taylor and Francis, 1985.

Grenier, Richard. "Yanqui, Si! U.N., No!" *Harpers* (January 1984).

Harrison, Selig. "A Break Through in Afghanistan?" *Foreign Policy* (Summer 1983).

Houghton, Robert, and Frank Trinka. *Multilateral Peacekeeping in the Middle East*. Washington, D.C.: Center for the Study of Foreign Affairs, 1984.

James, Alan. "Painful Peacekeeping: The United Nations in Lebanon 1978–1982." *International Journal* (Autumn 1983).

Keohane, Robert, and Joseph Nye. "Two Cheers for Multilateralism." *Foreign Policy* (Fall 1985).

Kirkpatrick, Jeanne J. *The Reagan Phenomenon—And Other Speeches on Foreign Policy*. Washington, D.C.: American Enterprise Institute for Public Policy Research, 1983.

Klare, Michael T. *American Arms Supermarket*. Austin, Texas: of Texas, 1984.

Luck, Edward. "The U.N. at 40: A Supporter's Lament." *Foreign Policy* (Winter 1984).

Lui, F. T. "Comments on the IPA Report." *Peacekeeping and Technology*. Ed. Hugh Hanning. Oxford, England: International Peace Academy, 1983.

Maynes, Charles. "A Cause Worth Fighting For." *The Nation* (21 September 1985).

Miller, Debra. "Contributions of the U.N. to International Security Regimes." *The U.S., the U.N., and the Management of Global Change* Ed. Toby Trister Gati. New York: New York University Press, 1983.

Nelson, Richard. "Multinational Peacekeeping in the Middle East and the United Nations Model." *International Affairs* (Winter 1984/85).

Newell, David. "On Morality in Foreign Policy." *Newsweek* (16 December 1985).

Nixon, Richard. *Real Peace*. Boston, Mass.: Little, Brown and Company, 1984.

Nye, Joseph S. "NPT. The Logic of Inequality." *Foreign Policy* (Summer 1985).

O'Brian, Conor. "U.N. Theater." *The New Republic* (4 November 1985).

Parson, Sir Anthony. "The United Nations and International Security in the 1980's." *Millennium: Journal of International Studies*

Platt, Nicholas. House. Committee on Foreign Affairs. *U.S. Participation in the United Nations*. 97th Congress, 2nd Session. Washington, D.C.: GPO, 1982.

Poneman, Daniel. House. Committee on Foreign Affairs. *Proposed Amendments to the Nuclear Non-Proliferation Act, 1983*. 98th Congress, 1st Session. Washington, D.C.: GPO, 1983. Puchala, Donald J. "American Interests and the United Nations." *Political Science Quarterly* (Winter 1982–83).

Raman, K. Venkata. "United Nations Peacekeeping and the Future of World Order." *Peacekeeping*. Ed. Henry Wiseman. New York: Pergamon Press, 1983.

Rikhye, Indar Jit, Michael Harbottle, and Bjorn Egge. *The Thin Blue Line*. New Haven, Conn.: Yale University Press, 1974.

Rikhye, Indar Jit. "Peacekeeping and Peacemaking." *Peacekeeping*. Ed. Henry Wiseman. New York: Pergamon Press, 1983.

———.*The Theory and Practice of Peacekeeping*. New York: St. Martins Press, 1984.

Ruggie, John. "The United States and the United Nations: Toward a New Realism." *International Organizations* (Spring 1985).

Scheinman, Lawrence. *The Nonproliferation Role of the International Atomic Energy Agency*, Washington, D.C.: Resources for the Future, 1985.

"Security Council Hears Views on Cyprus Efforts, Extends Mandate of Peacekeeping." *U.N. Chronicle*.

Sethi, J. D. "Steps Toward Reform." *World Press Review* (December 1985).

Spector, Leonard. "Proliferation: The Silent Spread." *Foreign Policy* (Spring 1985).

Stanley, C. Maxwell. House. Committee on Foreign Affairs. *U.S. Participation in the United Nations*. 97th Congress, 2nd Session. Washington, D.C.: GPO, 1982.

Tugwell, Maurice. "The United Nations as the World's Safety Valve." *A World Without A U.N.* Ed. Burton Pines. New York: The Heritage Foundation, 1984.

"UNIFIL Mandate Extended for Six Months." *U.N. Chronicle* (May 1985).

Urquhart, Brian. "International Peace and Security." *Foreign Affairs* (Fall 1981).

Vayrynen, Raimo. "Focus On: Is There A Role for the United Nations in Conflict Resolution?" *Journal of Peace Research* (1985).

Waldheim, Kurt. "The United Nations: The Tarnished Image." *Foreign Affairs* (Fall 1984).

Yeselson, Abraham, and Anthony Gaglione. *A Dangerous Place: The United Nations as a Weapon in World Politics*. New York: Grossman Publishers, 1974.

Appendix B
Important Debate Terms

Debate has a rather extensive lexicon or language. Major terms are defined here, with reference, when applicable, to the page where the term is discussed in greater detail.

Argument   Two or more people exchanging assertions and claims. (p. 4)

Assertion   A statement advanced without proof. (p. 16)

Burden of proof   The responsibility of the affirmative to present a prima facie case in favor of the resolution. (p. 109)

Burden of rejoinder The responsibility of all arguers to attempt to refute assertions and claims presented by opposing arguers. (p. 6)

Case   The position or stance the debater takes in defending or rejecting the resolution. (p. 20)

Claim   A statement advanced with the underlying proof supplied (p. 17)

Clarifying   A statement made to interpret ambiguous or misunderstood assertions or claims. (pp. 27–28)

Clash   Debater's responses to opposing assertions and claims. (pp. 92–93)

Constructive   One of the first four speeches in the debate, wherein debaters initiate issues into the debate. (pp. 19–20)

Counter-value   Standards of quality or worth that differ from those offered by an opponent. (pp. 133–34)

Criteria   A set of benchmarks or measures. (pp. 49–52)

Cross-examination   The four 3-minute time periods after the constructive speeches, during which arguers pose and answer questions. (pp. 19–21)

Debate	A structured form of argument involving a resolution, time limits, and agreed upon-speaker responsibilities. (p. 4)
Definitions	The meaning of words or phrases. (pp. 45–49)
Ethics	Standards of right and wrong. (pp. 187–88)
Evidence	The proof or documentation supporting an assertion, turning the assertion into a claim. (pp. 64–67)
Forensics	Legal or judgmental speaking. (p. 17)
Initiating	A statement introducing an issue into a debate round. (pp. 25–26)
Issue	General areas of dispute consisting of claims and assertions grouped around a particular theme or idea. (p. 17)
Overview	An issue presented outside of the existing case structure, highlighting an important assertion or claim. (p. 133)
Presumption	The preexisting beliefs of an audience, which determine their likelihood of accepting or rejecting new values or policies. (pp. 29–30)
Paradigm	A prototype or model. (p. 149)
Prima facie	A case that will stand on its own merits by meeting all the stock issues. (pp. 5, 108–09)
Proof	Any tangible and material support used to justify accepting a statement as true or valid. (pp. 61–83)
Questioning	A statement probing the logic or evidence presented by an opposing arguer by seeking clarification. (p. 27)
Rebuttal	Debate speeches during which opposing claims are refuted, issues are refocused, and debaters extend and refute assertions and claims already introduced in the debate. (pp. 19–20)
Refocusing	A statement designed to shift attention from one issue to another. (p. 28)

Refuting   A statement designed to overcome opposing statements and claims presented by opposing arguers. (pp. 26–27)

Signifying   An assertion of claim important enough to warrant the attention of the audience. (p. 26)

Signposting   Telling the listener what assertion, claim, or issue is being discussed. (p. 97)

Status quo   The present system, or things as they currently exist. (p. 152)

Stock issues   Traditional or expected issues that audiences use to evaluate arguments. (pp. 43–45)

Style   The speaker's language-related choices. (pp. 95–97)

Value   Standard of worth or excellence. (pp. 34–36)

Value Debate   Debate in which the speakers discuss the value or worth of ideas or policies rather than their workability or feasibility. (p. 10)

Index

artificial versus contextual, 128
relationship to burden of proof,
5, 29-30
relationship to negative, 128
Prima facie case, 5, 108-109
Principle
as a way of determining where a
value fits on a hierarchy, 39-40
Proactive debate strategies, 125,
132-133
Proof in debate, 16, 61-83
definition, 62
role in accepting or rejecting
claims, 63-64
standards for using in a debate, 64
substantive and motivational
proofs, 62-63, 90
Propositions, 40-43
of fact, 41
of policy, 42
of value, 42-43
Propriety
standard of evaluating evidence,
as a, 68-70

Qualitative harm, 141, 152
Quantitative harm, 141, 152
Quayle, Dan, 89
Questioning
type of debate statement, as a, 27,
111, 129

Reactive debate strategies, 125
Rebuttals, 19
Refocusing
type of debate statement, as a, 28,
111, 129
Refutation, 97-99
four-step form, 98-99
Refuting
type of debate statement, as a,
26-27, 111, 129
Rhetoric, 43, 88-90
Rokeach, Milton, 34-40

Scientific method, 70, 149
Second Affirmative Constructive, 29,
121-122
Second Affirmative Rebuttal, 29,
124-125
Second Negative Constructive, 29,
133-134
Second Negative Rebuttal, 29,
135-136
Shell arguments, 121, 134
Significance
rules for arguing significance, 53
stock issue, as a, 52-54
way of determining where a value
fits on a hierarchy, as a, 38
Signifying
type of debate statement, as a,
26, 111, 129
Signposting, 97
Situational expectations of debate,
22-23, 34, 65, 92, 110,128-129,
159
Solvency, 44
Speaker duties, 130-131
Speaking order, 19
Speaking skills paradigm, 164-165
Spread style of debate, 93, 160
Status quo, 152
Stock issues, 29-30
role in debate, 43-45
role in policy debates, 44-45
role in value debate 45-55
Straight refutation strategy, 121,
132-133
Structural limitations of debate,
21-22, 65, 108-110, 128-129
Structural paradigms, 128, 151-152
Style, 95-97, 112-113, 194-195
Sufficiency
standard of evaluting evidence, as
a, 67-68

Tabula rasa, 163
Toffler, Alvin, 12